AIKIDO

Basic and Intermediate Studies
Revised

by John Litchen

Technical Assistance : Graham Morris Sensei 6th Dan Shidoin

Yambu

**** *There's a lot of good stuff for the novice through Kyu grades. There are snippets and annotations throughout the book which are quite insightful and informative.*
...Clarke Bateman reviewing for Aikido Journal...

**** *A very nice approach. It is laid out in very logical fashion, and discusses core principles and basic techniques in considerable detail. The book is profusely illustrated with line drawings.*
...the Aikido Guy at Amazon.com

From www.aikido-chch.co.nz/reviews/litchen_basicandintermediate.html
...We particularly liked the digressions in the text into universal ideas such as reigi and musubi that underpin all aikido. For the Aikido students in their early training years this book will be a very good addition to their aikido library. It is more than just a technical text — a trap many books fall into. Read and enjoy...

***** *This is a fantastic book to supplement your class training. Author John Litchen has taken care to minimize the wear of hakamas in the illustrations and this really makes it easier to study the positioning and movement of the feet... This book is one of the better technical manuals out there and would be of interest to more than the Aikido student. If you study classical jujutsu or hapkido/ kuksool/hwa-rang-do, you'll find value as well.*
D.Nguyen "Goju Guy" (Round Rock, TX United States.)

合気道

AIKIDO

Basic and Intermediate Studies
Revised

by John Litchen 4th Dan Shidoin

Technical Assistance : Graham Morris Sensei 6th Dan Shidoin

Australian Edition ©2006 John Litchen
A CIP record for this edition can be found at the National Library of Australia: http://www.nla.gov.au
ISBN 1-9212-0704-3

National Library of Australia Cataloguing-in-Publication entry

Author:
  Litchen, John.

Title: Aikido : basic and intermediate studies revised /
  John
Litchen.

Edition: 2nd ed.

ISBN: 9780980410464
  (pbk.)

Notes: Previous ed.: 2006.

Subjects:
  Aikido.
Aikido--Training.

Dewey Number: 796.8154

2nd Australian edition published by Yambu, 2013
PO Box 3503, Robina Town Centre, Qld, 4230.
Australia

Table of Contents

Table of Contents

Table of Contents

Acknowledgements.

No book of this kind is ever written without the help both directly and indirectly of many people and I would like to acknowledge this.

I would like to express my gratitude to Graham Morris Sensei, 6th Dan Shidoin, who has been my primary instructor over the past fifteen years and whose advice and assistance throughout the time spent working on this project has been extraordinarily helpful. His willingness to be both Uke and Nage for me was much more than I expected at the commencement of this project, and the result is a much better book than I expected when we first started talking about it and taking the initial photographs.

There are other very important people who have profoundly affected my thinking in Aikido and I also offer them my thanks and gratitude.

The most important of these would undoubtedly be the late Seiichi Sugano Shihan, 8th Dan, (1939 – 2010) who was responsible for Aikido and its technical and philosophical direction in Australia. His inspiration still goes beyond what my inadequate words can express. He transcended a setback that would have flattened most people and was doing better and more profound Aikido than ever. He literally inspired awe in all who come in contact with him. Though no longer with us, his presence fills many dojos around the world.

I would also like to acknowledge and thank Nobuo Takase Shihan, 7th Dan, from New Zealand, and Yoshikazu Watanabe, 7th Dan from Tokyo, Japan, who through their example and teaching have inspired me to explore deeper aspects of the art.

I would also like to thank Jorge Rojo Gutierrez, 6th Dan from Aikikai Chile who was my very first instructor and who was the first person to demonstrate to me the wonderful potential that Aikido holds.

This book is a result of my continuing search for that potential.

I would also like to thank Tony Smibert Sensei, Shihan 7th Dan, President of Aiki-Kai Australia who through his tireless efforts has improved my Aikido as well as the way I see it in relation to a broader world context, and Robert Botterill 7th Dan Shihan who among others was one of my first teachers when I joined Aiki Kai Australia. I have been and continue to be inspired by all of them.

There are a number of people who assisted by taking photos as directed, or who allowed portions of the bodies to be used in demonstrating locks and pins and who occasionally acted as Uke. My thanks go to Ray Pedler, scenic artist, who took many of the earlier photos, David Griffiths, David Robinson, Russel Cosby and Andrew Wilson all of whom acted as Uke, and who on some occasions also took photos, and more recently Travers Hughes, Jurgen Zier, Clifford Coetzee,Lam Nguyen, Jerry Ormsby, and Yusuke Komiya.

Finally I would like to thank all the people with whom I have practiced and studied this wonderful art over the years; literally too many to name but their input is gratefully acknowledged.

Of course any mistakes, inadequacies, poor interpretation and shortcomings are a result of my incomplete understanding of Aikido and should not be taken as a reflection of anything my teachers have tried to impart. I can only do my best at any given point in time and sincerely hope that you can accept this.

This book is meant as a study guide, as a means of giving the reader (an Aikido student) some additional material and concepts to think about in addition to what is being studied with a qualified instructor in a dojo.

Some of the techniques depicted in this book are dangerous and should not be practiced without supervision of a qualified instructor in a formal class. The author and publisher can not be held responsible in any way for any physical injury, or damage of any kind, which may result from readers attempting the techniques depicted in this volume. Any one wanting to study Aikido needs to be reasonably healthy and fit and if not certain, a qualified Physician should be consulted before commencing training. Training must be taken in a proper dojo with a properly qualified instructor supervising at all times.

Part One

Introduction to Aikido

Reigi — Etiquette and Bowing

"Budo begins and ends with respect."

Morihei Ueshiba O-Sensei, Founder of Aikido
who always stressed the importance of etiquette and respect.

The Duality of Aikido.

As Aikido students we study conflict in order to understand harmony.

Conflict and harmony are opposites just as **Yin** and **Yang** (IN and YO) are opposites. Together they make the *Whole*.

Aikido practice is partner practice. By alternating the role of attacker and defender students of Aikido learn to see, feel, and understand each situation from both sides.

As Uke, we learn how to attack with conviction while at the same time trusting that Nage will not harm us, but will use our attack to study a technical response. We also learn how to take responsibility for ourselves and our actions, working on how to receive the technique by flowing with the response to minimise harm to ourselves, and learning control so that if Nage doesn't respond to our attack we can stop and wait until he is ready before trying again.

As Nage, we learn to harmonise and blend with Uke who is for the exercise lending us his body for those moments we need to practice our defence. We study how to be centred, to be calm amidst furious activity, and how to blend with a given action or situation to lead it to a suitable conclusion where neither partner suffers any damage.

The practice of being alternately attacker and defender (Uke and Nage) helps lead us to a greater understanding of the unity of Humanity and Nature. We can not escape **Nature** as we are a part of it, so we might as well embrace it.

Aikido offers us this opportunity.

"The essence of Aikido is to unite ourselves with the energy of the universe and to follow the dynamic flow of nature."

"In Aikido there are not a lot of rules. The simple act of bowing contains and maintains all the rules necessary."
Doshu Moriteru Ueshiba.

Good Manners

Good manners and respecting other people are as important in the dojo as they are outside and in everyday life.

It is common for people to ask about the practice of bowing in Aikido. In particular many people are concerned that bowing may have some religious significance.

It does not!

In western culture it is considered proper to shake hands when greeting someone, especially for the first time, or when saying goodbye. In Japanese culture, although handshaking is becoming popular, bowing fulfils these functions.

If one has reservations about bowing in the dojo, then by considering it to be the same as shaking hands should alleviate these concerns.

There are several times during an Aikido class when by tradition we bow. These are:
- On entering or leaving the dojo,
- When stepping onto or off the mat or training area,
- At the beginning and ending of the class,
- And in most dojos to each other as each person asks another to practice, or thanks the other person for training during that exercise.
- When the instructor personally demonstrates or corrects an individual's technique or practice.

When bowing to the instructor at the beginning of class, or to one's partner during class it is customary to say, **Onegaishimas**. (I request a favour, or more colloquially, shall we begin? or can I practice with you?)

When bowing at the end of the class one says, **Domo Arrigato Gozaimas,** or **Arrigato Gozaimashita.** (A polite form of saying hank you.)

Bowing during class familiarises you with an aspect of Japanese culture that is important if you wish to travel to Japan to study, to work, or even to take a holiday or to practice Aikido.
- It is an expression of respect, expressing an open mind and a willingness to learn from one's teacher and fellow student.
- It reminds you that your partner is a person, not a practice dummy.

A formal bow as you step onto the mat is a way of remembering the legacy and the teachers who came before you, who are passing on their knowledge to you, and:
- It is a sign of respect to O-Sensei the Founder of Aikido.
- It is an emptying the mind of one's outside everyday concerns in preparation for focussing on the practice to be taken during the class.

There are many other nuances to bowing in the dojo, and in time these become a part of your etiquette and respect.

Dojo Etiquette

The Dojo is where we study and practice Aikido

The word dojo means the place or location where we learn the way of — Aikido, judo, or any other art. This place could be anywhere: a hall hired for the day, a private room, a specific dedicated space, a permanent location, or even outside in a park or a garden or on the beach.

In Japan where people once came from different levels in society and who didn't under normal circumstances mix together socially, it was common practice so everyone training could be treated equally, to observe certain rules of etiquette.

In Japanese feudal society if people didn't observe strict rules of etiquette and behaviour, they quickly found themselves dead. It was a matter of survival to be polite, and to behave properly and appropriately towards members of the various levels of society. This behaviour has filtered through to modern Japan where there are still different levels in society, though it is not as obvious as it was in times past.

In Aikido dojos around the world proper etiquette (***Reigi***) is always apparent, though in some countries there is a more relaxed attitude towards etiquette than in others. Students should make an effort to be aware of proper behaviour as it reflects well upon them. If uncertain about how to behave, observe what the others in the dojo are doing and copy that. In a permanent dojo you may find a list of rules posted somewhere on a noticeboard where all of the students can see it.

Bowing

When entering or leaving the dojo, it is proper to bow in the direction of the Kamiza, which is at the front and is the focal point in the dojo. Here you will find a picture of O-Sensei Morihei Ueshiba, the Founder of Aikido. You may also find some calligraphy related to Aikido.

This is a standing bow.

A formal bow is made after stepping onto the mat. This is done from Seiza, which is a seated position. This bow is performed right at the edge of the mat by placing the left and right hands at the same time on the mat in front of you so that the two thumbs and the index finger form a triangle. It is a deep bow with the head almost touching the hands in front. This is a sign of respect for the legacy left by O-Sensei that is being passed on by the many devoted teachers and instructors all around the world. After this bow one should sit quietly in seiza for a few moments in order to empty the mind of outside concerns.

The student can now move onto the mat to wait for the training to begin.

Often students will do some light stretching or loosening exercises. A loud clap will signal class is about to begin and all the students will line up in **seiza** facing the **Kamiza**, with the highest ranked student on the right side of the dojo to the lowest ranked student in descending order to the left side of the dojo. Unranked students will sit at the very end of the left side of the line or if there is no room, will make another line behind on the left side of the dojo. When the instructor enters he may call for **Mokzu**, which is a quiet short period of meditation intended to calm the mind and focus it on the class about to begin.

Class formally begins with everyone following the instructor's bow towards the Kamiza. This is once again acknowledgement of O-Sensei's legacy. It also demonstrates our willingness to learn and shows respect for all the years of work and study others have made for Aikido to be what it is. The instructor will turn towards the students who will immediately bow to him, and he will respond in kind. In this bow the left hand is placed on the mat first followed by the right. (In some places the senior ranked student will call out Sensei or sempei ni rei before the students bow to the instructor. This is simply a call for students to show respect to the instructor by bowing.) As everyone bows they all respond with the phrase, **Onegaishimas**, which loosely means do me the favour of practicing or more colloquially, *shall we begin the practice?* This second bow to the instructor signifies the student's willingness to learn, and the instructor's response signifies his willingness to teach and is a way of thanking the students for being there. After the instructor has finished his bow the student will pull back the right hand while raising the body, then the left to finish again in the seated position.

After the loosening up exercises everyone will sit in seiza while the instructor demonstrates the first exercise or technique to be practiced. When he has finished every student bows to him. They then choose a partner for the exercise. The student may bow to the person being chosen who will respond in kind. This asking and acceptance is usually a standing bow, but in some places it could be a formal bow in seiza. (If uncertain just follow what everyone else does.) When the instructor claps to announce the end of that exercise the partners will again bow to each other as a way of saying thank you for practicing, then everyone drops into seiza to watch the instructor demonstrate the next exercise or technique. The rest of the class follows the same procedure.

At the end of the class everyone lines up facing the Kamiza exactly as they did at the beginning. The teacher leads everyone in a bow towards the Kamiza, then turns and faces the students. They all bow and the instructor responds. This is exactly the same as at the beginning of the class, except the students say **Domo Arrigato Gozaimas** a polite way of saying thank you. The students remain seated until the instructor leaves the mat. He may take a personal bow towards the Kamiza from the edge of the mat then another towards the students to thank them, or he may simply indicate that the students are free to go since class is over. At this point it is customary for the students to go about thanking each one of their training partners for the time spent practicing together.

Finally on leaving the mat each student should take a formal bow. This is not strictly imposed and often many students make an informal standing bow when leaving the mat.

> **Common sense rules.**

Since training is conducted barefoot students should wear sandals to and from the dressing room to the mat. The sandals are left at the edge of the mat during training.

Feet should be kept clean, the toenails cut. Hands too should be clean and the fingernails cut short. Aikido is a contact activity with students holding, grabbing and throwing each other. Being clean is important to maintaining good health.

Remove watches, rings, necklaces and other jewellery before training.

Make sure your keikogi or training uniform is clean. You should be wearing it, the **obi** or belt properly tied, when you step onto the mat. If you need to adjust your uniform during practice, bow to your partner and turn away from the Kamiza to adjust your uniform.

Please keep talking during class to a minimum, and then it should only be about the technique you are practicing.

If you come late to class wait beside the edge of the mat until the instructor indicates you can come on. Perform a proper kneeling bow. Move to one side and do whatever stretching and warming exercises you may need before joining the general training.

If you are having trouble with a technique, do not shout across the dojo for the instructor to help. Approach the instructor at a convenient moment and ask quietly.

If the instructor should teach you or your partner personally during class it is proper to perform a bow afterwards to thank him. While the instructor is working with your partner, kneel or sit on the mat to watch.

If you need to leave the class early or for any other reason, wait until the instructor is not demonstrating then ask for permission to leave. Remember to perform a proper formal bow before leaving the mat.

Always carry out the directives of the instructor promptly. Do not keep the rest of the class waiting for you.

Do not change clothes on the mat. There is a dressing room for that.
Remember, you are in the dojo to learn, not to gratify your ego.

Do not engage in roughhousing or needless contests of strength during class. There are no competitions in Aikido.

Take pride in your dojo. A few minutes of your time to help keep it clean is a pleasant way to begin or finish a class. If everyone helps the task is easy.

If you have a cold or the flu please refrain from training as these ailments are easily passed on the others.

In hot weather, don't forget to bring your water bottle. You are free to drink as much as you need when you need. Aikido uses a lot of energy and in hot weather it is easy to become dehydrated.

If everyone is mindful of his or her partner, then practicing Aikido should be a rewarding and fulfilling experience.

A NOTE ABOUT TERMINOLOGY.

There are many techniques practiced in Aikido; some of which have names, and many that do not. The names generally describe both the attack and the defence.

An example could be Yokomen Uchi (the attack: a strike to the side of the head using the edge of the hand, Tegatana), Shihonage (the defence or response: four corners throw) Omote or Ura (to the front or to the rear).

These names came about because the early students, who studied directly with the Founder Morihei Ueshiba – O'Sensei, and in particular the Uchideshi or live in students, needed a way to remember what O'Sensei was teaching them. By describing the attack and the response they could focus it in their mind and make it easier to remember when analysing and practicing it later. O'Sensei didn't give names to a technique unless pressed to do so by the students. He maintained that each technique was unique and could never be repeated so there was no point in naming it. However he sometimes named a technique when the students insisted, though there was no formalisation in this. It was simply a spur of the moment thing.

Eventually certain names became standardised in the minds of the senior students and these were used and passed on to newer students. Some years later as the numbers of students grew, a curriculum was devised by Kisshomaru Ueshiba (Head of Hombu Dojo at the time and later the 2nd Doshu after the death of O'Sensei) and Koiichi Tohei (Head instructor at Hombu Dojo). To all intents the names used then became standardised and are generally the names used today throughout the various Aikikai Organisations around the world.

There are however a number of Organisations (such as Yoshinkan Aikido, started by Gozo Shioda, a pre 2nd world war student of O'Sensei), which use slightly different terminology to describe the same techniques. The differences basically are dialectical rather than conceptual. The techniques are the same, just the words to describe them vary because the students came from different backgrounds, and had slightly different perceptions of what O'Sensei was demonstrating and explaining.

For example: In Yoshinkan Aikido a wrist-grab is called Tekubi Mochi or Katate Mochi, whereas in the Aikikai it is called Katate Tori. Both mean exactly the same thing. The first pinning technique (Osae waza or Katame waza) in Yoshinkan Aikido is called Ikkajo, and in Aikikai it is called Ikkyo. Again the difference for all practical purposes is dialectical. The technique is essentially the same.

In this volume, because my background is with Aikikai, I have used that terminology to describe the illustrations used throughout. A short glossary of terms can be found at the back of this book. For further and deeper explanation please ask your Aikido Instructor who is always willing to help.

Normally students **Shodan** (1st Black belt) and above wear a pleated trouser called HAKAMA. It is usually black though sometimes a deep navy blue is used.

Hakama were worn by most men in all walks of life and even by some women, although a particular style of Hakama is associated with Samurai. Mounted Samurai warriors used a Hakama of heavy cloth instead of leather leggings because it was easier to make a trouser from thick cotton type material. Leather was difficult to prepare and obtain so it was reserved for the complex flexible upper body armour. The idea of the thick trouser was to prevent damage to mounted warriors' legs from brush and grass and the pleats were there to allow easier movement.

The Samurai continued to wear the Hakama even when they became foot soldiers since by then it had become part of their dress code and the wearing of the Hakama instantly identified them as being different from everyone else.

There is a myth perpetuated by Westerners that the pleats or folds which number seven (3 in the front on the left, and 2 in the front on the right with one on each side at the back) came to have symbolic meanings with each pleat representing a variety of related concepts. They are:

Yuki — courage, valour, Bravery.

Jin — humanity, charity, benevolence.

Gi — justice, righteousness, integrity.

Rei — etiquette, civility, courtesy, obedience.

Makoto — sincerity, honesty, piety.

Chu — loyalty, fidelity, devotion..

Meiyo — honour, dignity, prestige.

I include this here for those who may be interested, since there is no real evidence in Japan that these symbolic meanings actually existed.

Wearing a Hakama today is traditional for many Budo including Aikido, Iaido, Kyudo, and Kendo, but unless an occasion is formal, such as a wedding for example, one rarely sees a Hakama worn as daily attire other than in a dojo.

It is one of the reasons why Aikido looks so elegant when practiced by senior students. The hakama adds to and emphasises the circular nature of the Aikido movements.

Having the ties and knots in front in line with one's centre (Seika Tanden or Hara) and a small back plate in the small of the back helps the Aikidoka focus on originating movement from the centre point.

It does however obscure the feet and legs, which sometimes makes it difficult for observers to see exactly how the Aikidoka is moving.

Since beginning (**Kyu** Grade) students do not in most places wear Hakama but only a training **dogi**, (*originating from Judo practice*) it was thought that the reader new to Aikido would be more comfortable seeing some of the explanatory pictures relating to basic Aikido without Hakama. Thus leg, foot and body positions for both Uke and Nage can be clearly seen.

The more advanced techniques and applications are shown with both participants wearing Hakama.

Preparation and Warming up

It is general practice in all martial arts and sports to do a series of warming up and stretching exercises before going into serious or strenuous training. Warming up is absolutely necessary to prevent injuries such as tears in the muscles or damage to ligaments and tendons which may be suddenly called upon to do fast and strong movements.

In Aikido we generally begin after the formality of bowing at the start of class with a series of breathing exercises. These help to clear the mind of extraneous thoughts and begin the process of focussing our attention on what we are going to do. They also help to fill the body with oxygen and energy. Originally from Shinto and Buddhist traditions they are commonly known as Misogi breathing exercises. They are often combined with light stretching, or with a movement that focuses on shifting our centre back and forth while remaining stable and grounded. (Funekogi or Torifune) Sometimes with this movement focus is emphasised by using Kiai.

Stretching in Aikido is light and usually done with movement. They are not deep static stretches but rather soft gentle stretching of the muscles and tendons in the legs while moving from side to side. The idea is not so much to stretch the muscles and tendons beyond where they can go but simply to warm them so afterwards during training sudden movements do not compromise flexibility or damage muscles. Particular attention is paid to joints; ankles, knees, hips, shoulders, elbows and wrists.

In relation to the joints the exercises are not extreme and only move the joints in the direction they are supposed to go rather than against this direction. This encourages them to become more flexible and stronger. It also encourages our bodies to follow this direction during application of a technique to take ukemi without damaging the manipulated joint.

Many of the warming up exercises used in Aikido are common in all martial arts and include: ankle rotation, knee bends and knee rotation, hip rotation, shoulder rotation, swinging arms to rotate shoulder joint, elbow rotation, and a series of wrist exercises that rotate the complicated wrist joint and stretch the tendons both on the inside and outside of the wrist.

Sometimes there are a number of sit-ups and push-ups practiced as part of general conditioning though in many places these are not considered necessary.

There are a number of exercises with a partner, various backstretches, and wrist exercises again but with a partner applying the stretch.

There are sensitivity exercises where one partner allows the other to lead him into a position where he can become unbalanced, teaching us how far we can be shifted before gravity makes us fall. This enables us to become aware of how much we can give to Nage to work with in developing technique before we are obliged to take Ukemi. This working together helps Uke and Nage develop trust, commitment and sensitivity to each other. This is part of learning how to harmonise with a partner, how to feel how our partner moves us, and how to adjust to that movement and position ourselves for falling (Ukemi), or going down into a position of submission to a pin or lock. (Osae waza, Katame waza)

Not all classes begin with the same exercises, and generally only a few of the many different exercises are used. Those used depend upon what the instructor has in mind as the focus for that particular class.

MISOGI BREATHING.

There are many different exercises involving breathing to help clear the lungs of stale air and to fill the body with fresh oxygen and energy. Some of them involve kiai, and some involve moving the body in unison with the breathing. They also help clear the mind of extraneous thought and thus calm the spirit.

Since most of the time our breathing is rather shallow using perhaps only the top third of the lungs, when we focus on a specific breathing exercise we are in effect utilising more of the lungs than normal to help increase the lungs' capacity to absorb oxygen and release carbon dioxide. People who suffer from problems such as Asthma have found these kinds of breathing exercises beneficial.

Some exercises are targeted at a specific area of the lungs; for example while the arms are held out at shoulder height, bent at the elbows so the hands reach towards the sky, slowly breathe in while drawing the elbows together in front of the upper chest area, causing the back half of the lungs to expand as air is breathed in. Breathe out as the arms are returned to the starting position. Repeating this exercise several times helps oxygenate the back half of the lungs. The exercise is then reversed, breathing in as the arms open up to fill the front half of the lungs with fresh air, then breathing out of course as we bring the arms together in front of the chest.

Other exercises focus on the bottom two thirds drawing air deeply down into the lungs into areas that are under utilised in normal everyday unconscious breathing.

A whole training session could be devoted only to breathing and focussing on drawing in and generating energy, but this would probably only occur at a week long training camp where deeper aspects of Aikido training are explored. Most normal classes will incorporate one or two breathing exercises at the start of class, with perhaps another at the end as part of a cool down period.

A typical exercise is to imagine drawing energy from the heavens down, compressing it into the body.

Begin with the hands in front of the **seika tanden** or central one-point. The arms are opened out to expand the chest and lungs. While slowly breathing in gradually raise the arms above the head. The feeling is as if we are trying to gather as much air and energy as we can. Imagine reaching far beyond the extension of our arms, as far as the edge of the universe. As we raise our arms above our head still breathing in we are attempting to grasp the whole universe around us.

When the fingertips are almost touching and we can't get any more air into the lungs we pause for a moment. Exhale slowly as the hands are lowered down along the body's centre line. We should have the feeling that we are compressing all the energy we have gathered down into our one point.

Before allowing the arms to drop down in front of our thighs this final position is held for a moment so the energy can settle into our one-point. The exercise is repeated perhaps four times before moving on to the next one.

Another exercise (**Hachi Wari**) is sometimes used at the start of a class, but more often than not at the end as the final part of a cool down is done in seiza.

Initially bending from the waist we stretch forward as far as we can comfortably reach. From this point while breathing in slowly we raise the arms as high above the head as possible. Close the fists to lock in the energy drawn up from the ground. Begin exhaling and draw the arms down sharply until they are parallel with the shoulders. While continuing to exhale loudly, the arms are raised slightly then brought down again. This is continued three or four times. Each time the arms are not raised as high as the first time and are brought down lower and lower. The feeling is like pumping the air out of the lungs.

When all the air is forced out of the lungs and the arms are at their lowest point reach out in front, again bending from the waist. Begin breathing in and repeating the exercise.

Funekogi undo is an important exercise and it is nearly always practiced near the start of a class either before the breathing exercises or as the conclusion of the breathing exercises.

It is a **misogi** breathing exercise whether done with kiai or without. In action it appears as a kind of rowing exercise and many people equate it with the style of standing-up rowing the fishermen of Japan's inland sea use while rowing their fishing boats.

In actual fact it teaches how to coordinate body movement with breathing while remaining stable and centred. An understanding of this kind of movement is essential not only for **Kokyunage** techniques but for most other techniques as well.

The movement begins in left stance **(Hidari Hanmi)**. The back leg is straight and the front leg bent. Weight is centred over the front leg and arms are extended with the hands open. It is essential to be aware of the

| FUNEKOGI UNDO —Tori Funi Undo |

hips (*which enclose the one point or seika tandan*), and to initiate the movement by shifting the hips back. As the hips move back body weight begins to transfer from the front leg to the back leg which accommodates the transfer of weight by bending. The front leg will now be straight. At the same time as the hips move back the arms are drawn back. The hands close into fists (*with the thumb inside the clenched fingers rather than outside the fingers as in a normal fist*) trapping the energy grasped in front and drawing it back towards the waist. The hands finish beside the waist at the same moment as the hips complete their backwards movement.

Remember, the hips move first to initiate the drawing back of the arms.

This drawing back movement is accompanied by inhaling sufficient air to fill the lungs. As the hands open to release the gathered energy the hips move forward. The arms rise up and extend forward as if propelled by the hip movement. They follow the hips forward using the energy from the centre to extend through to the open fingertips where it can be released. Energy is also drawn up from the earth through the back leg into the hips where it can be added to the energy extended through the arms to be released through the fingers. The breath that accompanies this forward movement is a strong exhalation.

If the exercise is repeated without **kiai** the breathing is timed to inhale as you draw back and exhale as you extend forward. When using **kiai**, sufficient breath must be inhaled in that first drawing back to enable a strong **kiai** over several back and forth movements. Also the **kiai** is timed to the movement. The sound of the extension is **iiiii,** and drawing back it becomes **ho. (iiiiiho).**

The second part of the movement begins in right stance (***Migi Hanmi***) and is exactly the same as for ***Hidari Hanmi***. This time however the **kiai** changes to **iiiii-** while extending and **sa** while drawing in. (**iiiiisa**). If a third set is practiced it is back to ***Hidari Hanmi*** and faster in execution than the first two sets. The **kiai** that accompanies this movement is an extended **iiiii** sound both forwards and backwards. (**iiiii-iiiii**). Since one leg bends while the other straightens as you move forwards or backwards the hips and the upper body should move without bobbing up or down producing a smooth, parallel, well grounded movement forwards and backwards.

Following the ***Hidari hanmi*** movement a non stance position is taken with the legs about shoulder width apart. The arms are raised above the head palms together, a deep breath taken, and exhaled as the hands are lowered and clasped (*left over right*) in front of the one point and vigorously shaken. This is called **Furitama**, which is part of an ancient Shinto ritual where the spirit is shaken down into the body. If the body is relaxed with the knees slightly bent the vigorous shaking of the hands should vibrate the whole body. It helps focus energy into the one point. This is repeated after each ***funegogi*** set.

Following the third time a slight stretch is done with the hands clasped. This stretch is used to make the student aware of the space around his centre, how far up, how far around, how far below he can reach into the sphere that surrounds the body.

Other stretching then follows. These are not usually the deep static stretches used in some martial arts, but rather they are moving, gradually extending stretches used to warm muscles and tendons so any sudden movement during training will not cause damage.

Beginning with the legs wide apart and gently rocking from side to side, the muscles and tendons of each leg are alternatively stretched and relaxed.

Each movement from side to side is deeper than the previous until finally the body is as close to the mat as possible. At this final point with the body weight on one leg while the other is stretched out, heel to the mat and toes pointing upwards, the stretch is held for a few moments before being shifted to the same deep stretch on the other side.

During the pause in this deep position the participant should try to relax as much as possible before changing across to the other side.

Following this stretch there could be one or two others, the most common one being sinking into the equivalent of a horse riding stance *(Shikko Dachi)*, and with a hand resting on each knee to help maintain the outward stretch of the legs, the upper body is turned first to one side as far as possible, then slowly back to the other.

The breathing pattern is to exhale as you extend to either side and to breathe in as you return through the central position.

There are many other stretches for the arms and shoulders, often practiced with one person assisting the other to stretch. We should be extremely careful doing partner assisted stretches as it is too easy for one person to overstretch the other, which could possibly cause severe damage.

The number and type of stretches used at the start of an Aikido class varies from class to class and from instructor to instructor, being a matter of personal preference along with movement and concepts the instructor may wish to explore in a training session.

HAISHIN UNDO
Back stretcching with a partner

There are many variants of Haishin Undo but two in particular are most often practiced.

This first one is used at the start of a class and is included in the various stretches and warming up and loosening exercises in preparation for the techniques of an Aikido class.

One partner gets down on hands and knees. The other stands beside, then squatting down so that the buttocks become level with the kneeling partner's hips; he gently stretches back across his kneeling partner. This is practically a whole body stretch. This position is held for a few moments before the stretching partner returns to the slightly squatting position. Remaining in the squatting position helps strengthen the muscles in the legs. The back stretch is usually repeated 10 times. The partners then change roles and the other person has the opportunity to do the same exercise.

The standing form of **Haishin Undo** is mostly used as a final exercise (the end of a cooling down period) at the end of a class.

Uke holds the hands or wrists of his partner. Both turn until they are back to back, then Nage drops his hips until they are just below Uke's hips finally leaning forward to draw Uke up onto the back for a long body stretch. Uke can let go at any time if he feels uncomfortable. After about 10 to 15 seconds Nage returns to a standing position, gently lowering his partner back to the floor. They then swap roles and repeat the exercise.

Other stretches done with a partner are often the first part of a specific technique.

They are practiced slowly as both a stretching exercise and as a body movement (*Tai Sabaki*) and used as preparation for the full technique. Typical examples are **Gyaku Hanmi Katatetori Tai no Henka**, or **Kokyuho** (See page 65, Responding to an attack and Application of Technique). Often **Shomen Uchi Iriminage** or **Ai Hanmi Katatetori Iriminage** is used as a backstretch where the technique is entered but the throw is not completed or taken past Uke's point of balance. The exercise is to prepare the body for the technique to be done later.

Shown below is an example from *Ryotetori*. (*Two hands grabbing.*)

This exercise, **Shiho Giri**, is in effect the same as **Ryotetori shihonage omote** as far as body movement is concerned, although the hand positions are slightly different to those taken if the throw is completed.

Tekubi Kansetsu Junan Ho
wrist exercises

These exercises help develop strength and flexibility in the muscles and tendons of the wrists. They are always done during the warm up period at the start of a training session, often following after other types of moving stretches have been practiced. They are a part of the conditioning process which prepares you for the techniques that could be practiced during class.

All the wrist exercises are used in throwing and pinning techniques, and each exercise has the same name as the technique it becomes.

Practicing these wrist stretches during the warm up period gives each student an understanding of how it will feel when that technique is being applied, and how far it can be allowed to go before having to take **ukemi**.

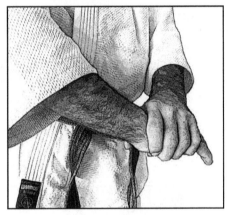

Ikkyo exercise

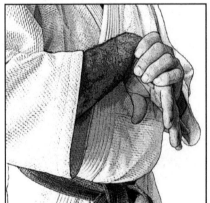

There should be no gap between the palm of the hand and the top of the other wrist.

The strongest part of the grip should be with the little finger and the thumb.

Keeping the arms close to the body the wrist is drawn up as far as possible. A substantial stretch should be felt across the top of the wrist.

A variation of this is to close the fist, then draw it up in the same way, but this time holding the closed fist from underneath rather than on top. This will give a much greater stretch.

In all stretching exercises one should only go as far as needed to feel the stretch. Overdoing it to the extent where it is painful is not necessary and will only cause damage.

The more often the stretches are practiced the more flexible and stronger the wrist becomes.

As in all the following exercises, the stretch is usually repeated five to ten times for each wrist.

In Aikido it is customary to work both sides of the body equally, so any exercise or technique done on the left side is repeated on the right.

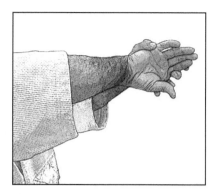 

Nikyo exercise

Nikyo begins by extending the arm with the palm turned outwards. The other hand grasps the extended hand as shown, making sure there is no gap between the grasping hand and the top of the extended hand. The extended hand is then drawn in as far as possible towards the approximate centre of the chest.

It is essential that the thumb of the extended hand is also trapped by the grasping hand or the exercise is not effective. The grasped hand is drawn in towards the centre of the chest and held for a few seconds. Arms are kept close to the body. Sometimes the hands are turned upwards slightly towards the face to put as much stretch as possible on the tendons and muscles. The arms are extended back out again, relaxed for a brief moment, then the drawing in is repeated.

 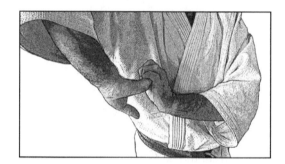

Sankyo exercise

With **Sankyo** the fingers of one hand are laid on the palm of the other. The fingers and the hand on top are then twisted inwards and back under the armpit. The palm of the twisted hand finishes facing outwards. This stretch also rotates the bones of the forearm against the elbow until they can not turn further.

As in all these exercises there are variations that can be used. Another variation is to hold one hand in front of your chest with the palm facing away from you, and then use your other hand to extend that palm further outwards as far as possible. This works the wrist while gently stretching all the muscles of the arm as you extend it forward.

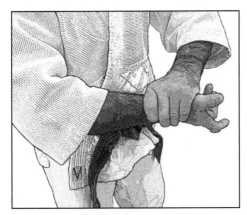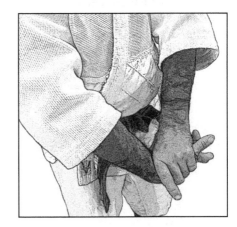

Yonkyo exercise

Yonkyo as an exercise is a downward wrist extension with the palm up. This is basically the opposite of the Ikkyo exercise. Here some pressure is applied to the radial bone as the hand is extended downward. The whole arm and shoulders should be relaxed so the only pressure and stretch felt is in the wrist. The knuckle of the first finger sits on the radial bone and exerts the pressure as the arm is extended downward.

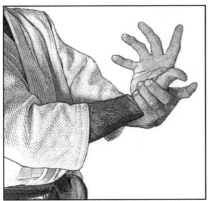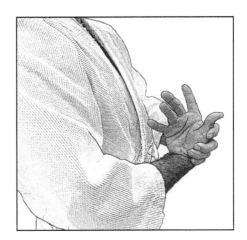

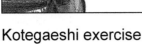
Kotegaeshi exercise

Hold the hand in front of your chest with the palm facing towards you. Grasp the wrist with the palm of your other hand making sure you grip the thumb area with the little and the ring fingers. The other fingers also grip but not as strongly. The thumb of the gripping hand puts pressure on the base of the little finger of the gripped hand to assist in turning the whole hand. The gripped hand is drawn down towards your centre while the gripped thumb area is turned outwards. Hold this positing for a moment before allowing both hands to rise back in a relaxed manner to the starting position.

This particular exercise is very similar to the **Kotegaeshi** but the grip is slightly different. The thumb rests in the palm of the gripped hand instead of against the base of the little finger as in the previous exercise. The hand is stretched out and extended over the shoulder. This works the bones in the forearm as well as the muscles and tendons. Note how it also helps stretch the tendons in the elbow area.

Shihonage exercise

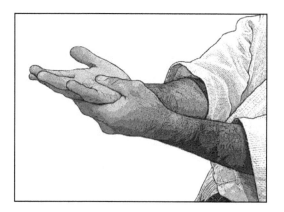

This opposite view shows how far over the hand and arm can be extended. By extending even further around and down towards the floor the body will naturally turn and bend over that way and a forward rolling ukemi can be practiced adding a further dimension to this exercise

This final exercise doesn't have a name but is always done as it is the only one that stretches the inside of the wrist.

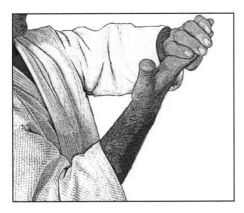 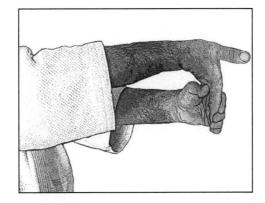

Hold one hand up in front of your face with palm facing towards you. Grip the fingers on the top with your thumb underneath. Stretch the arm outwards as far as it will go pushing forward with your thumb while pulling the fingers down at the same time. This should open up the wrist and stretch the tendons and muscles on the inside. This should also lock the elbow so the arm becomes as straight as it will go.

Whenever doing any of the wrist exercises we should at all times maintain a relaxed and receptive body. The shoulders especially should be relaxed. Focus on trying to feel how the muscles and tendons in the wrist, the forearm and the elbow are responding to the various exercises. Practicing them very slowly at home or before a training session is a good way to understand how they work and how they affect your body's response. Then when practicing the same exercises with a partner applying the technique it becomes easier to respond in a manner that doesn't allow damage to occur.

Another point to consider is that each of these exercises actually works the wrist joint in the directions it can turn, so with practice you develop flexibility and strength at the same time.

Some of these exercises are isolated from the technique and practiced slowly to give Uke an opportunity to learn how to allow his body to respond, and how to position to take appropriate ukemi.

Nage applying Sankyo   *Nage applying Kotegaeshi*

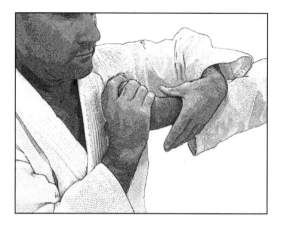 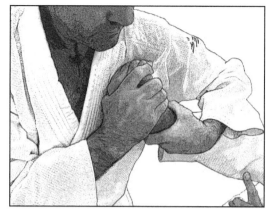

Nage applies **Nikyo** against his shoulder for leverage. By dropping his elbow and leaning forward slightly, as if taking a slight bow, pressure is applied to Uke's wrist at the point where the radial bones join the wrist bones. Uke will drop to the floor to alleviate any pain. Uke can also indicate he has received enough by slapping his side and Nage will release the pressure.

Both partners can practice carefully applying **Nikyo** in this manner to learn how much pressure to apply from Nage's point of view, and how much pressure can be received from Uke's point of view. The point of the exercise is to learn correct application of the wrist lock and at what point **ukemi** should be taken.

This is a more advanced application, and is basically the same as if Uke was practicing this exercise by himself. The extended arm position is the same except instead of applying the stretch himself by drawing in with his other hand Nage is applying the Nikyo stretch by gripping Uke's wrist with one hand and applying the stretch with the other. Dropping to the floor lessens the pain by undoing the stretch being applied by Nage. However, to maintain his control Nage will follow Uke's downward movement continuing to apply the **Nikyo** stretch. This eventually becomes an arm lock. To finish the complete technique Nage will spin Uke around and guide him down so he finishes face down on the mat. Nage then changes the wrist lock into an arm pin to immobilise Uke.

See pages 88 to 95, and page 106 for details regarding Nikyo and its application...

Nage applying Nikyo arm pin

Katame Waza

Katame Waza are techniques that involve pinning, locking or immobilising Uke in one way or another. Usually the arm, wrist or elbow are involved in these techniques after Uke is taken to the ground either by leading down, unbalancing enough to cause a fall, or by throwing. Nage follows Uke down to the ground to apply the immobilisation.

Most martial arts have a variety of methods for immobilising an opponent, and in many cases they appear to be the same; after all there are only so many ways a wrist can be twisted or an arm bent. The appearance of similarity however is superficial, as what underlies the application of the technique is the philosophy behind it — the reason it is applied and the effect it has on the person to whom it is applied.

If the reason is to do as much damage as possible then it is easy to dislocate shoulders, tear rotator cuffs, ruin elbows by snapping the joint, break wrists with excessive twisting, tear muscles and damage soft tissue, and there are martial arts that will teach this.

O-Sensei Morihei Ueshiba, The Founder of Aikido in one of his many aphorisms said: *"To injure an opponent is to injure yourself. To control aggression without inflicting injury is the Art of Peace."*

In Aikido we try to minimise damage firstly by exercising the wrists and arms individually and with a partner, and secondly when applying the lock or pin, working the joint only in the direction it naturally moves rather than against the way it moves.

There are some exceptions of course but these are only practiced when students are reasonably advanced and have an understanding of how the body's various joints work and exactly what their individual pain threshold is from practicing the previously described wrist exercises over a period of time.

Initially for the beginning student, the pins and locks may seem painful, but the moment the lock or pin is released the pain dissipates. The key to absorbing the apparent pain of a pin or lock as it is being applied is to remain as relaxed as possible and to allow the body to move just ahead of the pain threshold to receive and absorb it.

Some examples of pinning techniques are **Ikkyo**, **Nikyo**, **Sankyo**, and **Yonkyo**. These are very similar to the individual wrist exercises of the same name and are shown here as examples. (*The techniques that lead to these pins are described in "Application of Technique" beginning on page 81.*) Sometimes the following pinning techniques are practiced isolated from the technique that leads to them as an exercise in understanding where and how to pin.

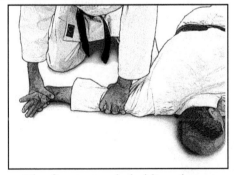

*Ikkyo
Ude Osae*

There are two holds for Ikkyo Ude Osae. The first is simply holding the wrist as the elbow is twisted forward to prevent Uke from moving the arm. The arm is held at an angle above the shoulder and Nage though square on to the arm is at a slightly oblique angle to Uke's body. The knee against the ribcage and the outward extension of the arm prevents Uke from moving. The second is the same as the first other than holding the hand in a Nikkyo type grip and turning the fingers back towards Uke's head. This is a much stronger pin and results from dealing with a grabbing attack rather than a striking attack.

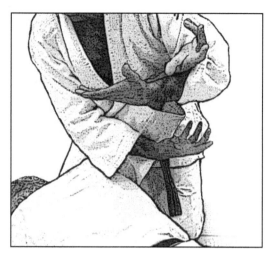

Nikyo
Kote Mawashi

Nage's knees trap Uke's shoulder preventing movement. Uke's elbow is drawn in tight against Nage's one point. The wrist is held tight against the chest.

Nage then rotates his upper body towards Uke's head. This applies the arm lock to totally immobilise Uke. If Uke is relaxed Nage will be able to feel the arm tighten and will know when to stop applying the lock.

When Uke feels he can't stand any more tightening or pain he taps the mat with his free hand indicating that he would like to be released.

Nage releases Uke and moves away.

Sankyo
Kote Hineri

With the **Sankyo** grip Nage cuts the arm down and taking the elbow he moves in front, stepping backwards to draw Uke down forwards. (**Omote**) The pin is similar to **Nikkyo** except the palm of Uke's hand is held against Nage's shoulder to apply the arm pin. This comes on much stronger than **Nikkyo** because the elbow is twisted and locked to prevent movement.

Note the arms are reversed for Sankyo compared to Nikyo.

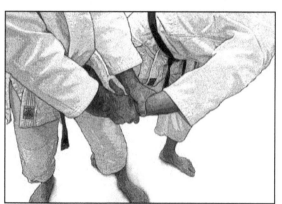

Yonkyo
Tekubi Osae

Yonkyo is applied to the inside of the fore arm on the radial bone. The arm is cut down as if wielding a **bokken**. Nage steps in and uses his shin against Uke's elbow to extend the lock and prevent movement.

Tai Sabaki — Body Movement

Usually after the wrist exercises and before any preliminary exercises such as partner assisted stretching Tai Sabaki or body movements are practiced. It is essential for beginners to practice these body movements so that they become natural and are performed without thinking because they will find these movements in various combinations in all applications of technique.

Initially feet should be shoulder width apart with weight evenly balanced. The centreline of the body should be over a point exactly between the two feet.

Knees are slightly bent so legs are not locked, and with arms hanging loosely by side of body. From this initial relaxed position (*Shizentai*) we move into left or right hanmi stance. From hanmi, we can move freely in any direction — Forwards, sideways, backwards, using either straight lines of entry or a circular motion forwards or backwards to enter into a position from which a technique can be applied.

Hanmi — Stance

Feet are shoulder width apart and body is slightly oblique. Vertical centre line remains as indicated by asterisk. Knees slightly bent to allow easy movement forward, backward, or to either side. Weight is slightly towards front foot.

One should feel a strong connection to the earth. While moving in any direction weight should be lowered and centred. The body should not bounce up and down but feel as if gliding along. *This means stepping on the ball of the foot and not on the heel.* Stepping on the heel tends to straighten the legs, locking the knees and produces a high centre of gravity which is unstable. Using the ball of the foot keeps the knees slightly bent and makes it easier to move quietly and smoothly, almost like gliding across a smooth surface while still remaining stable with a lower centre of gravity.

All movement begins from the centre (**Hara, Dantien, Seika Tanden**) so focus should begin here. This point is just below the navel in the centre between the hips.

When you move, *the hips move first*, the legs and body follow naturally. In time, moving from the hips rather than shifting the feet becomes natural and is done without thought.

left   right

Migi Hanmi — right stance

Practicing technique in a seated position (Seiza) and moving from this position is called suwari waza (seated techniques) and is excellent for developing the concept of moving from the hips.

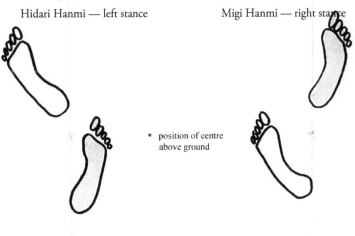

Hidari Hanmi — left stance   Migi Hanmi — right stance

* position of centre above ground

TSUGI ASHI

Sliding forward and follow up step

Moving to either side of the line of the incoming attack (Indicated by pencil drawn arrow) allows the defender to bypass the attacker and to be in an advantageous position to redirect the attacker's energy.

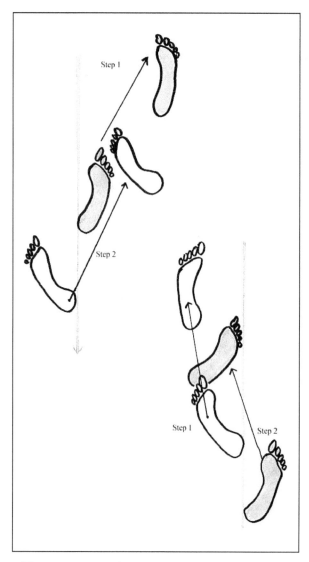

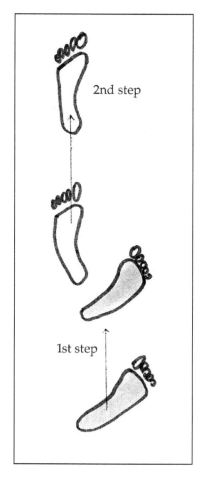

The upper example is **Migi Hanmi.**
The right foor moves first and the left follows. Hanmi is maintained off line to the right,

In the lower exampole *the left foor moves first with the right foot following.* **Hidari hanmi** *is maintained offline to the left.*

Sending step.
(Sometimes called **Okuri Ashi**)
Above is an alternative method of *Tsugi Ashi*. Here the rear foot moves up to just behind the front foot. The front foot then steps forward. This is the same for either hanmi though only the left hanmi is shown. Generally this movement would be more of a straight line forward rather than off line at an angle. However it is just as easy to move off at an angle once the back foot has been placed behind the front foot.

This **okuri ashi** or stepping movement can also be sideways, left or right, without changing stance. As with all movement the weight should be concentrated through the balls of the feet with the heels barely touching. Never settle all weight flat on the feet as this prevents easy movement. In all these movements, the body should appear to glide forward or backward or sideways at various angles depending which way the movement goes. There should be no obvious stepping, or bouncing up and down. Also the feet should not be dragged so they make a sliding sound. If the foot is light enough and just barely touching the mat there will hardly be any noise at all.

Tsugi Ashi — front foot stepping, back foot following...

step forward   *bring up back foot*   *step forward*

Tsugi Ashi — back foot stepping up to front, front moving forward...

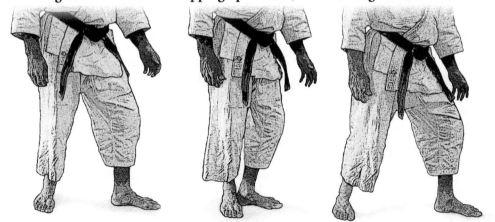

bring back foot forward   *and step forward with front foot*

These two ways of stepping look exactly the same for someone watching, but the feeling for the person doing them is totally different. Stepping forward and bringing up the back foot has the feeling of almost dragging the foot forward, whereas bringing the back foot up to the front allows the person to push dynamically forwards. It does seem to have more energy...

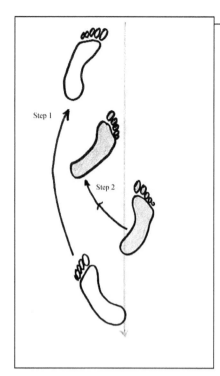

Issoku Irimi

Stepping through and changing stance.

With this movement, beginning in right **hanmi** the left foot moves around and past the right foot. The right foot then drifts across and slightly forward to finish in left **hanmi,** or the opposite stance, and on the left side of the incoming attack. **This is a deeper entry than Tsugi Ashi, finishing behind rather than next to the attacker.**

To move to the other side one begins in left **hanmi** and steps firstly with the right foot.

Every movement in Aikido is practiced on both the left and right sides. This develops the ability to move either left or right unhindered by preference, and after practicing for some time the ability to move and react without even thinking about it.

Moving either side becomes as natural as walking down the street. In fact all movements in Aikido eventually become as natural as walking, which we do all the time without even considering how we do it. It is something we have learnt with the core of our being. In time Aikido movements will also emanate from our core in a spontaneous and unhindered fashion.

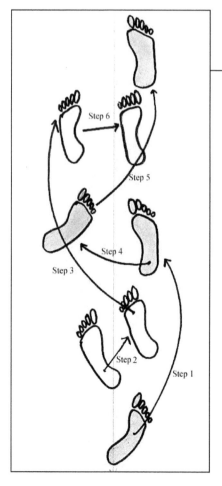

Irimi Ashi

Moving forward and changing stance.

Moving forward (**Irimi**), entering and crossing to either side of an imaginary line. This is basically the same as **Issoku Irimi** except more than one step is taken. Each time, the **foot movement originates from a movement of the hip.**

Step 1. The hip moves right side forward and the right leg follows to step. As the hip realigns itself in relation to the stance the back foot then drifts across to the correct position. (Step 2.)

Step 3. The left hip then turns forward and the back left leg steps forward into the opposite stance with the right foot following. (Step 4)

Step 5 is a repeat of step 1, and so on.

The forward movement is from Hidari hanmi to Migi hanmi to Hidari hanmi etc.

This movement can also be done backwards. It is the exact reverse of the forward movement.

Once again, **the hips initiate the movement.** As the hip turns backward the front leg naturally follows and this then becomes the backward step into the opposite stance.

Ayumi Ashi *— This is basically the same movement as Irimi Ashi, but there is less movement to either side of the forward line of movement.*

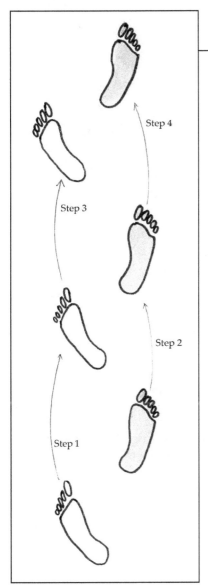

Step 4

Step 3

Step 2

Step 1

Ayumi Ashi

Moving forward with gliding steps while changing stance

This is not unlike normal walking forward, except that the arms swing in line with the legs, (r*ight arm with right leg, left arm with left leg*), thus alternating between left **hanmi** and right **hanmi**. The knees are kept bent so the movement forward is almost like gliding across the mat. It should be smooth and the body should not bob up and down.

This is generally straight moving forwards rather than moving from side to side as with ***Irimi ashi*** and ***tsugi ashi***

Note that one complete half of your body moves forward at a time, followed by the other half.

Two variations of this movement are where the stance stays the same rather than alternating left and right. This is achieved by firstly moving the back foot behind the front foot, then stepping forward with the front foot. This is repeated each step so the stance stays the same and the body is slightly angled sideways. Generally the movement will be slightly diagonal.

The other way is the back foot moves across in front of the front foot, which then moves forward. Again the one stance is maintained and the body moves forward slightly sideways.

Ayumi Ashi is basically the same movement as **Irimi Ashi** though there is less movement off line to either side.

Ayumi Ashi variations

Stepping across in front allows Nage to enter behind Uke when the second step is completed.

Stepping behind and moving forward allws Nage to enter deep behind Uke.

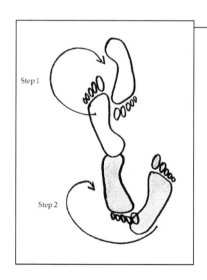

Step 1

Step 2

Tenkai

pivot 180 degrees on balls of feet...

Pivot 180 degrees to face opposite direction.

Both feet almost pivot at the same time and at the end of the turn, stance (*Hanmi*) is opposite to the start.

If starting position is **Hidari Hanmi**, finishing position is **Migi Hanmi**. If **Migi Hanmi** is the start then **Hidari Hanmi** is the finish.

In this exercise however, the position of the arms in relation to the stance is reversed after the first move. That is instead of right leg and right arm forward (*Migi Hanmi)*, finish position is right leg forward with left arm extended. Turning back again continues this opposite arm and leg position; left leg forward right arm extended.

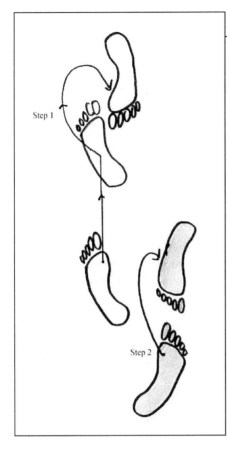

Step 1

Step 2

Kaiten

step forward and pivot 180 degrees ...

This is the exact same move as **Tenkai**, pivoting 180 degrees on the balls of the feet to face the opposite direction.

But in this instance one enters slightly first by taking a sliding step forward, or to the side, before commencing to pivot. Again the finish is in opposite stance with reverse arm extended.

Both these exercises are often used against a mid level punch and by stepping to the side and turning 180 degrees with the opposite hand forward this hand can be used to take hold of the punch or to deflect it and redirect it.

It should be noted than when practicing kaiten with a partner or against an opponent one should step off line first before making the turn.

Remember, your opponent is coming towards you, so there is no need for you to step towards him. Rather you should step to the side as his attack arrives at the position you originally were standing. Your opponent will suddenly find himself entering into an empty space and perhaps momentarily becoming disconcerted. This gives you time to redirect the attack to unbalance or throw him.

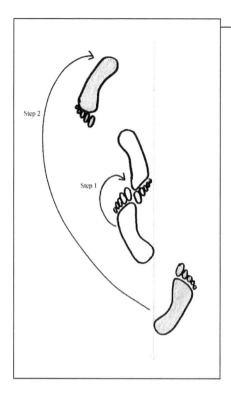

Tenkan

a backwards turn around the front foot

Turn backwards 180 degrees beginning with hip. As front foot begins to pivot, allow back leg to swing around behind front foot, to finish facing the opposite direction.

Finish in the same stance as the start. *Hidari Hanmi to Hidari Hanmi or Migi Hanmi to Migi Hanmi.*

The finish position is parallel to, and a mirror image of (*the attacker's*) Uke's position.

This turn naturally shifts Nage (*the defender*) at least one shoulder width off the line of attack,

However *many students fail to remember to step off the line so as not to impede the incoming attacker which can leave them open to being grabbed or struck.*

The very first movemnet should be a slight step off line without making it obvious. (*In effect, Irimi*) This way when Nage disappears it catches Uke by surprise.

Shift weight forward enough to allow pivoting on the front foot. **This movement begins by turning the hip.** As the hips turn backwards control the moveement of the back leg and continue to step around to the rear. Once the step is complete, readjust stance.

Irimi Tenkan

step forwards and turn backwards 180 degrees...

The back foot steps forward to become momentarily the front foot. The rest of the movement is the same as **Tenkan**.

Pivot on the front foot and allow the back foot to swing around behind, so body has turned 180 degrees.

Note that *Hanmi* is now opposite to that of the starting position. *Hidari Hanmi* start to *Migi Hanmi* finish.

In the finish position Nage is also facing same direction as Uke, but is behind rather than parallel to Uke.

With *Tenkan* one simply shifts to the side and turns to avoid an attack. With I*rimi Tenkan* one enters first (*at an oblique angle off to the side*) then turns to avoid, finishing slightly behind the attacker, preferably behind Uke's leading shoulder, which in effect is his blind spot, a position from which he cannot reach you no matter which way he turns.

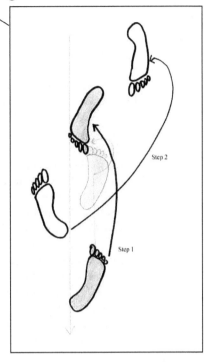

Hantai Tenkan

step through and turn 90 degrees...

This is the same start as *Irimi Tenkan*.

That is the back foot moves forward to become the front foot, but instead of turning 180 degrees, the turn is only 90 degrees.

The finish position has Nage facing towards the side of Uke.

The stance (*Hanmi*) is once again the opposite of the commencing stance.

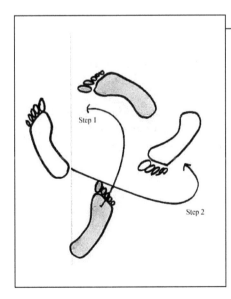

MOVING AIKIDO.

One of the most important aspects of Aikido is movement.

Moving in — *IRIMI*
Moving around — *TENKAN, IRIMI TENKAN*
Moving beside — *TENKAI, KAITEN, HANTAI TENKAN*
Moving behind — *USHIRO*

There are no backwards movements in Aikido: every movement begins with the intent of entering (*Irimi*).

All movement can be done to the left and the right side. Often combinations of two or three movements are blended together without conscious thought. It simply happens in a natural way.

Even when grabbed forcefully, if Nage (the person being grabbed) is relaxed, a variety of movements can be done without any strength being necessary. It is this ability to move which allows Nage to unbalance Uke and thus execute a throw or a takedown and pin.

The Reasons for moving are:
To avoid being overwhelmed by a strong attack…

By allowing the energy of the attack (*Ki*) to flow past, giving time to control this energy by redirecting it so that it dissipates and Uke is unbalanced at which point Uke can easily be controlled or induced to fall.

To redirect the energy into a circular pattern so Uke spins further away and can easily be thrown or pinned. (*Centrifugal force applies here.*)

To draw Uke's attack in to your centre usually in a partially circular pattern (*Centripetal force applies here.*) where you can easily control the aggression.

Simply to evade so the attack is dissipated into nothing.

Evading an attack doesn't mean running away. It means entering into the attack in some form to destabilise it, at which point Uke can be given extra impetus by a slight body movement from Nage, so that Uke must take a fall, or Nage just continues to move past so the attack is rendered ineffectual because the target is no longer there.

Evading also means leading the attack from its point of full commitment to beyond its natural limit at which moment the attacker becomes unbalanced and a throw or pin can be applied.

This is more difficult to do than it seems. **The general tendency to pull or drag Uke into a throw will be resisted, so Nage must focus on not doing this, but by using a subtle leading movement at the moment of contact may well induce Uke to overextend to the point where he is vulnerable to being toppled over or thrown.**

Movements are practiced individually, in pairs, or in groups with one person taking a turn to be Nage while the others are Uke. Each partner or group member takes a turn to be Nage as well as Uke.

Most of the movements shown in this section are practiced as part of the body preparation done at the beginning of a typical class. Not all of these movements are used all the time. Generally only those that will apply to the techniques the teacher wishes the student to practice during that class will be used during this part of the class.

The concept of IRIMI and the concept of TENKAN are two most important and fundamental concepts in Aikido.

Irimi means entering and *Tenkan* means turning to the rear.

We always enter directly in towards Uke's centre at a slightly oblique angle to the line of attack to be either inside or outside of the direction of attack. — Or we turn around the line of attack from a fixed point in front but off the direct line of attack to enter to the rear of Uke.

Variations and combinations of these two fundamental concepts give us all the movements we need in Aikido. There is no stepping backwards, there is only entering (*Irimi*) or turning around to the rear (*Tenkan*).

Combining these gives us *Irimi Tenkan,* or variants such as *Issoku Irimi Tenkan, Tsugi Ashi Tenkan, Hantai Tenkan, Tsugi Ashi Kaiten, Tenkai,* and so on.

There is always an *Irimi* movement, no matter how small, before the *Tenkan* or variant of *Tenkan*. **Even if there isn't a physical Irimi movement to initiate Nage's response, there is the intention of Irimi before the actual physical Tenkan movement takes place.**

If the concepts of Irimi and of Tenkan are kept in mind at all times while practicing then we are less likely to make the mistake of entering and stepping back in an attempt to drag Uke around. We are more likely to step forward and blend with Uke's movement as we turn. Blending and turning will lead Uke around in our desired direction with little effort as the movement is a continuation of Uke's own natural forward movement. If the timing and blending is right Uke may not even feel what is happening to him until his legs go out from underneath and finds himself taking a gravity assisted fall.

It takes a long time to achieve this harmonious smooth blending and leading. Much patience and perseverance along with regular practice is required.

SHIKKO (Knee Walking)

Moving from a formal seated position (*Seiza*) is probably the most difficult way of moving for students beginning Aikido. Even for advanced students, doing seated techniques that require movement on the knees is difficult and many do not practice in a seated position, especially if they have had problems with their knees, or have arthritis or other age related injuries, or sports injuries that have in some way damaged the knees.

There are some benefits from practicing *Suwari Waza* or seated techniques. These include strengthening of the large leg muscles, learning to move by using the hips, teaching the student how to be focussed on one's centre and its development of *Ki* energy, learning how to extend one's energy, and finding how to do a technique in a manner that is economical and efficient because one doesn't have use of the legs. All of these benefits help improve ability to perform standing techniques (*Tachi Waza*), which is probably the greatest benefit of all.

In ancient times Warriors at court during formal occasions at all times had to be ready to defend their Daimyo or Lord. They had to be able to move freely, to fight and draw their weapons, to move from a seated position to a standing position, or anywhere in between. Their ability to fight from a seated position is legendary, and although of not much practical use today, this tradition of *suwari waza* has been maintained as an important element in Aikido training.

A few schools however don't do *shikko* because they consider it irrelevant to today's times.

There are three approaches in general training and these are: *Tachi Waza* or standing techniques, *Hanmi Handachi Waza*, techniques which have one person (Nage) seated and one person (Uke) standing, and *Suwari Waza* where both Uke and Nage are seated and perform techniques on their knees.

The moving Triangle
Shikko

Beginning in seiza...

There is a triangle formed with the point being where the feet are, and with the knees representing the two other points.

Movement is not done as if walking when standing but as if moving this imaginary triangle. The whole triangle moves forward by swivelling on one point (the right knee in the diagram), then alternatively swivelling around the other point (the left knee). The two feet should stay together for effective movement.

In some traditional dojos, as an initial way of teaching the importance of keeping the feet together they were loosely tied with an old obi or a piece of rope around the ankles so the legs couldn't be used as one would in normal walking.

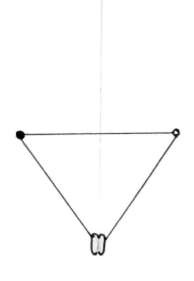

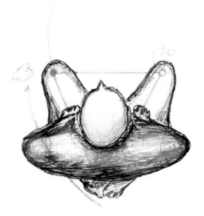

A triangle or a triangular base is extremely stable with the body's weight pressing down just behind the centre of the triangle and evenly distributed between the three points, which represent the left knee, the right knee, and both feet held together.

As the left knee moves forward in an arc swivelling around the right knee, the two feet follow together in the same arc as indicated by the arrows in the diagram.

Before any move can be made one must raise one's centre and sit back on the balls of the feet.

By shifting the weight onto the right side the left hip can move forward. The left knee will naturally move as well and so will the feet.

When enough distance has been covered, approximately one body width, the weight is settled back onto the balls of the feet and the left knee slowly lowered until it touches the floor.

The weight is then shifted to the left side allowing the right hip and leg to move forward, this time swivelling around the left knee. Again when sufficient equal distance has been covered weight is settled back and centred on the balls of the feet, allowing the right knee to be slowly lowered to the floor.

These steps are repeated as often as needed.

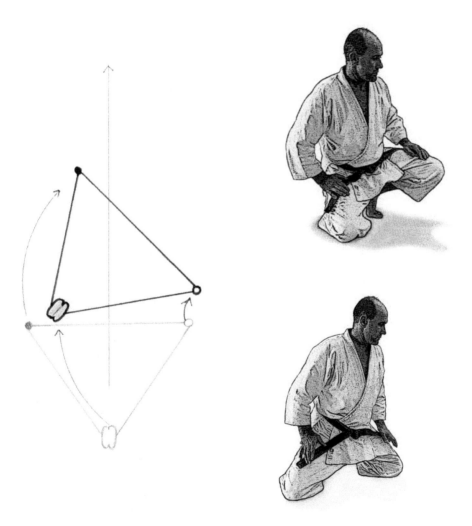

Moving forward with the left knee and swivelling on the right knee...

Moving forward with the right knee while swivelling on the left knee...

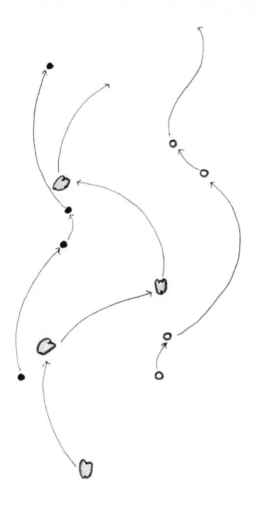

This final diagram to shows the combined arcs the knees and feet make while moving forward in **shikko**. The photo diagrams clearly demonstrate how **shikko** should look in practice.

We can also do most of the standing *Tai Sabaki* moves as well while in a seated position: *Irimi tenkan, Tenkan, Hantai tenkan, Ayumi ashi, and Tsugi ashi.*

Just as in *Tachi Waza* various ways of moving are combined while doing a technique, so too in *Suwariwaza* and *Hanmi Handachi Waza* various ways of moving are often combined during execution of a technique.

Moving fluidly while practicing *Suwari Waza Shomen Uchi Iriminage* against two attackers (*Futari Nin Gakko.*)

With **Hanmi Handachi Waza** Nage is seated while Uke is standing.

Hanmi Handachi is usually practiced at more advanced levels because of the difficulty in doing a technique with Nage disadvantaged by sitting and having to use **shikko** to move while Uke is comfortably standing and can move more freely.

All the techniques one can practice standing (**Tachi Waza**) can also be practiced in **Hanmi Handachi** and **Suwari waza..**

(See page 212 for more about Hanmi Handachi waza).

Part Two

UKEMI
The art of receiving — falling safely

There is no Aikido without Ukemi...

Everyone who studies Aikido must learn Ukemi so that a throw (**Nage Waza**) or a pin down (**Osae waza, Katame waza**) can be studied without injury occurring.

Ukemi is protection against the serious damage that a powerfully executed technique can do. Aikido is one of the few martial arts where practice in the dojo at a senior level can approximate the same technique being done as it would in a *life or death* situation because of the ability to take ukemi.

Ukemi means to receive with the whole body. (It also means to attack while being prepared to receive.) It involves movement of the entire body in response to the application of a throwing, pinning, or joint locking technique: moving with the technique to diminish its effect to prevent damage occurring. Since there are different **ukemi** for various applications attention needs to be focussed on following the natural movement of the technique to create the best **ukemi** suited for that technique.

We practice forward and backward rolling **so we can receive nage and katame waza,** and so both partners can practice with ever-increasing intensity of commitment and energy in studying a technique and its outcome.

With **Osae waza** there is no roll. A break fall is usual when Nage doesn't let go. This is because Uke feels Nage is going to apply **Katame Waza** and thus prepares for the pin or lock to be applied without damage.

The importance of ukemi is that it develops suppleness; quick reflexes, removes fear (*of falling, of being hit*), and allows you to give yourself in trust to your partner. Since both partners take turns at being Uke (the person receiving) as well as Nage (*the person doing*), trust and cooperation are essential components of training.

Ukemi is not only receiving. It is also about attacking correctly with strong determination and intent. By extension, at advanced levels, it could also be about resisting Nage's attempt to apply a technique especially if a weakness in the application is perceived. (*Uke should also look for a possible Kaeshi waza —counter attack—here.*) However, once Nage applies the technique correctly Uke should stop resisting and allow his body to receive it with a roll or breakfall to dissipate the energy of the technique. To continue to resist to the bitter end will result in Uke getting hurt, especially if Nage decides to apply an entirely different technique than the one Uke thinks he is resisting.

Uke should remember the **energy of the response comes from his attack.** The more energy (Kinetic or moving energy) there is in the attack the more explosive will be the response.

Attacking correctly is preparation for receiving, so you should never attack harder or faster than your ability to receive or take ukemi.

Attacking should be done using the whole body with energy extended from the centre, and not just using arms or hands. Nage's response must also extend from his or her centre using the whole body. Only in this way can Uke's centre and body be moved effectively or unbalanced. The moment Uke feels balance or energy being redirected or taken away; Uke should relax and follow this movement, which will determine the type of **ukemi** for that situation. Uke needs to be relaxed even while resisting, so any change, no matter how subtle, in Nage's intention can be felt.

Being Uke is possibly more important than being Nage, as this allows for a deeper understanding (*with one's body rather than one's mind*) of the effect of a technique's application. **Ukemi** is the primary means of learning technique. Taking a turn as Nage completes the understanding of the technique. Uke and Nage both work together to create the technique and the appropriate **ukemi**.

Ushiro Ukemi — backwards rolling...

From a static start:

step 1...Lower yourself to one knee making sure the back leg is positioned at right angles to the front leg so when (step 2...) you sit down onto the hip you do not sit on your foot. Step 3...Push with front foot raising the extended leg up and over the head. This gives you the momentum to roll over.

Make sure the body is at a slight diagonal angle to the direction you are rolling so you do not roll over your head but go over the opposite shoulder from the hip.
Step 4...The finish position is identical to the kneeling position before sitting on the hip to commence the roll over.

Stand up and change hanmi to practice the same steps on the opposite side.

Initially we practice these steps, finishing in a kneeling position, but after a few attempts, subsequent practice should be flowing and continuous, each step blending into the other so the complete backward roll becomes a single movement rather than a series of steps.

When stepping backwards make sure the step is across and behind the front leg, and as you lower yourself to your knee this leg should be at right angles to the front leg. This ensures the body is angled correctly to go over the hip and diagonally across to the shoulder on the other side. The rolling steps are the same only continuous. The finish position should be standing, using the momentum of the roll to propel you back up onto your feet.

Uke should remember that Nage isn't in control of the backwards roll, **Uke is,** and can thus adjust the speed of the lowering down and the roll back. It can start fast and finish slowly or the other way, starting slowly but finishing fast.

Breakfalls

If a technique is executed at high speed there often isn't time to roll backwards. In these instances the **ukemi** needs to be different in order to lessen the impact (*and possibility of damage*) when hitting the ground or floor.

This type of **ukemi** is called a breakfall. Basically it is a roll that is stopped before the roll happens.

There are a number of ways to take breakfalls, some which can be practiced alone, but others need to be done with a partner.

It is always good to practice these ukemi as much as possible so your body learns to react and do them without you having to think about them. These **ukemi** should become second nature. Just as we don't think about how our feet move when we walk or run — we just do it — so should our body react when we find ourselves in a position to take **ukemi**.

Directly backwards

Lower your upper body as if squatting down.

Finally sit down and roll back.

As you roll back, keep your head tucked in and your mouth closed. Allow your hands to slap the ground or mat on both sides. This dissipates the impact of falling and sends the downward energy away from you.

Allow the legs to kick out so as to prevent rolling back onto the neck.

Keeping the head tight against your chest lessens the chance of damaging the neck muscles. Keeping the mouth closed prevents you from biting your tongue if by chance you roll back far enough to hit your head on the mat.

Backward fall to one side

With this breakfall backwards to one side, the front leg is extended forward as if continuing to walk forward while the upper body is suddenly stopped.

Weight should be transferred to the other leg which bends as the body is lowered, as if doing a one legged squat. The arm on the same side as the extended leg is also extended ready to slap down.

Lean back until the balance is gone and there is no option but to fall. Turn your head towards the same side so you can see where you are falling.

At the instant your hip touches the mat; allow your bent leg to fly forward. This assists in turning you towards the side you have chosen to fall.

As your hip touches the mat so too should your right hand (*at an angle no greater than 45 degrees*) slap the mat allowing some of the energy from falling to dissipate.

Roll back along the right side from the hip to the shoulder. This allows the energy of the impact to completely dissipate along the side of the body from the hip to the shoulder and from the hand along the arm to the shoulder. By the time you have rolled back to your shoulder the energy of the fall should have completely disappeared.

The other hand should be raised above your face for protection. Remember the keep the head tucked in and the mouth closed so there is no chance of biting your tongue if you accidentally bump your head on the mat.

> **Backward side fall rotating around a trapped leg...**

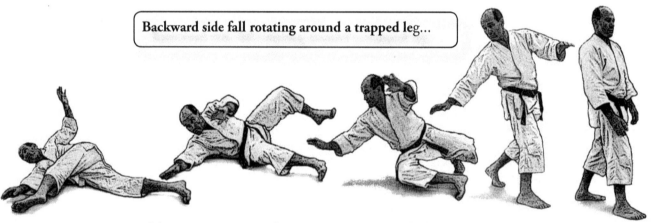

If during an exercise with a partner Nage traps the leg so Uke can't roll backwards a side fall can still be taken by rotating the body around the trapped leg

Turn without moving the front leg and look at the point where you are about to fall.

Allow the body to continue turning as you drop to the knee and hip.

Strike the mat with your hand the moment the hip touches the mat. Allow the body to roll slightly from the hip to the shoulder. This shifts the force along the side of the body and out along the extended arm.

Allow the rear leg to roll over the front leg. This turns the whole body to the side dissipating the force of impact. It also allows the possibility of rolling away onto forearms and knees to stand up again. As good as this method is, many repetitions become tiring.

A less tiring aspect of this type of fall is to step around the trapped leg to use the free leg to take your body weight as you lower yourself down to the mat thus lessening the impact. Finish position is more or less the same as already described. As the rear leg rolls over the front leg this momentum can be utilised to roll further away to get up again.

Stepping around the trapped leg also allows much greater distance to be gained by using the step to push away from Nage.

A **double breakfall** is a more effective way of taking *ukemi* because instead of the energy dissipating along one side from the hip to the shoulder and from the hand to the same shoulder, Uke uses the first slap and initial impact to push away and roll across the shoulders and back to finish with a second breakfall on the other side. This can also be practiced continuously using the slap from one side to push back to the other.

> **Double breakfall practice with a partner assisting...**

In application, instead of falling to the side away from Nage, Uke falls initially on the same side as Nage then propels his body away from Nage, lessening the impact as he rolls away across his back.

For this exercise Nage is simply holding out his arm at shoulder height so Uke can practice side break falls as he walks into the extended arm at face level. (*A response to perhaps chudan tsuki iriminage.*)

Uke enters and allows his body to partially pass under the arm. At the same time he turns to look down to the mat where the initial fall will occur.

The first fall will occur just in front of Nage, then using the energy of the fall as well as flinging the top leg over to the other side Uke will roll away from Nage into a second breakfall which terminates some distance away from Nage.

Double breakfall practice without a partner...

The idea of studying break falls is to get used to different ways of falling so any possible disadvantageous position can be accommodated with some kind of **ukemi**. The more they are practiced the easier and more natural they become.

When Uke is sensitive to the way Nage is leading and projecting him an appropriate fall is automatic and done without thinking. It just happens.

Lean back, turn to the side you wish to fall, let that arm hang down in a relaxed manner. Drop to the knee on that side while at the same time reaching towards the mat with your hand. The hand should make contact at the same time as the knee. As you roll back the energy of the fall travels along the arm to the shoulder and along the side of the body from the knee to the hip to the shoulder.

The fall can finish at this point and is an excellent method of falling around Nage's leg if it has trapped your leg to prevent movement backwards.

As you roll away from Nage you use the energy that has collected in the shoulder to propel you back to the other side. Rolling across your back releases the energy and totally negates any impact on the mat. It also allows you to make some distance from Nage giving you time to get up again before Nage can reach you.

Breakfall with partner holdidng Obi...

Another way of practicing this fall is to have Nage hold your **obi** (*belt*) to support you as you lean back. He will be holding you up. You don't know when he will let go, but the moment he does you are already falling and will only have a fraction of an instant to decide which side to fall and whether it will be a breakfall or a step back into a roll or a combination of both.

Leaning back far enough to fall if Nage lets go Uke prepares to fall to either side. He looks in the direction he anticipates falling and lets his arm on that side drop down to reach towards the mat.

Until Nage releases Uke there is nothing Uke can do. This exercise is primarily to accustom Uke to **take a fall at the instant he feels he has no choice.** When Nage lets go, Uke must fall; gravity will make certain of this.

Uke could also step back to make a backwards roll, or twist around into a kind of forward roll. The easiest is a simple fall to one side.

Below, Uke has chosen to take a breakfall to the left side. It could easily have been to the other side

The object of the exercise is to teach the body to react at the instant it is dropped or projected, to react without anticipating which way to go. Through practice and repetition of various methods of falling the body learns at a core level how to react naturally to projection, or to the sudden removal of balance.

> **Partner assisted flip-over sideways breakfall...**

Another partner assisted method of practicing a sideways breakfall. This particular exercise is good practice for falling out of **Koshinage** (*Hip throw where Uke is rotated across Nage's hips*), from **Jujinage** (*Crossed arm rotating throw*) where Nage keeps hold of Uke's arm to prevent a forward roll, or from **Kotegaeshi** *where Uke must roll over his wrist as it is twisted outwards.*

Uke assumes a push up position, then passes one arm under his body so Nage can take hold from the opposite side.

Nage grips Uke's proffered wrist with one hand while holding just below the elbow with the other hand.

Nage pulls Uke's arm right through to rotate Uke's body completely over. Uke allows his now free arm to fling over as his body is suddenly turned.

The arm should strike the mat a fraction before the body lands on its side.

At the same time Nage will lift up Uke's arm that he his still holding so the impact of hitting the mat is considerably lessened.

This exercise is repeated several times on each side before Uke and Nage change positions.

Years ago, students were not taught how to fall since they often came to Aikido after training for some time in other Martial Arts. It was up to them to figure out how to fall safely as they found themselves being thrown.

If they were young and athletic this was not too much of a problem, but even though many could react instinctively to protect themselves from injury enough could not, so teaching methods of falling safely became necessary. Today, because of the extraordinary spread of Aikido worldwide, and the fact that many students come to Aikido not from a martial arts background, a fair emphasis is placed on teaching the beginning student how to fall before moving on to any of the throwing and pinning techniques.

Mae Ukemi — forwards falling and rolling...

Perhaps the easiest way to begin learning to do a forward roll is to start from a seated position swince you are already on the mat and don't have to fall.

From seiza lean forward and reach back with one arm past the opposite knee. In the picture above the left arm reaches back past the right knee.

Reach back far enough so the left shoulder almost touches the mat. This position creates an oblique angle to the line of direction the roll will take.

Straighten and raise the right leg. This rolls the body forward over to the back of the shoulder. Looking back at the right foot angles the head and upper body so the head and point of the shoulder will not touch the mat as you roll over.

Raise the right leg higher so it goes up in a large circle over the head while at the same time pushing with the left leg. This should give enough momentum to roll the body over.

If the body position is correct it should roll from the left shoulder diagonally across the body to the right hip with enough momentum to carry forward back into a seated position.

If we examine the way the body moves for this forward roll we will soon see that it is exactly the reverse of the backwards roll, and in fact the two are often practiced together, rolling forward to a seated position then backwards again finishing in the same seated position as the start.

Looking at the pictures above, if we go forward from left to right, then we simply go back from right to left. Then we do the other side, starting right to finish coming across the back of the left shoulder, then reversing it going left to right.

The next step is practice the same fall from a position where Uke is kneeling on one knee.

Uke leans forward to reach towards the mat **inside his front leg.** The next step is to straighten the back leg while continuing to extend forward. By raising the back leg he will slowly tip himself over into a forward roll, falling in this case onto the back of the left shoulder and rolling across to the right hip. The roll is the same as above also finishing in the same starting position.

Forward roll from a standing position — Zempo Kaiten Ukemi...

Rather than dive into the fall as some people like to do because it looks spectacular, it is much better to lower the body as close as possible to the floor to lessen the distance to fall before making contact.

Breaking it down into steps Uke leans forward and lowers his upper body on the inside of the front leg, curving the arm and reaching back towards his back foot. This turns the body to the best angle for rolling without the head and neck touching the floor. Another reason for lowering inside the front leg is that if Uke doesn't do this his front leg will be in the way, forcing him to dive over the top of it. This results in a fall to the floor from a much greater height and possibly more potential to damage the shoulder if it makes contact at aless than perfect angle.

Once the arm makes contact with the floor the back leg is raised upwards to the point where Uke is tipped forward. As the roll commences the raised leg is thrown over in a vertical arc above Uke's centre line.

Uke will roll along the arm, past the back of the shoulder and diagonally across the back to the other hip. Again in this example Uke commences by rolling along the left arm and shoulder across to the right hip.

The momentum of the roll should carry the body forward into a seated position which is only a transition between sitting and standing. There should be enough forward momentum to carry Uke into a standing position with hardly any effort on his part needed to stand up.

When practicing alone Uke will simply step forward and repeat the roll starting on the other side. *(This time the right side)*, or he will turn back to face the direction he came from and roll back on the other side.

Sometimes these rolls are practiced in various directions. Starting by facing forward Uke will turn left and roll, or to the right and roll, or even 180 degrees to roll in the opposite direction. This is to accustom the body to make a forward roll after being spun around, as often happens in applications of **Kokyunage**. This turning around into a roll is of course practiced commencing both left and right sides.

Forward roll over a partner...

A more advanced method of practicing a forward roll is with Uke rolling over the back of Nage to finish in a side breakfall. This is quite difficult to do and is not for beginners until they can comfortable roll forward on their own without making much impact on the floor.

The roll commences about half way across Nage's back and finishes in the air on the other side of his body. Uke then drops to the floor to finish with a side breakfall. Most of the time, the arm making the outside arc over the top will strike the mat first to absorb some of the impact.

This is useful in multiple attack scenarios where Nage simply drops in front of one attacker forcing this kind of roll over his back.

Front Breakfall — Zempo Mae Ukemi...

This kind of fall is not used very often but it is useful to practice it, especially from a standing position, as it could be necessary for Uke to receive this way if being projected from a front kick (Mae Geri), where the attacking foot is twisted over so Uke is flipped forward onto his face.

Initially practice this from a kneeling position.

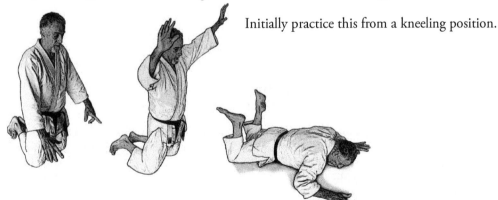

Uke raises his centre from seiza, then continuing to raise his arms he slowly leans forward and falls flat.

Both **forearms and hands** should hit the mat together a fraction of time before the rest of the body. Because the arms are extended at right angles to the upper body and the elbows bent the impact of the fall should be absorbed through the arms and be dissipated across the shoulders. The body should move slightly forward at the moment of initial impact to dissipate the downwards energy forward rather than up into the shoulders. The weight of the body is then lowered to the mat with the head turned to either right or left side so there is no chance of bashing the nose against the mat.

The finish position is not unlike a push up position except that the upper body is much closer to the surface than it would be for push up exercises because both forearms are in contact with the mat.

The next step, after becoming accustomed to this hard fall, is to try from a standing position.

As shown here, Uke simply leans forward and falls over. Sometimes one leg will go down as if to kneel which sometimes seems to make the fall less daunting.

It is not a natural fall and no one likes to do it. It seems more natural to roll rather than fall flat onto your face. But there could be a time when this type of **ukemi** is needed.

Some people whose arms are very strong from doing regular push up exercises actually dive face forward into this fall. This is not recommended for the beginning student.

In fact this kind of fall is rarely practiced even at senior levels because of the possibility of damaging the collar bones and the shoulder sockets.

However on the rare occasion that the defence to Uke's attack is for Nage to get behind to wrap his arms around Uke's upper legs to prevent him from moving forward (*a grappling attack*) or dropping down to grab both ankles from behind, he will then project Uke by simply leaning his shoulder against Uke's back. Since he is unable to move his legs, Uke will have no choice but to fall face forward into the **ukemi** described above.

Ukemi for Ikkyo...

Ikkyo is a fundamental technique involving an arm pin (Ude Osae), although it can be used to initiate a throw (**Ikkyo Nage**). Learning how to receive **Ikkyo** is as important as learning how to roll forwards and backwards.

There are many different ways **Ikkyo** can be initiated and implemented. It can be soft and fluid or it can be hard and elbow breaking.

One older way was for Nage to enter catching Uke's elbow from underneath while grabbing Uke's wrist at the same time. The elbow was then snapped upward. Uke would respond by rising up onto his toes in order to take away the strain on the elbow. The moment Nage felt Uke's centre rise he would twist the arm over forward rotating Uke's upper body completely over. The arm would be dropped right to the floor in front of Nage and Uke would come crashing down.

If Uke inadvertently took a step forward, a common and automatic reaction to being twisted over, he would come crashing down onto his own leg and quite possibly would crack one or two ribs in the process or even give himself a blood-nose.

Receiving **Ikkyo** done in this manner is hard on the body, but these days it is rarely practiced in that way.

The following method of preparing for **Ikkyo omote** can be practiced alone and can be done slowly and comfortably, taking time to accustom the body to being turned (*without stepping*) and receiving the technique in a relaxed manner.

> **Receiving Ikkyo Ude Osae — Omote form...**

Imagine as Uke you make a **shomen** strike and that Nage has entered to counter this strike. His forearm near the wrist area will have extended against your wrist (*without grabbing*) and turned your upper body to face the opposite direction. Alow your body to rotate on the balls of the feet without changing position of the feet.

Imagine now the elbow is rotated up and over and that at the same time Nage is entering with a single step into your centre to disturb your balance and to shift you slightly sideways. As the arm continues to turn over you will drop down on to the outside knee leaving the inside leg to remain straight. You support yourself with the other arm. (*Left arm shown here supporting...*) This is a strong stable position and to get you to fall over further to that side would require a considerable nudge or push or a kick into the ribs from Nage.

Nage needs to take you all the way to the mat to apply the arm pin. There is an empty

space in front of your still raised arm and the logical thing for Nage to do is to step sideways away from you rather than trying to push you over against the resistance of your supporting arm and leg.

Because Nage is still holding your arm, you will have no option but to fall into that empty space.

When practicing this **Ikkyo ukemi** alone visualise that what you are doing is a response to Nage doing ***Ikkyo Omote.*** Keep this in mind as the fall is finished by simply leaning across and falling flat into the empty space. There should be very little impact as most of your body weight is supported by the outside arm and leg.

> **Receiving Ikkyo Ude Osae — Ura form...**

Uke is attacking Nage with a **shomen uchi** strike. But this time imagine that Nage has slipped to the **Ura** side of the attacking arm, allowing the arm to continue descending, rather than turning the arm back over into Uke's face to turn him completely around as in the previous exercise.

As Uke's arm descends in front of Nage's centre line, Nage takes control of the elbow and wrist and extends the elbow slightly forward so he can draw the wrist back towards his centre (*Seika Tanden*). Maintaining the arm in front of his centre he continues to move **Irimi Tenkan**. As soon as Uke feels his arm being guided to the rear he will drop gently down onto the knee nearest Nage, thus positioning himself to be spiralled around in a circle to the rear.

In solo practice Uke will step forward and as he strikes **shomen uchi** he will lower himself gently down onto the knee of the same side as the striking arm. Turning the striking arm over and back towards the rear he will pivot on his knee. As he gets about half way around the circle his other arm will extend out to support his weight. He will then begin to lower himself towards the mat.

Finally, imagining that Nage has control of his arm and will draw him out and forward at an oblique angle Uke allows himself to fall at an angle in the direction of his extended arm.

This is the empty space in front of the extended arm. The position of the arm at the finish is exactly the same as shown previously in the **Ikkyo Omote** exercise. Note: ***In this Ura example, because Uke has turned approximately 180 degrees the other arm can't be seen.***

Both the **Omote** and **Ura** forms for receiving **Ikkyo** are practiced equally on the left and the right side. Over time these exercises will accustom Uke's body to receiving **Ikkyo** with control, rather than just allowing himself to be dumped and pinned.

Uke has no choice in taking ukemi, but what he can do is control how he takes ukemi in order to minimise damage, and to use the least amount of energy possible in the circumstances. Practicing these forms will enhance fluidity and make receiving an unconscious core body reaction that is perfectly natural.

> ### Receiving during hanmi handachi practice...

Attempting to minimise damage to the lower back...

Movement in Aikido not only involves entering at oblique angles or directly into the line of attack, or making circles to enter to the rear of the attack all in a parallel plane — it also involves moving down and up in a vertical plane while doing the other entering and avoiding movements which when combined create up or down spiralling movements as Nage and Uke come together to create a technique.

Training in **Hanmi Handachi** where Nage is seated (*beginning in seiza*) and Uke is standing when attacking, an often practiced technique is **Shomen Uchi Iriminage**.

Uke makes a strong **shomen** strike down onto a seated Nage. Practicing alone, visualising he is attacking a seated Nage, Uke steps forward and strikes down.

As he steps forward to strike Uke must take an extra smaller step with the other leg for support as he immediately lowers himself down onto the knee on the same side as the striking arm.

Uke must imagine that Nage has slipped to the side to avoid the downward strike and at the same time has reached up to grasp the back of Uke's neck with one hand while with the other he has cut Uke's elbow down towards the mat, accentuating Uke's own downward movement.

If Uke drops to his knee as if stepping down to pick up something he will keep his back straight and avoid bending from the waist as so many do during this technique. Stepping down this way will minimise the likelihood of strain and damage to the lower back.

Uke allows his striking arm to reach the mat where it can help support him. He allows the other leg to step out creating a wider circle.

Using this leg to help push, Uke spirals around the knee on the mat imagining he is being turned by Nage who is making a **half Tenkan** movement or a slight **Irimi** followed by a **Tenkan** (*as it is done in the standing Ura form of iriminage*).

Having gone perhaps half way around a full circle Uke can then use his extended leg to push back into a back roll (*as shown above*), or a breakfall.

In the example below with a partner...

Nage has taken Uke far enough around so he can enter for the final throw. This is accomplished by using the arm that originally cut Uke's elbow down, to strike towards Uke's face tipping his head over causing him to take a back fall or a backwards roll whichever is the most appropriate in the circumstances.

In solo practice Uke will simply push back with his extended leg causing him to roll backwards. This may not be possible when training with a partner so Uke must be prepared to take some kind of breakfall.

The important point to focus on during this ***ukemi*** practice is to lower the whole body down in a controlled movement rather than simply crashing onto the knee or allowing the body to bend over at the waist. Bending over from the waist puts a lot of stress on the lower back and in time will cause problems that are difficult to rectify. Even when doing ***Shomen Uchi Iriminage*** as ***Tachi Waza,*** *(or standing technique)* if Nage cuts Uke down very low, using this method of receiving will protect the lower back from possible over stretching and consequent damage.

Please note that the beginning of this solo exercise is the same as that shown for receiving **Ikkyo Ura,** until the knee touches the mat. From that point on it differs as described.

With the ***Hanmi Handachi Iriminage*** two finishes are shown here with a partner.
Left: Uke has slipped through far enough to finish with a back fall rather than a roll.
Right: Uke has pushed back as Nage completes the application, taking a backwards roll.

Setting up to take Ukemi by attacking correctly...

Aikido is primarily taught as a defensive art based on harmonising and blending with an attack, and then redirecting it so it passes by and is in effect dissipated or defused.

In order to understand how to blend or harmonise with an attack — **studying certain specific attacks is essential**.

By studying a specific attack Uke (*the person attacking*) is given the opportunity to practice how to receive the defence applied to that attack. What Uke is really doing is setting up to take a specific **ukemi** suited to the attack committed.

There are many different ways of taking **ukemi** and the student who practices these will be more adept and relaxed when a technique is applied as a defence against an attack.

Relaxation is the key to receiving if Uke wants to feel how Nage is shifting the energy flow to create the technique that leads into a throw or pin. Once Uke feels the way in which the energy is being redirected, taking an appropriate fall is much easier.

Nearly all attacks in Aikido require partner participation. One can practice strikes alone but not any of the attacks that involve grabbing in various ways; there must be something to grab hold of, a wrist, an elbow, a shoulder, and so on.

The most commonly used grabbing attacks...

Gyaku hanmi katatetori

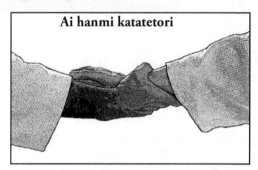

Ai hanmi katatetori

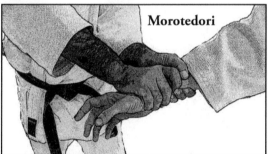

Morotedori

Gyaku hanmi hijitori

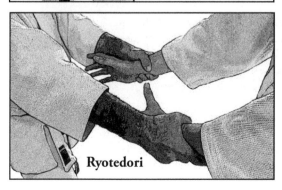

Ryotedori

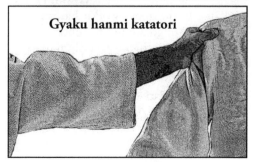

Gyaku hanmi katatori

Standing in Gyaku Hanmi — working with a partner who is grabbing the wrist, the elbow, or the shoulder

The exercise here is to be aware of the point of contact and that in order to move Nage must not fight against the grip but remain relaxed so the rest of the body is able move around it.

Uke must grab with the body not just with the hand. The energy of the grab should come from Uke's centre, travelling from the ground up through the body and into the hand. The grip is firm but without the rigidity of muscle power. If Uke is relaxed while maintaining a firm grip, when Nage applies a technique Uke will feel the way the movement is going and be able to position himself to take appropriate **ukemi**.

Katatetori — single wrist grab

Hijitori — elbow grab

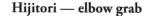

Katatori — shoulder grab

Morotedori — two hands grabbing forearm

Again the stance is **Gyaku Hanmi** although the legs here are not shown.

In the above **gyaku hanmi** grabbing attacks Nage must move by using a **tenkan** movement to go around the obstruction of the grab. This turning backwards leads Uke forwards and starts to unbalance him to the point where a slight shift forward by Nage will cause Uke to take a fall, (*Mae ukemi)*. If the exercise is stopped at this point it is called **Tai no Henka.**

Alternatively one can enter directly towards Uke's centre line by taking a sliding forward step (*Tsugi Ashi)* and extending the grabbed arm forwards into Uke's face. This will tip Uke backwards and make him take a back fall (*Ushiro ukemi*). If practiced to the point of unbalance before the fall the exercise is called **Kokyu Ho.**

Ai Hanmi Katatetori.

Here the stance is **Ai Hanmi** with a single cross hand grab to the wrist. Sometimes this grab is called **Kosadori.** *Here the grab is inside the wrist. Usually it is from the outside of the wrist.*

Note ***this is the opposite side compared to the previous gyaku hanmi examples.***

As always, the response is to remain relaxed and deal with this attack by moving around it, or entering in such a way as to unbalance Uke.

*In the case of the **Ai Hanmi** grab Nage can make either an **Irimi tenkan** movement which means he steps behind Uke and turns to lead Uke forward in a circular path, or he can slide across in front of Uke then make a **kaiten** move to lead Uke straight forward to a point of unbalance.*

Ryotedori, which is grabbing both wrists from in front, is generally Ai Hanmi...

Ryokatatori, is grabbing both shoulders from in front...

Kata Men Uchi, is grabbing one shoulder while striking with shomen to the head. Sometimes the strike is *men tsuki* instead. (*Punch to the face.*)

Munadori — grabbing the collar or lapel/lapels with one or both hands from in front.

With one hand the the **hanmi** is usually **gyaku** hanmi, whereas with both hands grabbing the **hanmi** is almost always **ai** hanmi.

one hand grabs lapels
gyaku hanmi munadori

both hands grab lapels
ai hanmi munadori

Grabbing attacks from behind — Ushiro...

Ushiro Ryokatatetori

Grabbing both wrists from behind.

Ushiro Ryohijitori

Grabbing both elbows from behind.

Mundakeshime — bear hug

Ushiro Ryokatatori — grabbing both shoulders from behind...

The attacks shown here are from a static position.

With movement these positions are transitory positions between Uke completing the attack, and being shifted to a position of unbalance where Nage can apply a technique.

Both Nage and Uke often practice these attacks from the rear in a static form at first before attempting the extra dynamic of movement.

With movement, distance and timing become particularly important since there is no static starting point, consequently the practice becomes more demanding and focussed.

These **attacks from the rear are generally much more difficult to deal with and are considered advanced.** Nage must step around Uke either by leading Uke forward if he pushes, or by stepping back if Uke pulls. Using Uke's pushing or pulling energy and moving to either side are essential to draw Uke into an unbalanced position where a technique can be applied. (*See page 202: Ushiro Ryokatatori Kokyunage.*)

The collar can be grabbed with one or both hands from behind without the wrist grab shown here. Uke can push Nage forwards, or pull Nage backwards.

Ushiro tekubi mochi eridori — wrist and collar grabbed from behind

Katatetori Ushiro Kubishimi, a wrist grab combined with a strangle hold from behind. Sometimes it is called *tekubi mochi ushiro kubishimi.*

*It is often shortened to **ushiro kubishimi**, which only means a stranglehold from behind without a hand grab. Each dojo or association has its preferred name for this attack.*

Striking Attacks

*These include various punches —**Tsuki** — to head, chest, or stomach level... **Jodan Tsuki, Chudan Tsuki**, or **Gedan Tsuki**, strikes that simulate sword cuts — **Shomen Uchi, Yokomen Uchi, Kiri Otoshi**, as well as kicks like **Mae Geri** and **Mawashi Geri**.*

Punches in Aikido are not like those found in Karate, but are based on the way you would use a spear or a short staff or a knife (**tanto**). The body movement when using a weapon is the same kind of movement used when striking without the weapon. What changes **without the weapon is the Maai or distance at which the strike is used and responded to.** There are a number of other kinds of punches, and combinations of grabs and punches that are used in more advanced training. These will not be shown here as they are beyond the scope of this text. (*Examples are Uraken, Seiken, Hiraken, Haito, Nukite.*) **Shotei** or palm heel strike is often used in **Iriminage**.

Kicks such as variations of front kicks (**Mae Geri**) and turning kicks (**Mawashi Geri**) usually to mid (**Chudan**) or lower (**Gedan**) levels are not practiced very often because of the difficulty of taking **Ukemi**. It is also thought that to take one leg off the ground to kick leaves the person in a vulnerable position where balance can easily be taken away.

Senior students who are Dan grades (**Yudansha**) sometimes practice defences against kicks. Front kicks and other straight kicks are treated the same way as a straight punch, and similar techniques can be applied. Turning kicks are treated similar to a **Yokomen** attack.

Open handed strikes, are cutting strikes using the side of the hand (**Tegatana**). The two most commonly used are both based on sword cutting and are **Shomen Uchi** and **Yokomen Uchi**. In **Shomen uchi** Uke raises his arm, steps forward, and cuts vertically downward as if using a sword to cut into Nage's head. The point to strike is the middle of the forehead. This strike should be completed in one fluid movement and not in separate steps.

Yokomen uchi begins the same way but as Uke steps forward he moves to the side, which alters the angle of the strike. The target is the side of the head or the neck. The angle of the strike is slightly less than vertical but not as much as 45 degrees. If looking at a clock face, the position of the minute hand somewhere between 1 and 2 for the right arm and between 11 and 10 for the left arm would be the correct angle.

Strikes (**Ate or Atemi**) are made with the fleshy side of the hand called **Tegatana**. (*Translated as sword hand*). Punches are made my closing the fist in such a way that the joints of the index and middle fingers protrude slightly. This is so these points will penetrate the target area (eg. the ribs).

Stepping forward with
Shomen Uchi

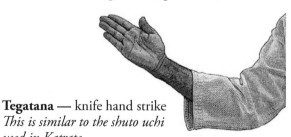

Tegatana — knife hand strike
This is similar to the shuto uchi used in Katrate

Tsuki — straight punch with index knuckle protruding — *Nakadate Ipponken.*

Shomen Uchi showing line of attack B   **Yokomen Uchi** showing line of attack B

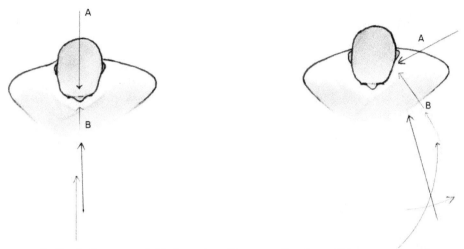

In both diagrams A is the point of contact by the striking open hand.

The line of attack B in the **Shomen uch**i example is directly towards Nage's centre. The striking hand (***Tegatana***) should impact in the centre of the forehead. With **Yokomen uchi**, although Uke begins from the same position, instead of entering in a straight line he moves to the side and enters from an oblique angle. The striking hand impacts the side of the head, or the neck.

With the Shomen uchi attack the movement is Irimi ashi. The arrows show both the direction of the movement toward Nage as well as the direction of the strike.

With Yokomen uchi the movement is also Irimi ashi, but because the first step is not directly towards Nage, but off line towards Nage, Uke repositions his body by allowing his back leg to swing across in a slight arc, so that he still finishes lined up towards Nage's centre. The bottom circular arrow shows the direction Uke's back foot moves, while the upper circular arrow shows both the direction of the initial step as well as the angle of the striking hand. The straight arrow shows the approximate angle of the attack. *See pages 71-72 for details regarding Yokomen Uchi attack and response.*

Shomen Uchi attacks the centre of the forehead

Yokomen Uchi attacks the temple or side of the head or the neck below the ear...

Chudan Tsuki

Mae Geri

Chudan tsuki or mid level punch is a straight punch off the front leg rather than a reverse punch off the back leg. When stepping forward to punch the whole same side of the body is used which gives considerable force to the punch. The arm is not locked at the elbow by twisting the wrist at the point of impact, but rather the arm acts in a springlike manner allowing the fist to bounce back once impact has been achieved and the energy of the punch dissipated. The same kind of punch is used to head level (**Jodan Tsuki**) or to the lower abdomen area (**Gedan Tsuki**).

The same movement to enter and punch is also used to enter and grab the wrist in **Gyaku Hanmi**. Dealing with the punch is virtually the same as dealing with the hand grab. The front kick (**Mae Geri**) shown above is also dealt with in exactly the same way as the mid level or lower level punch.

Mae Geri from seiza is sometimes used to initiate an entry when practicing **Suwari waza Ikkyo** to **Yonkyo**. *Though this is not practiced very often it can be seen in some old video footage of O-Sensei where he clearly disconcerts his Uke with a kick to the ribs as he initiates entry for Ikkyo in response to a shomen attack while seated.*

Practicing this kick from **seiza** has benefit in that it helps to develop movement from the **seika tanden** or **hara** while strengthening the large muscles of the legs.

To kick Uke raises up so his weight is centred over his knees. This also allows space for the lower leg to come through for the front kick and to return. During the kick the weight is obviously centred over the other knee. After the kick the weight is again shifted over both knees and Uke lowers himself back down to **seiza**. The kick is practiced on both sides so both legs are worked equally.

Part Three

> **Responding to an Attack**
>
> **Training with a partner and dealing with attacks**

Practicing with a partner is what makes Aikido truly interesting. Learning to deal with someone grabbing you right from the start is far more challenging than simply practicing movements alone. Although this is fine in order to improve basic **Tai Sabaki** and **ukemi**, it is practicing with a partner and taking turns at being both Uke and Nage *(attacker and defender)* where true understanding begins. It has been said that to be Uke is more important than to be Nage, as being Uke allows for a deeper understanding with one's body the effect of a technique. How well one receives the application of the technique depends upon one's ability to take the appropriate **ukemi**.

What makes the whole process more difficult is that each time two people practice a technique *(attack and response)* it's never quite the same. Uke could move faster or slower than before, enter at a different angle, could respond in a way unexpected, turning more or less than before, perhaps even stopping to move— any number of minor differences, all of which make the practice slightly different each time. Nage constantly has to readjust to accommodate Uke's movement, just as Uke also needs to readjust his receiving each time Nage applies a technique, because the same things are happening with Nage's response as are happening with Uke's attack. Changing partners makes it all more complicated since new partners will again move differently and respond differently than the previous partner. **Each time you practice something you should try to maintain the idea that this is not only the first time you do it, but the only chance you have to get it right. Each time is unique, and should not be considered as part of a sequence that is repeated** on each side.

A fundamental exercise is Tai No Henka, practiced from **Gyaku Hanmi Katatetori**. It is used to study timing, distancing, harmonising and blending of one's movement with that of another person.

Initially **Tai No Henka** is practiced from a static position with Uke grabbing Nage's wrist and standing in *Gyaku Hanmi* as shown here.

Note that Uke is not front-on but angled to one side to avoid the possibility of a strike by Nage who has one hand free.

Since Uke also has one hand free as well as both legs available Nage must now move in order to avoid the possibility that Uke will use some kind of strike coupled with the grab.

As a basic exercise, Uke simply holds Nage firmly while trying to maintain a relaxed body. The actual grip is the point of contact and is the point that determines the **Maai**, or correct distance. In this static exercise Uke has grabbed strongly and feels some resistance from Nage who is holding his centre stable and is grounded. Nage must not pull Uke around but if Nage suddenly turns with a **tenkan** step an empty space will be created where the grip is. With the resistance suddenly gone Uke will find himself falling forward.

Alternatively, Nage leaves the wrist that is being gripped where it is and moves slightly forward bringing his body closer to the handhold, and then when it is lined up exactly in front of his centre, he turns around it with a **tenkan** movement. This creates an empty space and because Uke is still gripping firmly he is drawn forward to a point where he is unstable and can easily be toppled.

The next stage is to practice Tai No Henka with movement.

Nage extends a hand towards Uke who possibly perceives it as a threat rather than an offering, so his response is to step forward, his intention to counter whatever Nage has in mind. He grabs the wrist, to follow up with a strike or perhaps to pull Nage towards him. As he reaches for the wrist his focus is on grabbing. At the moment his fingers touch and begin to grip Nage leads Uke's hand forward. Instinctively Uke will extend a little further to complete the grip. Nage moves off the line of attack and around the point of contact with the tenkan movement just as Uke completes the grab only to realise he is becoming unbalanced. Any slight forward shift by Nage will now cause Uke to fall.

Practicing this way introduces timing to the equation, which in turn allows both partners to study distancing and harmonising with each other's movement.

Classes often begin with Tai No Henka, as a way to prepare the body for movement. It should not be forgotten however, that this is a fundamental exercise and focus should be on moving one's centre offline and around the energy of the attack with a view to unbalance Uke so a throw or a pin (Osae waza) can be affected. In actual fact one doesn't simply tenkan, it is irimi tenkan with the irim step offline to the side to allow space for Nage to pass by as he over-extends to complete the hold on Nage's wrist.

With **Morotedori**, the movement is exactly the same as the previous **katatetori** grip. Nage steps unobtrusively offline and moves his centre around the two hand grip, (*Irimi Tenkan with a irimi to the side*) and raises his arm upwards along his centre line as if wanting to touch his forehead with his thumb or as if preparing tpo raise a **bokken** for **shomen uchi**. This twists Uke into a position that is totally unstable and he can easily be thrown. Again **the practice here is not the throw but learning how to move around this very strong two-handed grip.**

Morotedori

In moving practice rather than static, the moment Uke moves threateningly towards Nage, Nage initiates by striking towards Uke's face. Uke naturally steps aside and grabs the striking arm with both hands and attempts to force it down. The moment the grip tightens Nage moves around it to unbalance Uke by taking control of Uke's centre and twisting him into an unstable position, ready for a throw.

Once again this exercise is body preparation for a series of techniques from that particular (*Morotedori*) grip.

Note that the position at the start of this exercise is **Gyaku Hanmi** and again Uke is angled to one side out of the way of a possible kick or punch from Nage.

There are a number of other similar exercises that are used as preliminary training for moving around incoming energy and harmonising with this energy in order to use it, but the examples shown are the most often practiced and lead to many different techniques.

Note: In these and the following images the roles of Uke and Nage are changed just as in normal practice — each taking a turn to do both roles. It should be clear which person is Uke and Nage.

Shomen Uchi — Irimi Tenkan response...

Commencing in **gyaku Hanmi,** both partners face each other.

As Uke steps forward and raises his arm to strike **shomen uchi,** (*a strike with the hand blade to Nage's forehead*), Nage steps forward and off line at the moment Uke has committed to the strike.

Nage then turns 180 degrees to finish slightly behind Uke. Nage is now in the opposite stance or hanmi to the stance he had before moving.

This is the same body movement as shown for gyaku hanmi Katatetori Tai no Henka as well as Morotedori. The movement is **tenkan** with a small step forward at an oblique angle before turning around that foot to the rear (**tenkan**).

Shomen Uchi — Isoku Irimi Kaiten response...

This is a combination of two movements: **Issoku Irimi** — a sliding forward step, and **Kaiten** — pivoting 180 degrees on the balls of the feet.

Uke and Nage face each other in **Ai Hanmi.** As Uke steps forward to strike shomen uchi Nage takes an oblique offline step forward with the front foot, bringing the back foot forward to maintain a stable stance. This shifts the whole body forward without changing the stance.

As Uke finishes the strike Nage finishes with a **Kaiten,** pivoting 180 degrees on the balls of the feet to face the same direction as Uke and in the same stance as Uke, which is again the opposite stance to the one he started in. Nage is now in an advantageous position parallel to and slightly behind Uke.

Please note how this differs from the previous **Irimi Tenkan** example. Though the middle position is more or less the same, the beginning and end positions are different.

*Many reponses in Aikido contain two or more **Tai Sabaki** which flow smoothly together and are done without thinking about them. This only comes about after much repetition, so Tai Sabaki is always practiced at the beginning of every class to reinforce muscle memory of the movements so in time they become natural.*

Chudan Tsuki — Tenkan response...

Chudan Tsuki — Punch to mid level.

Uke steps forward and punches to stomach level. Once the strike is committed Nage shifts his front foot offline and turns **tenkan** at the moment the strike almost touches him. Turning tenkan shifts Nage one shoulder width to the side so he finishes in a parallel almost mirror image position to Uke avoiding the punch and ready to redirect it.

Nage could also respond with **Irimi Kaiten** or any other **Tai Sabaki** that takes him off the line of attack and positions him to counter or redirect.

reminder:
the punch here is not like a karate punch which has a twist on the end and locks the elbow... it is more like stabbing and cutting upwards with a knife. The elbow is bent so the arm is flexible and can be retracted quickly.

Gyaku Hanmi Katatetori Kokyuho

Kokyu Ho is a fundamental exercise to develop breath power — Kokyu.

This is an exercise to prepare for a breath throw to the rear (*Kokyunage Ura*) or a side entry throw (*Sokumen Iriminage*) in which Uke must take a back fall or roll (*Ushiro ukemi*).

From the final position shown above and used in this exercise as a way of stretching and warming muscles and tendons, to actually fall Uke cannot step backward but must fall to the side around Nage's leg. This will become a side breakfall, or a partially circular breakfall around to the rear of Nage. *see page 44.*

Gyaku Hanmi Morotedori Kokyuho

It is the same for the **Morotedori** sequence. Both Nage's entry to unbalance Uke, and Uke's response and fall is exactly the same as above. In both of these Nage has entered with **Ayumi ashi** stepping in front variation.

To finish with a throw Nage would have to extend further around by turning his upper body causing Uke to fall, or by dropping his centre which will also cause Uke to fall.

As in the **Tai No Henka** exercises these two **kokyuho** are first practiced from a static position, then when the movement is understood, practice is for timing and **maai**.

As Uke starts to grab Nage enters directly in towards Uke's centre at the moment of contact, and extends through to unbalance Uke in preparation for a throw. In both these examples Nage has stepped behind Uke's leading leg so Uke cannot step back and must take a breakfall if the exercise is continued into a throw.

We generally have two levels of practice that we study in most Aikido classes.

1. **Static.** This is where Nage waits for Uke to attack, then responds with a defence.

2. **Leading**. Where Nage leads Uke into overcommitting himself and uses Uke's energy with some added momentum to defeat him.

There is a third level of training for advanced students, and this involves Nage understanding or reading the intention of Uke to attack, and moving in to catch Uke off guard before the attack begins, or slightly after the attack has commenced, but before Uke can complete his attacking movement and is forced to defend instead of attacking. Nage doesn't think of what he will do, he just moves in and does something that seems appropriate.

This is often how it works with multiple attackers. The moment Nage looks at one of the Ukes that person will immediately attack. How he starts his attack will determine how Nage responds with a technique. Nage will not have time to think about what to do. His body has been trained by countless repetitions of a variety of techniques and it will know what to do without consciously thinking about it.

At a an advanced level this third concept is taken one step further. Nage reads the intention of Uke to attack and in an instant decides that if an attack is going to happen then he wants it to happen in a specific way. **Nage enters with his own attack before Uke can commence his offensive action** and is forced instead to defend. Nage now uses this defence as if it was an offensive action and applies a technique to throw Uke.

An example of this would be: Nage reads Uke's intention to be offensive, but doesn't know how he is going to attack. Rather than wait to see what Uke does and then have to defend, Nage enters into Uke's space with a strike towards Uke's face. Uke responds instinctively by raising an arm to protect his face. Nage treats this response as a *shomen* attack and enters to do *Ikkyo* or perhaps some form of *Iriminage* or *Kokyunage*.

This could be called offensive defence rather than passive defence, which is usually the way Aikido is practiced. Classes that use the offensive defence training are highly focussed and fast moving.

Practicing with a partner often involves studying the entry movements of a given technique. For example if **Ai hanmi Katatetori** is the beginning (a cross hand grip), Nage steps off to one side and enters towards Uke from Uke's outside (**Ura** or **Soto** side) raising his hand up outside of Uke's grip , and using his hand blade (**Tegatana**) cuts towards Uke's face. This has the effect of unbalancing Uke and making him lean backwards.

From this point a number of techniques can be used. Enter deeper and in front (**Omote**), take the elbow to revolve the upper arm across in front of Uke's head which will turn his whole upper body over to allow *Ikkyo, Nikkyo, Sankyo* and *Yonkyo omote* versions; or cut the arm down until it is in front of Nage's centre at which point Nage enters behind (**Ura**) Uke with an I*rimi Tenkan* movement to affect the Ura versions of the same techniques. Nage could also enter in front spiralling Uke's arm around across his face to spin him around into *iriminage omote*, or again enter behind to take Uke's neck with his free hand to help turn him into *Iriminage Ura.*

Entering (*irimi*) Ura against Yokomen Uchi...

Entering (*irimi*) Omote against Yokomen Uchi...

Most techniques have an Omote and an Ura form. Which one is used is dependant upon the timing of Nage's entry to counter the attack and redirect it.

For Ura techniques with **Yokomen uchi** attack Nage has to catch the strike before it is fully committed, before Uke begins to step forward with a strike. Timing is essential to enter early enough to turn Uke towards the back. The entry movement is a deep Irimi (*Tsugi Ashi*) to the attacking side with one hand encountering Uke's striking arm about elbow level and extending to the rear while at the same time making an **atemi** (strike) with the other hand towards Uke's face. The effect of this entry is to bend Uke over backwards leaving him unbalanced and vulnerable.

With Omote Nage has more time and can catch the striking arm as Uke is stepping forward to strike. Nage steps across and slightly towards Uke's centre with the lead arm making atemi towards Uke's face while the other arm cuts Uke's striking arm down and around to turn Uke so his back is now facing Nage, who again has the option of various techniques. The movement here is **Issoku Irimi** slightly to the side allowing the back foot to drift across to maintain **hanmi**, or a sideways **Okuri Ashi** movement. Nage then drops his striking hand and catches Uke's wrist as Nage sweeps this arm across his centre. The effect of this movement is to draw Uke forward and around slightly to an unbalanced position where a variety of techniques can be exploited. This turning of Uke's body is called **Tenshin** and is a fundamental movement used against many different attacks to position Uke ready for a technique to be applied.

Learning to deal with **Shomen uchi** is also similar to **Yokomen uchi** in so far as the timing is concerned. Catching the strike with Uke's arm at its apex before the strike actually commences, (**In**) or redirecting it while it is striking down (**Yo**) are the two timings that determine which way a technique will be practiced. **In** and **Yo** here is in relation to Uke's attack; Nage's response is the opposite responding with **Yo** to Uke's **In** and In to Uke's **Yo**.
Note: In and Yo are the Japanese equivalents to the Chinese Yin and Yang.

There are other timings such as stepping offline to avoid the strike and entering the moment it has finished with **atemi** or some form of destabilisation, or catching the arm at the end of the strike and continuing it all the way down to the floor to cause Uke to take a fall.
These timings are often practiced as separate exercises before attempting techniques related to them.

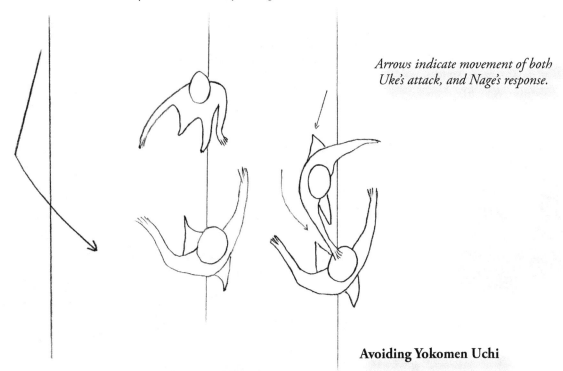

Arrows indicate movement of both Uke's attack, and Nage's response.

Avoiding Yokomen Uchi

Above: The line along which Uke and Nage are standing. The arrow indicates the line Uke takes to attack Nage with **yokomen**. If Nage doesn't move he will be struck on the side of the head or neck.

Below: four examples of shifting offline to avoid being struck. The first two are to either side of the line but back, the third is circular around Uke but just beyond reach, and the last is a direct **irimi** to attack Uke's arm and centre before the yokomen actually begins.

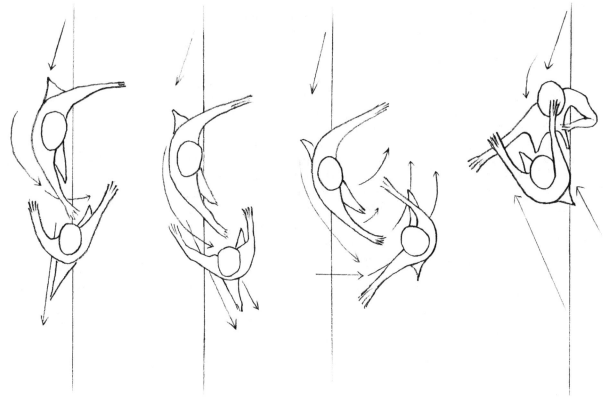

**Responding to a
Yokomen uchi attack**

**Entering (*irimi*) Ura against
Yokomen Uchi...**

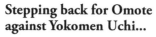

**Stepping back for Omote
against Yokomen Uchi...**

*Arrows indicate movement
of both Uke and Nage.*

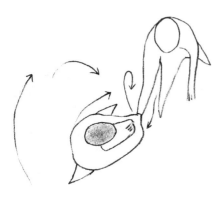

The final application here for both the **Omote** and **Ura** examples will be **shihonage**.

It would be just as easy to do **Kokyunage**, or **Iriminage** or **Kotegaeshi**. Nage's hand positions will vary depending on the technique he wishes to do.

What is important here, and is the same for all the **omote** forms of the techniques mentioned, is the sweeping body movement (*Tenshin*) which is used to turn and open Uke using the energy of his attack to draw him forward to position him ready for Nage's defence.

In all the **Ura** form it is to enter and tip Uke over backwards to take balance away and position him for a technique (**Shihonage**).

In the **Omote** form it is to draw Uke forward before turning and tipping him back over.

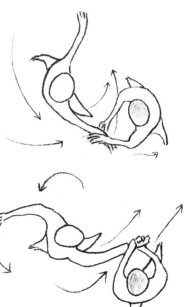

Responding to Yokomen Uchi attack from the Soto or Ura side.

As Uke commences the strike Nage takes a sliding step offline at an angle and redirects the attacking arm backwards while simultaneously attacking Uke 's centre. This is a direct Irimi movement where one enters instead of stepping back or stepping around. *Too deep an entry will knock Uke over backwards far enough to fall, so the amount of the entry needs to be exactly what is needed to tip Uke over and take away stability which will allow Nage the opportunity to get around behind Uke.*

This direct Irimi entry will bend Uke over backwards.
see photo page 70...

In this **Ura** form the timing has to be early enough to catch the arm before the strike really commences otherwise Nage must step across and continue the swing to open Uke.

As Nage enters one hand cuts the attacking arm down (between the wrist and the elbow) while the other hand cuts into Uke's face. **This is a very strong Irimi movement.**

As Nage continues entering the hand used to make the **atemi** to Uke's face crosses over and under Uke's wrist. Uke's forearm is rotated upwards while Nage rotates to the rear around the point of contact.

As Nage enters behind Uke he extends Uke's elbow forward and over to create a circular movement, turning Uke away and exposing Uke's back. This is a more difficult **tenshin** movement than the **omote** form because of the timing of the entry.

If the timing is right Nage can virtually slip behind Uke with Uke hardly feeling anything other than surprise to find his target behind instead of in front of him.

The beginning of two possible finishes shown are the **omote** and **Ura** forms of. **Iriminage**. *See pages176 to 181.*

This is the basic form looked for at a Kyu test...

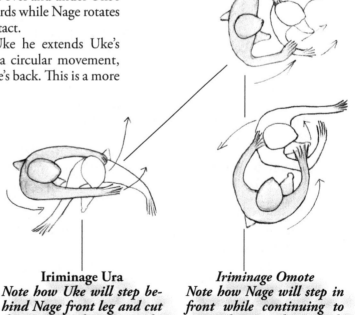

Iriminage Ura
Note how Uke will step behind Nage front leg and cut down in the direction indicated by the arrows.

Iriminage Omote
Note how Nage will step in front while continuing to twist Uke around in a circle as indicated by the arrows.

One further Yokomen attack is Gyaku Yokomen Uchi.

After stepping forward to strike **Yokomen uchi** to the side of the head Uke realises that Nage has stepped back so the strike has missed. Uke immediately slides forward to follow Nage's backward movement and strikes again with the back of his hand... **Tegatana**. This strike is **gyaku yokomen uchi**.

Nage's response to this would be to enter and take the striking arm from underneath while rotating the elbow forward leading Uke down into **Gokyo Ura**.

Oddly enough, Gokyo is the only application generally practiced from Gyaku Yokomen Uchi. Rarely is the importance of this strike emphasised when it is used by Nage within a technical application. Nage uses it to change sides during the progress of an application. It is also the opening move to counter **shomen uch**i leading Nage into the application of **Ikkyo** and those that follow from **Ikkyo**, such as **Nikyo, Sankyo, Yonkyo...**

> ### Dealing with wrist grabs...

At the very beginning Aikido practice is usually from a static position involving a wrist grab of one kind or another. Cross hand grip (**Ai Hanmi Katatetori** – or **Ai Hanmi Tekubi Mochi** or **Katate Mochi**), and gripping the same side (**Gyaku Hanmi Katatetori** – or **Gyaku Hanmi Tekubi Mochi** or **Katate Mochi**) are the usual ones practiced at first. Once the student is comfortable in dealing with these two kinds of grabs other grabs are introduced. **Morotedori** or two hands on one (called **Ryotemochi** in some dojos) and **Ryotetori** (or **Ryo-tekubi-dori**) which is both hands grabbing one on one.

Learning to respond to a grabbing attack is essential basic training. It is the groundwork to understanding how to deal with punches and strikes. It teaches us spacing and distance or **maai**, connection or **musubi**, and awareness of the energy flow coming from Uke. It teaches us how to go around or to lead that energy by making use of the connection we have with Uke when he grabs us.

Ai Hanmi Katatetori

Gyaku Hanmi Katatetori

Breaking the grip in various ways is part of how we deal with grabbing attacks.

Another way of dealing with a grab is moving and leading Uke into a throw during which he will let go in order to take **Ukemi**.

We have already looked at **Tai No Henka** so this following movement is similar. Instead of turning **Tenkan** so Nage finishes parallel to Uke while leading Uke forward to an unbalanced position, Nage steps across in front of Uke to lead Uke into a sweeping half turn (*another form of Tenshin*) to again finish parallel.

Note that Nage steps forward with the foot nearest to Uke while maintaing extension through his leading arm where it is grabbed.

***Above*: Beginning in Gyaku Hanmi,** the moment Uke grabs Nage's wrist, Nage repositions his body so it faces Uke at an oblique angle. With his gripped hand lined up with his centre Nage then steps across in front of Uke which turns Uke completely around so they both face the same direction but Uke is unbalanced. Note that Nage doesn't change the position of his arm (and hand) in relation to his body. He doesn't push with his arm. **He simply moves his whole body forward as a single unit, maintaining a relaxed but firm attitude.** Uke cannot stop this movement because he is not dealing with a single arm but with the whole body mass of Nage moving forward. Even if the grip is the much stronger **Morotedori** the movement and end result is exactly the same.

From this unbalanced position Uke can be thrown forward if Nage continues to extend or even shifts further forward, or sideways or backwards if Nage rotates his extended arm up over Uke's head.

***Below*: Moving outside (ura or soto)** and slightly to the rear while making use of Uke's need to maintain his grip.

Beginning in gyaku hanmi stance Nage shifts his whole body slightly to the rear of Uke's body line. This has the tendency to make Uke lean a little backwards. At the same moment Nage rotates his hand around so the **Tegatana** or hand blade is cutting Uke's wrist in towards his centre. This will tip Uke further backwards. As he continues to extend his arm towards Uke's face Nage completes a **Tenkan** step and is now aligned behind Uke with Uke's balance now shifted forward.

Uke subconsciously maintains his grip on Nage's wrist as he feels himself being unbalanced. This is a natural reaction to prevent himself from falling over, and it is this reaction that Nage has made use of while they remain connected. If Nage continues to extend, Uke will become completely unbalanced and will be forced to let go and take a forward **ukemi**. Uke will take the forward roll on the outside arm because he is already in a position to make this a comfortable **ukemi**.

Moving inside (*uchi or omote*) and using atemi to Uke's face to distract his attention and to unbalance him slightly to the rear, is another method of dealing with a grabbing attack.

We begin in exactly the same **gyaku hanmi** stance as for the previous exercise.

This time however entry is made inside (**uchi or omote**) with the strike directly towards Uke's centre (**atemi** to the face), while Nage's body moves slightly offline. As Uke momentarily attempts to deal with this **atemi**, Nage slips under the extended arm by stepping forward. Turning with a **Kaiten** move Nage finishes by extending the gripped arm slightly forward which causes Uke to be unbalanced to the front. He can be thrown forwards or backwards from this point with a **Kokyunage** (breath throw), or Nage could step back and cut Uke's arm all the way to the mat and up behind in a large circular move ready to do a **Kaitenage** (circular throw).

This finish follows from the **soto** or **ura**
form on the previous page...
Nage steps forward and cuts down
Uke lets go as he steps forward to escape
with **mae kaiten ukemi** or forwards roll...
A similar finish would occur from the example above except Uke may roll on the
same side as the hand grip instead of stepping forward to use the other side...

Breaking the grip.

There are many ways of breaking a grip to enable application of a technique...

Starting from **Ai Hanmi Katatetori,** the moment Uke grabs, Nage turns his palm upwards. Looking at the pictures above it can be seen that the knife blade (**Tegatana**) side is resting on Uke's wrist, and it is a simple matter to rotate the hand over cutting Uke's wrist down to break the grip.

Continuing to turn a point is reached where Uke can no longer hold on and the grip is easily broken. This is one of the ways entry can be made for **iriminage** or **kokyunage**.

If Nage's palm is facing down when Uke grabs on top and from outside instead of inside the wrist, the **Tegatana** is rotated upwards against Uke's wrist to break the grip. Nage can now enter around this grip to the rear of Uke allowing the possibilities of **iriminage**, **kokyunage**, or the **Katame waza** from **Ikkyo** to **Yonkyo** can follow from this **ura** entry.

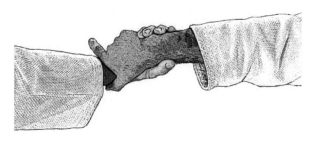

Starting again from the same Ai **Hanmi Katatetori** attack, but without turning the palm up, turning the palm slightly towards Uke's wrist as he grabs will allow the grip shown here.

This again allows entry for **iriminage**, **shihonage**, **kokyunage** or as shown here , entering with application of **Yonkyo**, *a grip that attacks the radial bone and the nerves along it...*

In this **ai hanmi** example as Uke grabs Nage's upturned wrist, Nage leads him forward while entering behind to do **iriminage**.

Gyaku Hanmi Katatetori

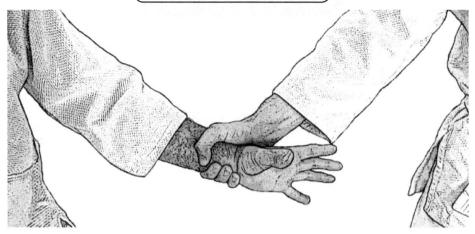

From **Gyaku Hanmi Katatetori** there are also many different ways to break the grip which can be done at **Jodan**, **Chudan** and **Gedan** levels.

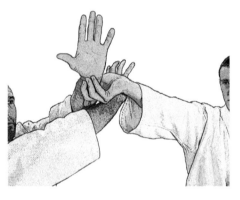

Jodan — upper level

Raise the grabbed hand up as if to cut **shomen uchi**. As Uke's wrist opens and the fingers loosen cut underneath with the other hand initially using **Tegatana**.

As the grip breaks, grasp Uke's wrist and step behind ready to lead him into any one of many techniques. (**Irimi-nage, Kokyunage,** etc.)

Raising Uke's hand should also be combined with drawing Uke forward so balance is disturbed, making it easy to enter behind while Uke is trying to recover.

Chudan— mid level

Nage turns so that Uke's grip is situated in front of his centre.
This is part of a small circle created with Nage's arm to loosen Uke's grip. Nage rests his other hand or forearm against the back of Uke's hand and steps sideways to enter behind. This movement releases Uke's hand so Nage can enter behind.

Gedan— lower level

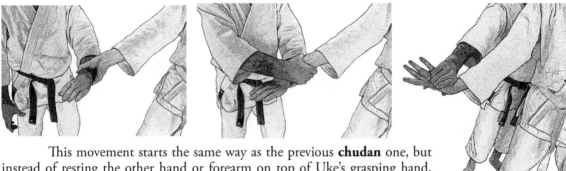

This movement starts the same way as the previous **chudan** one, but instead of resting the other hand or forearm on top of Uke's grasping hand, Nage reaches in front to grasp Uke's wrist and literally peels the hand away before entering sideways behind Uke.

Instead of entering behind Nage could step forward as Uke's hand peels away to do **Shihonage Omote**. Entering behind will of course facilitate **iriminage** or **kokyunage**.

Chudan variation

Instead of raising high as shown for **Jodan** Nage raises his hand a short distance before rotating his hand outwards over Uke's wrist. Using the knife blade side of his hand (**Tegatana**) Nage cuts Uke's wrist down and around in front to bring Uke's hand in line with his centre. He grasps Uke's wrist with his other hand break the grip. Nage could step forward to do **shihonage omote** or step behind for **iriminage** or **kokyunage**.

These basic grasping attacks are usually practiced from a static position at first so an understanding of how not to resist but to move when dealing with these attacks can be learned. Once an understanding of the movement is embedded, static practice is no longer needed.

Moving practice.

Nage begins moving at the moment Uke's hand makes contact, not too quick but enough to make Uke feel he has to finish grabbing. If Nage moves too soon Uke will simply stop. There is no point in grabbing at something that isn't there. Nage must allow contact to make the connection between himself and Uke, before leading Uke forward into an over committed unbalanced position. In effect Nage makes Uke reach further than normally needed to complete the grip. As a consequence he is more likely to hang on to prevent himself from falling rather than gripping in order to control. **This is a momentary subconscious psychological effect,** and before Uke is even aware of this Nage throws him or moves in a way that will further unbalance Uke's centre making him fall. The movement adds impetus to the fall, and gravity makes certain it will happen.

> ### Two Ways of dealing with Katatori — shoulder grab

A one handed shoulder grab will be from **Gyaku Hanmi.** If both shoulders are grabbed then Uke will tend to be more front on even though it may still be **gyaku hanmi.**

As Nage commences his shift to the Ura side his arm swings underneath and outside of Uke's arm, raising up until the forearm rests against Uke's elbow.

As Nage shifts further to the **Ura** side he moves forward bringing his lead foot close to Uke's lead foot. The movement is completed with a **Kaiten** turn which extends Uke's elbow forward to unbalance him. He can now be thrown forwards or backwards.

Starting from the same shoulder grab Nage strikes towards Uke's face to make him lean back. This time as Nage slips to the side and enters he rotates his arm over and around to the outside of Uke's grabbing arm, coming back up from underneath as the **Kaiten** turn is completed. This raises Uke's elbow and takes away his balance. It also traps Uke's hand so he can't let go and a lot more pressure is exerted in extending the elbow. This is more painful than the one above so caution is required when practicing. Again Uke can be thrown forwards or backwards.

Part Four

Basic Katame Waza
Applications of technique in response to an attack

Ikkyo — Ude Osae

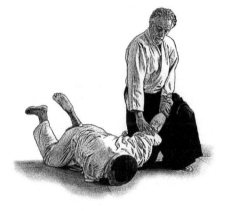

Sometimes referred to as **Dai Ikkyo** or simply just **Ikkyo** (**Ikkajo** in some styles), **Ikkyo** is the first technique taught to beginning students. Sometimes it is called the *first principle* since it is the first of a series of takedowns that employ an arm pin or lock as a way of immobilising Uke. It is essential to learn **Ikkyo** as it is embodied in **Nikkyo, Sankyo, Yonkyo**, and all arm pins or locks (**Ude Osae** and **Katame Waza**). It also a part of what underlies many other applications so if a mental block occurs while attempting one of the other arm pins, or related techniques, especially if the attack that leads to it is different or unusual, or something unexpected, it helps to go back to **Ikkyo** as a way of leading into those other applications.

Ikkyo, as simple as it appears to be, is extraordinarily effective.

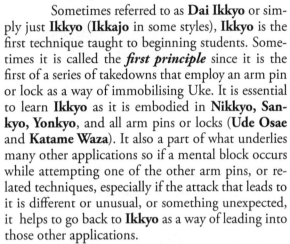

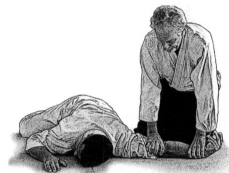
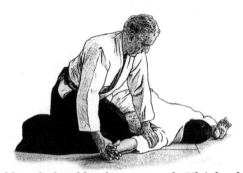

Ikkyo has two finishes, a pin holding the wrist — a pin holding the hand bending it towards Uke's head

Of course, it depends on precise timing of the entry which differs slightly for the **Omote** and **Ura** forms, the angle or line of entry towards Uke's centre which will unbalance or destabilise him for either **Omote** or **Ura**, and the way in which Uke is taken down to be pinned.

The pin is the same for both **Omote** and **Ura** and should have Uke's elbow and palm turned outwards and extended at an angle of slightly more than 90 degrees from the perpendicular line of Uke's body.

With **Ikkyo** hold down, Nage finishes square on to Uke's extended arm and at an obtuse angle to Uke's centre line. Both the extended centre line of Nage and of Uke will intersect somewhere at an invisible point in front of Uke's head. This triangular and square connection makes a strong finish.

Nage has one knee against Uke's ribcage and the other near the wrist. Uke's energy is extended out through his arm which has the elbow and palm turned forward. It is difficult for Uke to get up as any attempt can be thwarted simply by extending his arm further away from his body while holding the knee firmly against his rib cage.

Gyaku Hanmi Katatetori Ikkyo Omote

Step off line slightly outside of Uke's arm, and as you step back cut Uke's elbow down to draw him off balance. Extend up the back leg, through the hip and along the arm as you reach for Uke's elbow. Extend the elbow up and over towards Uke's face, turning him around to face the other way.

Ikkyo is often taught at first from **Ai Hanmi Katatetori** (*Kosadori*) *or as above from* **Gyaku Hanmi Katatetori.**

Uke grabbing creates a point of contact where the flow of energy can be felt. It is easier to deal with this energy than to deal with the energy coming from a punch or a strike.

To finish, Nage extends Uke's elbow towards his face, continues to rotate the elbow over as Uke turns, steps in with a slight sliding step to take Uke down until he touches the mat with his free hand, then finally steps slightly out to the side while dropping to the knees to prepare for the pin. This leads Uke down into the open space Nage initially created by moving in at an angle. He has no option but to fall into this space. Finally the hold down described earlier is applied.

Katatori Men Uchi Ikkyo Omote

With **Katatori Men Uchi** (*Shoulder grab and shomen strike to the face*) Nage intercepts the **Shomen** strike at the same time turning backwards (**Tenkan**) to allow the force of the strike to dissipate downwards. This causes Uke to lose balance by falling slightly forward. Nage immediately re enters as Uke tries to recover his balance. Nage cuts Uke's striking arm back upwards and in towards his face turning him back in the same way as in **Gyaku hanmi Katatetori ikkyo omote**. The **omote** finish is then exactly the same as that shown above.

Ikkyo Finish position...

With **Katatori Men Uchi,** if Nage waits for Uke to make the strike the only option is to turn **tenkan** as shown above, to allow it to pass. On the other hand if Nage counters with a strike towards Uke's face the instant the shoulder is grabbed, Uke's strike doesn't occur but becomes a defensive attempt to block being struck in the face. Nage also has the other hand free to stike elsewhere below Uke's head.

Continuing his forward movement he will tip Uke's elbow over through his centreline to take Uke down for **Ikkyo Omote.**

> **Shomen Uchi Ikkyo Omote**

With **Shomen Uchi Ikkyo Omote** the timing of the entry is important. Nage must enter with his arm raising to meet Uke's rising arm. Contact is made with one forearm against the other forearm and not by grabbing the wrist. Nage's other hand rotates Uke's elbow up and over and in towards his face to turn Uke around and over. At the same time Nage takes a sliding step in towards Uke's centre to tip him over sideways. Uke will fall over and support himself with his free hand. Nage brings his back foot forward to join the front foot then steps out sideways to draw Uke across into the empty space, dropping to one knee to take Uke down completely to the mat. As Nage lowers himself into position for the pin he slides Uke's trapped arm over his knee while rotating the elbow and palm forward. Again the finish is the same as previously described. (*page 81.*)

Ikkyo Ude Osae is also practiced from **Hanmi Handachi** (*Nage seated with Uke standing and attacking*) as well as **suwari waza** (*both Uke and Nage seated — shown below*). It is also practiced against attacks from the rear such as both hands, wrists or shoulders grabbed from behind, one hand grabbed with a simultaneous choke hold (***tekubi mochi kubishimi***), collar grab, and various attacks from the side and in front.

With both partners seated, as Uke attacks with **shomen uchi,** Nage slides forward a fraction to intercept Uke's striking arm.

Extending Uke's elbow back towards his face Nage tips Uke over sideways, and moving in with the inside knee, Nage lowers his weight down then swivels slightly away from Uke, drawing Uke back over into the space created. The finish is again the same as before, square on to Uke's extended arm with one knee held against Uke's ribcage and the other near Uke's wrist. Uke's elbow and hand are rotated forward.

Ikkyo finish from strikes...
After cutting the forearm up and over to lead Uke down, Nage finishes by grabbing the wrist while the other hand maintain a firm grip on the elbow which is rotated forwards to turn Uke's shoulder down pinning him to the mat.

Ikkyo Finish from grabs...
*will always finish with Nage holding Uke's hand in a **nikyo** grip and turning the palm in towards Uke's face as it is pinned.*

Practicing techniques in a seated position (**suwari waza**) is difficult because the legs are restricted. However, **shikko** practice teaches us how to move comfortably in a seated position (from **seiza**) and should be practiced regularly. The benefit is that it teaches us how to move from our centre utilising the hips and takes focus away from relying on moving the legs first. It develops full body coordination and improves the same techniques practiced from a standing position (**tachi waza**). It also helps strengthen the large muscles in the legs, and over time increases flexibility in the ankles and toes.

The same result applies to techniques practiced from **Hanmi Handachi** in that the person seated must move to avoid the attack and draw the standing person down into the space created so a technique can be applied.

See pages 234 to 244 for techniques in Hanmi Handachi and Suwari waza.

*It should be remembered that **Ikkyo** is a way of controlling Uke's upper body by rotating the elbow over and in towards the face and centre line to unbalance and turn Uke enough to allow Nage to lead Uke down into a position enabling a pin. By controlling the elbow Nage can manipulate Uke with little effort and this principle applies to many different techniques as well.*

Ushiro Ryokatatori Ikkyo Omote

As soon as Uke grabs the shoulders from behind Nage slides a little to one side, disturbing Uke's upper body balance and giving enough room to allow Nage to step back under one of Uke's arms to position himself partly behind Uke.

This has the effect of drawing Uke forward to a more unbalanced position. It also places Uke's elbow right in front on Nage's head. Nage now uses his head to extend Uke's elbow forward, in effect rotating the elbow over enough to tip Uke into a forward fall.

As Uke falls Nage takes the elbow with his inside arm and continues to extend downwards. At the same time he grips Uke's hand which is loosing its grip on the shoulder and using this second grip to extend along Uke's arm towards Uke's shoulder he enters with a slight step forward in at an angle towards Uke's shoulder. This takes Uke down onto the mat. Nage then finishes by stepping out away from Uke so Uke will fall into the empty space created. The hold down is finished as previously described making sure that the elbow is rotated forward to prevent any attempt by Uke to escape. In this example Uke's palm is gripped with a **Nikyo** hand hold. To finish the fingers and palm are turned towards Uke's head.

Angles and lines of movement for Ikkyo Omote and Ikkyo Ura

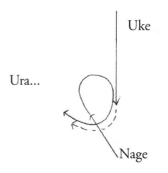

Omote...

The straight arrow indicates Uke's original line of attack. The dotted arrow shows the direction Uke is turned by Nage's entry.

The arrows for Nage indicate the triangular nature of Nage's entry and movement in towards Uke, then out again to create a space for Uke to fall into.

This triangular entry pattern is repeated for many techniques but is particularly important for initiating the **omote forms of Ikkyo and other Katame waza such as Nikyo, Sankyo, and Yonkyo.**

Ura...

The straight arrow and the continuing dotted arrow indicates Uke's movement is not turned back but continued forward and around to the rear thus making a circular movement.

Nage's entry is also circular after the initial step in to the rear of Uke. By turning **Tenkan** he will draw Uke completely around in a circle. Sometimes far enough so Uke is facing the same direction as he was when entering to attack.

Usually the finish position is about two thirds of the way round the circle.

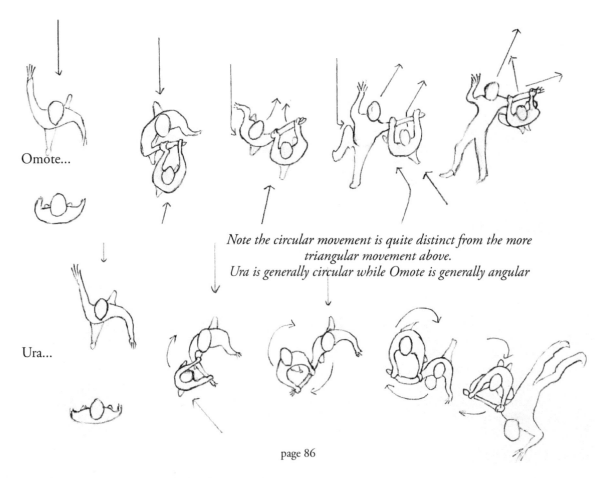

Omote...

Ura...

Note the circular movement is quite distinct from the more triangular movement above.
Ura is generally circular while Omote is generally angular

Shomen Uchi Ikkyo Ura

Nage meets Uke as Uke's strike commences to come down. Nage enters by taking an **Irimi** step to the rear of Uke's front leg, at the same time redirecting Uke's striking arm down in a semi circle to the rear. The moment Uke's arm is lined up along Nage's centre line he commences to make a **Tenkan** turn (*to the rear*) while continuing to cut down the arm at the same time. Uke will feel this turning backwards movement which begins to spiral him downwards.

He will drop down onto the knee of the leg closest to Nage, (*his inside leg*). This will allow him to spin further around with the least resistance. As Nage spins Uke around he lowers himself to the mat taking Uke all the way down. Finally the **Ikkyo Ude Osae** (*arm lock*) for the **Ura form is applied in exactly the same way as it is applied for the Omote form.**

Shomen Uchi Nikyo (*Kote Mawashi*) Omote

Shomen Uchi Nikyo Omote begins the exact same way as for **Ikkyo Omote**,. From shomen uchi, Sankyo Omote and Yonkyo Omote also begin in exactly the same way.

In order to facilitate the change from the *first principle* (Ikkyo) to the *second principle* (**Nikyo**), *the third* (**Sankyo**) and *the fourth* (**Yonkyo**), it is imperative that as Nage enters to take control of Uke's striking arm **he must not grab the wrist — he uses his forearm or the base of the side of the hand (Tegatana)** to redirect the striking arm.

Only after he has entered and deflected Uke's arm downward and across in front of Uke to turn and lead Uke down towards the mat (*as he would for Ikkyo Omote*) does Nage change the hand position into the required grip for whichever technique he is going to do.

It can be clearly seen here how the forearm is used to deflect the **shomen uchi** strike while at the same moment Nage commences to enter and take Uke's elbow in preparation to rotate it up and over as well as across in front.

In this case the Nikyo grip is already applied because Uke had grabbed Nage's shoulder. As the hand is freed Nage reaches for Uke's elbow to rotate it over exactly as for Ikkyo Omote, but maintaing the Nikyo grip.

From strikes such as Shomen Uchi, Nage enters as for Ikkyo Omote but needs to apply Nikyo hand grip as he rotates Uke over. So he changes grip from cutting down with his forearm into the Nikyo grip which is then maintained until Uke is on the mat and can be pinned down.

Refer to Receiving Ikkyo Ude Osae Omote Form (page 53) for method of receiving safely.

If Uke resists he will be forcibly turned by the simple fact that Nage's whole body will move forward into Uke's centre which forces Uke to turn or he will be end up flat on his back.

By allowing his body to turn, pivoting on the balls of the feet but without stepping forward, Uke can then go down onto the outside knee while supporting himself with the other arm. This stops him from being slammed down face first into the mat. At the same time Nage's downward extension prevents Uke from getting up and gives Nage time to change the grip before proceeding with the final pin.

This entry and initial take-down is the same for **Sankyo** and for **Yonkyo omote** until the point where the grip is changed. Since each pin is different the final move to get into the pinning position is also different.

A close look at **Nikyo Omote** hand change...

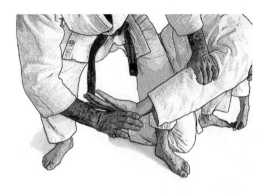

Nage, because he hasn't gripped Uke's wrist, slides his hand over and down along the top of Uke's hand. Note that forward and downward extension is maintained through Uke's elbow which makes it difficult for Uke to get up.

Nage continues to maintain extension Through Uke's elbow while turning Uke's hand back. At this point Nage has his thumb hooked behind the other side of Uke's hand ready to grip at the base of Uke's thumb.

Nage finishes the rotational movement finishing with a firm grip having turned Uke's hand over so the palm is facing forward.

Nage is now ready to lead Uke forward into a face down prone position where he can apply the **Nikyo** pin to Uke's arm. Note that Uke is down on the inside knee which is a position that allows him to be either taken forward or turned backward. Nage's leg in front of Uke's knee however indicates that the movement will be forward from this position.

Nage can either take Uke down as for **Ikkyo** then bring the arm back to the **Nikyo** pin position, or as he takes Uke forward he can draw the hand upwards and move around it so his knee drops in front of Uke's shoulder first to prevent forward movement while he positions the arm for the pin. The second way is a better option since it is unlikely to damage Uke's shoulder by trying to bring it back up against the joint which may not be as flexible in some people as it is in others. In either case ***Nage does not let go of Uke's hand until he has positioned himself to apply the arm pin.***

Shomen Uchi Nikyo (Kote Mawashi) Omote...continued

It can be clearly seen how **Nikyo** resembles **Ikkyo** in the takedown above. Note however the **Nikyo** hand-hold is maintained until Nage places it in the crook of his arm to cradle it.

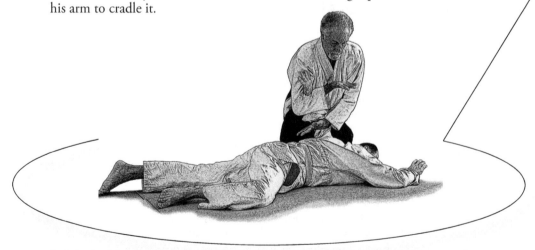

It is locked in place by the elbow. Nage's other hand draws Uke's elbow in close to his body so full contact with the arm is maintained through the hold-down. If the arm lock is applied correctly, Uke will be unable to move forward or backward nor will he be able to twist out of it.

A gentle twist towards Uke's head by Nage will convince Uke to submit.

Shomen Uchi Nikyo (*Kote Mawashi*) Ura

The Ura form differs from Omote. Entry is to the rear (Ura) as the **shomen uchi** strike comes down. At the moment Nage's forearm contacts Uke's wrist **Nage takes Uke's wrist** *instead of the elbow*. Nage steps further around to the rear (**Tenkan**), leading Uke downwards into an unstable position. While doing this Nage wraps his hand around Uke's hand the same way as described for Omote while maintaining the grip on Uke's wrist. He brings Uke's wrist up to his shoulder and locks it firmly by keeping his elbows down. With a slight forward movement towards Uke's unstable centre, Nage applies a downwards pressure on the elbow while keeping the wrist locked. This causes Uke to drop to his knees to avoid the pain.

The Ulna and the Radius bones are rotated and locked at the elbow and wrist, but the shoulder remains flexible. Applying downwards pressure on the elbow causes intense pain., but because the shoulder is not locked Uke can drop to his knees to avoid it — an instant reaction the moment the lock is applied.

The moment Uke's knees touch the mat Nage makes another but smaller *Irimi Tenkan* move. Stepping just behind the level of Uke's knee and as he completes this **2nd Tenkan** move he leads Uke's trapped arm around to Uke's rear all the while maintaining his firm grip on Uke's hand.

Uke will spiral on his inside knee which he has placed down appropriately to allow easier receiving, finally falling onto his face as Nage positions himself to apply the Nikyo pin.

Again, at no time does Nage release the hand grip he has on Uke until he is ready for the pin, whereupon he locks Uke's wrist with his elbow so he can release the grip on the hand and use that arm to draw Uke's elbow in tight to apply the pin described above.

Shomen Uchi Nikyo (*Kote Mawashi*) Ura continued...

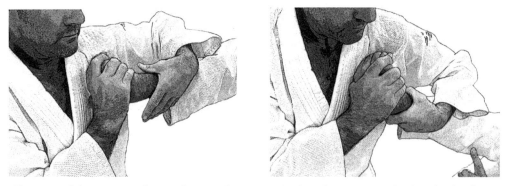

Close up of the position for applying **Nikyo Ura.** And as the pin is applied and Uke drops to his knees, Nage enters again slightly to the rear of Uke for the second **Irimi Tenkan** movement to lead Uke around and down so the final arm lock (**Katame Waza**) can be applied.

Gyaku Hanmi Katatori Nikyo (*Kote Mawashi*)

At the moment Uke grabs the shoulder Nage strikes with an **atemi** to Uke's face to distract him from the attack while at the same time making a slight **Irimi** to the **Omote** side and then allowing the back foot to drift across to the rear.

As Uke deflects the atemi to his face Nage allows his hand blade (*Tegatana*) to cut Uke's elbow down further unbalancing him. Nage then rolls the elbow over to lead Uke down to the mat for the finishing arm bar.

Gyaku Hanmi Katatori Nikyo (*Kote Mawashi*) continued...

For **Nikyo Omote**, instead of gripping the wrist and dropping the elbow he takes Uke's elbow from underneath and rolls it up and over (*as in **Ikkyo Omote** or **Nikyo Omote** from **Shomen Uchi***), extending downwards across the front of Uke while maintaining the grip on Uke's hand which will come off from the shoulder quite easily.

Nage now extends Uke's elbow forward as the grip is released from the shoulder. He maintains the grip on Uke's hand as he leads him down to the mat to finish in the same manner as for **Shomen Uchi Nikyo Omote.**

For the **Ura** form Nage also applies **atemi** to Uke's face but enters not on the inside of Uke's grabbing arm but slightly to the outside of the arm. It is more **stepping sideways rather than backwards at an angle**. This will tip Uke over onto one side thus making him unstable.

Nage then cuts it down at the elbow, rolls Uke's hand over and locks it in the position against his shoulder making sure the thumb is trapped. The elbow is dropped and Uke will drop to his knees to receive the pain, at which point Nage enters **Tenkan** and spirals Uke in a circle to the rear. **The arm pin is the same for both the Omote and Ura forms.**

Once Uke has dropped to the mat and is on one or both knees, Nage enters behind with an **Irimi Tenkan** pivoting Uke around to his rear but **without letting go of the Nikyo hand hold**. Nage then drops to his knees and applies the pin to immobilize Uke.

The finish for Nikyo Ura is the same as shown on page 90 and 91.

A slightly different way of doing **Gyaku Hanmi Katatori Nikyo** etc is to step back after the **atemi** to draw Uke forwards and down to an unbalanced position.

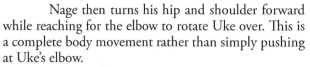

Nage then turns his hip and shoulder forward while reaching for the elbow to rotate Uke over. This is a complete body movement rather than simply pushing at Uke's elbow.

As Uke continues to rotate his shoulder forward and extending Nage's elbow, the grip will come away from the shoulder. Nage can now step forward to take Uke down to the mat for the finish with the **Nikyo** arm lock as already described.

Gyaku Hanmi Katatetori Nikyo (*Kote Mawashi*)

This movement is exactly the same conceptually and internally. The only obvious difference is instead of grabbing the shoulder Uke is grabbing Nage's wrist and there is slightly more distance between them. It would be the same if he grabbed Nage's elbow (*Hijitori.*)

Entering slightly to the inside with **atemi** to the face, Nage cuts down the elbow when Uke deflects the **Tegatana.** This unbalances Uke forwards.

Nage must only cut down enough to unbalance Uke so he can follow through with the technique as required. If he cuts down too far, Uke may fall over or take a step to compensate and thus try to counter Nage's **Nikyo**.

Taking Uke's wrist with a strong **Nikyo** grip Nage rotates Uke's hand over while at the same time extending Uke's elbow forward. Uke is now ready to be taken down to the mat in exactly the same way we previously did for **Shomen Uchi Nikyo Omote**. (*page 90.*)

For the **Ura** form, the initial entry is made slightly to the outside of the grabbing arm. As the grip is taken instead of rotating the hand and elbow forward and over down towards the mat, Nage will make a small **Tenkan** move to position himself just behind the line of Uke's centre, bringing the grasped hand up and locking it to his shoulder so he can drop Uke with the **Nikyo** hand lock, before completing the technique with another **Irimi Tenkan** movement to lead Uke around to the rear where the final arm lock will be applied. (*page 91.*)

Sankyo (*Kote Hineri*)

Shomen Uchi Sankyo Omote

For **Shomen Uchi Sankyo Omote** the beginning is the same as for Shomen uchi Ikkyo Omote and Shomen Uchi Nikyo Omote. Remember not to grip the wrist at this initial entry. Nage extends his arm upwards exactly as he would for shomen and this shifts the line of Uke's strike enough to allow the rotation of Uke's elbow over and down with his wrist (not grabbed) as the pivot point...

As Uke is taken forward and down to the mat Nage allows his hand to slide back along the edge of the inside of Uke's hand which has been turned up because of the rotation of the elbow forward.

The grip is taken palm against palm with Nage locking Uke's little finger into a tight grip. (*Compare with the close ups shown for Nikyo Omote to see difference*).

Nage extends Uke's hand and elbow forward then changes hands by taking the hand away from the elbow to grasp Uke's hand from the other side. The hand that itinally grabbed the sankyo grip is now free to make an atemi to Uke's face as Nage comes around the front of Uke's arm. He can now walk backwards, cutting the arm downwards from the elbow to take Uke down to the mat for the sankyo arm bar or pin.

In some cases using the Sankyo grip to control Uke Nage can bring Uke back up onto his feet in order to reposition him before coming around in front to take him down for the pin or arm bar.

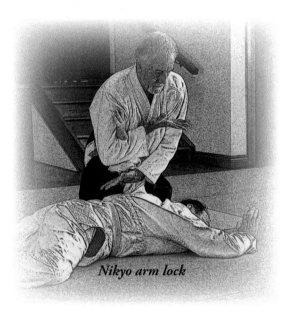

Nikyo arm lock

Sankyo arm lock

Comparing the **Sankyo** arm lock with the **Nikyo** there are two obvious differences. The most obvious is that for **Sankyo**, Uke's hand is grasped and held to maintain the inwards wrist twist and the palm is held flat against Nage's shoulder. This results in Uke's elbow also being twisted so pressure when applied is against the direction the joint moves rather than in the same direction. *It is a much more painful and restricting arm bar when compared to Nikyo.* Also Nage's arms are in the opposite position when applying **Nikyo**. The arm that would have held the wrist in **Nikyo** is now ready to draw the elbow in while the other hand holds Uke's hand against the shoulder.

The similarities are that Nage locks Uke in position with his knees on both sides of Uke's shoulder to prevent movement forwards or backwards, and a slight leaning forward posture will ensure Uke can not roll away or counter the immobilisation (*Katame Waza*).

As the student's experience and understanding of basic aspects of the technique increase, more complex methods of attack are introduced. **The end result is the same**: how we get there can vary considerably depending on the degree of difficulty or complexity of the attack.

The following example is from an attack considered to have a degree of difficulty to circumvent.

> ### Katatetori (*Katatemochi*) Kubishimi Sankyo Omote

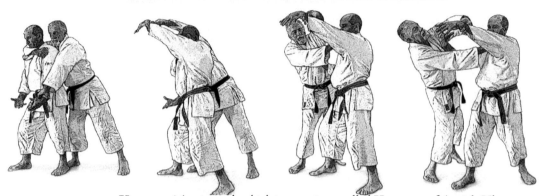

Katatetori (*wrist grab which is sometimes called **Katatemochi***) with Uke coming around behind to choke Nage with his other arm, **Kubishimi** can be difficult to escape from if Uke really applies a strong strangle hold on Nage's neck.

Nage must drop his chin to prevent Uke from crushing the throat. At the same instant, Nage drops his centre to create a more stable base then raises his grabbed hand up directly in front as he would for **shomen uchi**. This will allow him to slip back underneath the raised arm with one step after realigning his hips (centre) to create what is in effect an **ai hanmi** stance in relation to Uke's now twisted forward and unbalanced position. Uke is still hanging on to Nage's shoulder where he grabbed when applying the initial choke. Nage uses his free hand to make an **atemi** to Uke's face, forcing Uke further back into a more unstable position.

Nage now takes the **sankyo** grip with both hands extending it towards Uke's centre to continue destabilising him. To finish the technique from this point is the same as if doing it from **Shomen Uchi**. **Nage cuts Uke's forearm down as if it were a bokken.** This tips Uke over causing him to reach down to the mat to support himself. Nage immediately comes around in front of Uke's extended arm and uses one hand to grasp Uke's elbow. Nage steps back, dragging Uke forwards down onto his face, and finishes the technique with exactly the same arm bar (*Sankyo Pin or Katame Waza*) already described for **Shomen Uchi Sankyo Omote.**

Katatori Sankyo Omote

The moment Uke grabs the shoulder Nage enters slightly with an **atemi** to Uke's face. Stepping back Nage draws Uke forward while cutting the elbow down, and taking hold of the hand against the shoulder. As soon as Uke starts to lose balance Nage turns his hip and shoulder forward, at the same time using his other hand to extend forward through Uke's elbow. This turns Uke over and breaks his grip on Nage's shoulder.

Nage lets go of the elbow allowing his hand to slide down along Uke's arm to take the **sankyo** grip in exactly the same way as already described for **Shomen Uchi Sankyo Omote**.

Having taken a strong **sankyo** grip Nage comes around in front of Uke and uses an **atemi** to further destabilise Uke. The final move is to take Uke's elbow and by stepping backwards Nage leads Uke forwards and down onto his face to apply the **sankyo** arm lock.

Nage follows Uke down to the mat, locks Uke's shoulder with a knee on either side, and changes hands so he can hold Uke's palm against his shoulder to apply the arm lock.

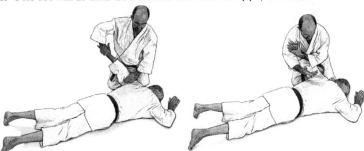

Shomen Uchi Sankyo Ura

Nage intercepts the **shomen** strike and entering slightly to the rear of Uke's front leg, turns Uke's elbow over and leads it towards the rear. He extends the elbow out at the same time as the entry is completed, allowing his hand to slide down to take the initial **sankyo** grip. Once Uke is turned over he changes grip and reaches for the elbow with the other hand.

Continuing to bring Uke's arm down Nage enters again behind Uke turning the elbow completely around towards the rear. Uke has no option but to drop onto the inside knee to make it easier for him to receive the technique. Nage continues to lead Uke around to the rear until he falls face down onto the mat.

Nage should exercise extreme caution when applying Sankyo or any arm bar, since too fasst an application or too much force suddenly applied will seriously damage Uke's elbow and shoulder...

Practitioners should remember that they are lending their body to their partner for the purpose of practicing application of technique, and that neither should wish to cause harm when it is their turn to be Nage...

Nage drops to his knees trapping Uke's shoulder while preparing to change grip once again for the final pin. This is exactly the same pin already described for the Omote form. Uke's palm is held against Nage's shoulder which twists the elbow and locks it in an immovable position tight against Nage's centre. Any twisting movement now will cause severe pain for Uke who will have no choice but to submit.

Yonkyo — Tekubi Osae

Shomen Uchi Yonkyo Omote

Yonkyo is the fourth **Katame waza** in the series beginning with **Ikkyo**, and is one that most students have some difficulty with. Perhaps this could be because the student focuses on inflicting pain rather than creating a movement that will control Uke and take him down to the mat.

Once on the mat if the **Yonkyo** has been applied correctly Uke will not feel much until he tries to escape or get up. Any attempt to escape will put the **Yonkyo** on with its accompanying nerve tingling pain. Effectively in this situation Uke puts the technique on himself by trying to get away from it.

This begins the exact same way as Ikkyo Omote. Remembering not to grasp the wrist Nage enters using his forearm (**Tegatana**) to deflect Uke's **shomen Uchi**. He reaches for the elbow and turns it over and across in front of Uke. This is still exactly the same start as for **Ikkyo**, **Nikyo** and **Sankyo** as well. This effectively turns Uke around and begins to take him down towards the mat.

Once Uke reaches for the mat and is supporting himself with his free hand and his knee, Nage extends the elbow and changes to the **Yonkyo** grip. *This grip is the same one used to hold a Bokken,* and Uke imagines Nage's forearm as the hilt of a **Bokken** (*Wooden training sword*). Cutting down with this imaginary sword takes Uke flat onto the mat. Nage steps forward and with his inside leg applies pressure to extend Uke's elbow forward. This extends the elbow enough to cause convincing pain both in the elbow and along the nerves adjoining the radial bone.

With the **Ura** form (not depicted) the entry is to the **soto** or **ura** side of the **shomen uchi exactly as if entering for Shomen Uchi Ikkyo Ura.** Nage enters with a small **Irimi Tenkan** movement and as he extends Uke's elbow he changes the grip to the **Yonkyo** grip and enters further behind Uke with a larger **Irimi Kaiten** movement while at the same time cutting down with Uke's forearm as if it were a **bokken**. Uke will fly around the perimeter of this circle to the rear to finish flat on his face at which point Nage enters and applies the knee pressure to extend the elbow exactly as he would in the omote form.

Yonkyo — up close...

A close look at the hand positions shows clearly how the forearm is held as if weilding a bokken...

Nage cuts the forearm down as if doing shomen uchi with a bokken. This takes Uke all the way down to the mat...

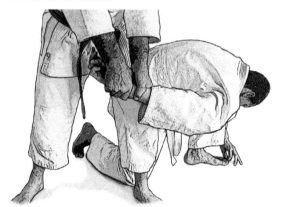

Nage allows his lead leg to slide forward into Uke's elbow. As pressure is maintained on the radial bone with a firm grip (*Nage's is energy extending through index finger knuckle into Uke's radial bone.*) Nage continues to extend Uke's elbow forward with his leg. Extreme caution should be used in applying this lock as Uke's elbow can easily be seriously damaged. Compare this standing finish to the finish applied from a seated position. (**Suwari Waza**)

Standing finish for Tachi Waza

Seated finish for suwari waza

Gokyo — Ude Nobashi

Yokomen Uchi Gokyo

     Gokyo is the fifth technique in the series which begins with Ikkyo. In the initial part of the movement it almost appears to be the same as **Ikkyo** and many people make this mistake when doing **Gokyo** for the first time.

The important point to notice is that Uke's wrist is taken from underneath for Gokyo and not from on top as it would be for Ikkyo.

     From **Yokomen Uchi** it is easier to learn the application than it is from **Shomen Uchi** (*where confusion with Ikkyo is often made*).

     Nage enters with direct **irimi** to the **Ura** side and opens up Uke with an **atemi** to the face at the same time as he cuts Uke's attacking arm to the rear. This has the effect of turning Uke's upper body slightly rearwards and taking away some of his stability.

     Uke will almost inadvertently push the **atemi** to the side which gives Nage the opportunity to reach across and take Uke's wrist from underneath.

     As Nage continues to enter slightly to Uke's rear he lines up his centre so it is facing Uke's side. Nage allows his hand that that originally cut Uke's arm to rear to now slide underneath Uke's elbow without having lost contact with the arm.

     From this point Nage will rotate Uke's arm completely over until Uke's palm is facing upwards. This will turn Uke's upper body over bringing his head and upper body down towards the mat.

     Nage's hands are now gripping on top of Uke's elbow and on top of the back of Uke's wrist which is facing upwards.

     With Uke's arm now lined up exactly in front of Nage's centre, it is a simple matter for Nage to lead the completely unbalanced Uke down at an oblique angle (*in the directiocn his arm is pointing*) to the mat to finish with a pin.

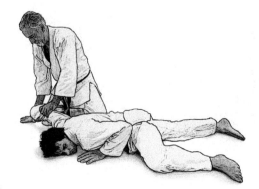

Usually Gokyo is practiced as a defence against a knife attack. By taking the wrist from underneath and rotating the arm over until the palm faces upwards helps prevent the knife from cutting Nage's wrist and makes it easier for Nage to disarm Uke. The pin that is applied for **Gokyo** is quite painful and almost always causes Uke to open his fingers and loose the grip on the knife, making it easy for Nage to take it away.

Before taking Uke face down onto the mat it is possible to snap the elbow while leaning sharply on it while the wrist is resting on Nage's knee. *Of course we don't do this in training or we would have serious legal and medical consequences.* We should however be aware of the danger of damaging Uke's elbow and take extreme caution when practicing to make sure nothing like this happens.

T*echniques like* **Ude Nobashi** *and* **Hijijime** *should only be practiced under the supervision of a qualified instructor.*

As Nage takes Uke completely to the mat he will relax the pressure (without releasing the grip) on Uke's elbow. Uke will naturally try and pull his Arm back. This is a subconscious reaction and Nage immediately assists this movement by drawing Uke's elbow up and sliding Uke's wrist in so that it sits underneath the raised elbow.

The pain Uke feels will depend upon how far in Nage has taken the wrist, and how much downwards pressure from on top of the raised elbow is applied to force Uke to open his fingers (releasing the grip on a knife if he has one.)

This is the basic from practiced by advanced Kyu grades. *There are other methods from Shomen Uchi and other attacks but these are not relevant for this volume.*

below: At this point the wrist is pulled up while pressure is put on Uke's e;lbow (to break it) to release the knife or y**onkyo against the thumb** can be used to open the fingers ,or the arm can be pulled back and downwards pressure on the elbow will stretch the wrist and open the fingers. All of these methods are quite painful and Uke is encouraged to release the knife.

Rokyo — Hijijime

Rokyo, is the sixth in the series beginning with Ikkyo.

It is sometimes called **Hiji Jime** or **Hiji Gime**, which means elbow Lock or bar. This also is usually practiced at higher Kyu grades or by **Yudansha**. It is not really for the beginner but it is shown here from a mid level punch as a matter of interest and to complete the series from one to six (**Ikkyo to Rokyo**).

Chudan Tsuki Rokyo

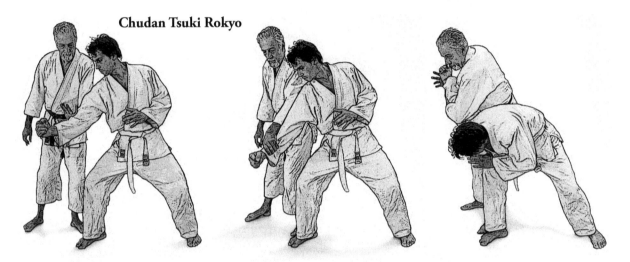

Nage enters to the Ura side of the punch and deflects it slightly before allowing his hand to slide down to grasp Uke's wrist. Nage's body position is **Hantai Tenkan**. (*see page 33 for description...*)

Resting his elbow on top of Uke's elbow, Nage can now rotate Uke's attacking arm over and draw it up towards his outside shoulder while all the time maintaining pressure against Uke's elbow to keep it locked and unable to be bent.

Superficially this resembles **Nikyo**, but in reality is nothing like it. (*It is sometimes considered to be a variation of Nikyo.*)

Nage's free hand takes Uke's wrist and accentuates the twisting to make sure the arm is rotated enough to apply pressure against the elbow.

If Nage makes a sudden turn to the rear with his hips and upper body he will snap Uke's elbow, so application is always done slowly and carefully allowing Uke time to move back slightly in order to receive this arm lock without damage. There are other ways more devastating to finish this lock, as well as applications from **Bokken**, **Tanto**, and **Jo** attacks, but again none of these are relevant to this volume.

A qualified instructor should be present when practicing this technique.

A comparison of the basic arm pins used in general Aikido practice.

There are six arm pins or *Katame waza.* Some are more difficult than others. All of them are effective if used properly and in the right context. They are **Ikkyo, Nikyo, Sankyo, Yonkyo, Gokyo, and Rokyo** (also called **Hijijime or hiji-gime.**).

Ikkyo is perhaps the most important of all the pins as it forms the basis to understanding all the others that follow. **A thorough understanding of Ikkyo and how it is done in varying circumstances is essential** to gain insight into many other and varied techniques.

Nikyo holds Uke down by applying pressure through the upper arm and the shoulder. Nage's energy extends from his centre through Uke's elbow and down along the arm to the shoulder. The forearm is able to rotate and as Nage turns his body towards the Back of Uke's head the lock is applied.

With **Sankyo, Nage's hand positions are the opposite of that held for Nikyo.** Also Uke's arm is turned so pressure is applied against the elbow joint, consequently there is little movement and the lock comes on very suddenly. ***Always apply this lock with caution.***

This seated finish for **Yonkyo** is also much more difficult to receive than the standing finish. A lot more pressure can be applied to Uke's upper arm to open up the elbow joint. ***It should be practiced with caution and the moment Uke taps the mat Nage should release the hold.***

Gokyo is usually practiced as a method of defence against a knife attack. The downwards pressure from the elbow onto the wrist will open up the fingers and release the knife.

Rokyo is rarely applied from a seated position. *In Tachi waza the Katame waza is the same but Nage will be standing and Uke will usually be down on one knee with the other leg stretched out behind so he can receive it more comfortably, that is with less stress. (see page 105)* The seated finish shown here is more devastating and certainly more difficult to receive.

This particular finish is sometimes used as a variation when doing **Iriminage**.

Instead of a throw Nage stretches Uke's arm across his thigh as he kneels behind Uke. Uke's head is turned the other way and downwards pressure is applied to the elbow joint and the head at the same time. This is a quite dangerous hold down which is why it is usually only studied at a senior level.

There are quite a few other arm locks and holds which are basically extensions of the arm with pressure applied to nerve points or the points where muscles meet and are connected to the bones, (*variations of Gokyo or Yonkyo and sometimes Sankyo*) as well as locks that compress the elbow joint and wrist. There are also arm locks that tie up both arms behind Uke's back, but none of these are for the Aikido novice and will not be shown in this book.

One other pin sometimes used is with **shihonage**.

Instead of allowing Uke to roll away he is taken down to the mat. His wrist is twisted outwards as it touches the mat while Nage uses his knee or shin to extend Uke's elbow in towards the side of his head.

This pin is used to release a knife Uke may have been using, or it is simply used as an alternative finish with Nage making a strike to Uke's face while holding him immobile.

Duality in Aikido

Hard or soft — Geometric or Organic

Regardless of style, in whatever way we study Aikido we often see two ways which can be thought of as the Geometric and the Organic. I have chosen these two terms to distinguish straight line principles and responses from the more circular responses and principles. This has nothing to do with being hard or soft.

As a basic means of distinguishing them, geometric ways are precise, angular and square, and these elements are often displayed in the Omote versions of Ikkyo, Nikyo, Sankyo, Yonkyo, Iriminage Omote, Kaitenage Omote, etc, whereas the organic way appears vague, circular and without precise shape. The forms are fluid and change continuously, spiralling and circling within an imaginary sphere that encompasses the two practitioners. These elements are more often than not displayed in the Ura versions of Ikkyo, Nikyo, Sankyo, Yonkyo, Iriminage Ura etc.

There are others (Kaitenage for example) where both the omote and ura forms display more of the organic than the geometric, so there is no hard and fast rule. What is most likely is that both aspects of form are used together in various degrees regardless of whether the technique is omote or ura. Katame waza are examples where the response is initially organic but the finish is geometric.

Often at a beginner level what is studied is very geometric, broken down into steps taken one after the other in order to understand the concept and the result being practiced. Later when understanding is apparent the techniques of the attack and response are studied more with movement that is continuous rather than broken down into steps and the whole practice becomes more fluid and thus more organic.

Sometimes however people categorize straight line responses as hard and the circular responses as soft. In truth hard and soft do not really describe degrees of hardness or softness but describe the perceived result as Uke feels it. People confuse a strong muscled approach that is stiff as hard, while they think a more relaxed body response is soft. In reality some of the hardest ukemi I have ever taken have been the result of techniques so soft that I felt nothing until I found myself flying through the air or falling with incredible force down onto the mat.

Soft is a misnomer that disguises internal power that can not be resisted. Similarly, hard describes physical strength which can be resisted. Sooner or later the exponent using hard physical strength will come up against another stronger person who will simply stop him from doing anything. But the soft internal approach gives Uke nothing to resist and no way to fight against it.

From an observer's point of view, apart from the obvious omote or ura approach to creating a technique, there is little to distinguish whether Nage is hard or soft other than equating Uke's hard ukemi as the result of a hard technique. The only way to really know is to experience the result physically by attacking and then receiving.

It is a mistake to assume because it is omote it will be hard, or if it is ura it will be soft. Both forms can be hard or soft with the end result the same for Uke no matter which approach Nage takes.

Two Ways?

Although there are as many ways of studying Aikido as there are teachers teaching it, not to mention students studying it, I believe all systems fall into two basic approaches. It comes back here to the duality of hard and soft, or geometric and organic, mechanical or fluid, or whatever contrasting categories there are that can describe it.

Whatever the way, a strong foundation is essential. Some teachers believe that this can only be built by learning the mechanics of movement initiated from a static position. To start from a static position helps develop precision and proper awareness of the relationship between the two partners. It teaches how to circumvent the power of the other with precise movement and exact physical technique. It employs body mechanics, scientific principles of leverage, and movements that can be measured and quantified to determine success. It has whole groups working together in steps that are easily studied and understood. A number of Aikido teaching systems have evolved around this method of studying.

Other teachers in other systems of Aikido prefer to teach and study movement, encouraging the student to move around the power of a confrontation. This is more amorphous and free. The precision of the technique can be refined over time. Moving to avoid is the first priority. Then there is moving around, leading, and so on until an opening becomes apparent and a technique can be utilized. Once the student can relate to two bodies moving and interacting, technique can then be refined and improved upon. But physical technique, and body mechanics are not the main priority, it is the creation of movement that can be manipulated.

Whatever the way used to study we are constantly refining technique and movement, and that should be apparent to any teacher and student.

Other teachers employ an amalgam of both ways.

One way is more geometric, straight line, hard, while the other is more organic, circular, soft, but in reality both ways contain elements of the other. Both ways are equally valid as is any possible combination of them. Therein we find the duality of Aikido. Nothing is fixed. Everything is open to re-interpretation based on the practitioner's understanding at any particular moment in time. It is always hard and soft, internal and external, geometric and organic; it is all one Aikido.

Which method of study the student prefers, and therefore which school or association they choose is inevitably determined by that individual's personality and temperament and what it is they seek within the study of Aikido.

Duality in the one moment

At a more advanced level there is only simultaneous attacking and defending.

Rather than waiting to see what Uke is going to do then defending against this by deflection and entering, Nage considers that at the instant Uke attacks his own response must be to simultaneously attack Uke's centre.

Forget about defending, just attack. The attack launched towards Uke's centre will turn Uke's attack aside (in effect defending against Nage) while Nage destabilizes Uke's balance, predisposing him to fall.

If Aikido came from fighting with katana then it should be obvious that the only defence is to attack, there is no deflecting in sword fighting. Any response is an attack, and only one attack is all that is needed to penetrate to the other's centre.

To be effective Aikido needs this concept of the duality in the one movement: the response to an attack is an attack which is both then a defence and an attack at the same time. Any other response will fail, and effective Aikido is not being practiced.

It should be remembered that Aikido is a martial art and not a system of exercises that appear martial (which is what many people practice while convincing themselves they are actually studying a martial art). Aikido evolved from several deadly martial arts that had been proven on battlefields over centuries. When O Sensei first started teaching Aikido it was an art that could have devastating effects on an opponent, resulting in severe injuries or even death. That they practiced it with a degree of control is obvious or there would not have been followers who could go on to teach it. The duality here is that the possibility of those deadly effects are still there in the techniques we practice, but because we don't know we are practicing them, we tend to be too casual and so the practice often becomes an exercise without a real focus. If exercise is all we want then that is fine, but please don't think we are doing otherwise.

If practical application is what we seek then it is there also, hidden within the exercises, but focus needs to be more precise along with awareness, timing, distance and all other aspects that make an art truly martial.

Aikido is both things: an exercise system that helps improve body and mind as well as an art that can devastate an opponent. We should try to be aware of this duality at all times, and as we practice, we should seek exactly what is we are individually trying to achieve with our practice.

MUSUBI

We often hear the term Musubi mentioned in the dojo while practicing and we are told that it means joining or connecting our energy with that of our partner.

When we begin training with our partner grabbing the hand, wrist, elbow, shoulder and so on there is an obvious connection. This is where we feel the energy of one person impacting upon another. This is where we attempt to blend our movement and energy with that of our partner, so we can lead and control the other person's movement and balance.

But this is also Awase which means blending and is easily confused with **musubi**. **Awase** however is more a physical blending of energy and movement, a mechanical aspect of two bodies working together to study a technique. So too is **Wago** which means peaceful joining or harmony.

Musubi is more that that.

Musubi is about understanding and communication on a non verbal level. It is about the tying together or the joining of opposites, and the reconciliation of these opposites into balance. **Musubi is about tying Uke's intent to attack to Nage's intent to defuse** and control that attack, to create some form of balance.

Musubi is about the balancing of opposing forces such as Centripetal force where an object is drawn in towards a central point (spiralling inwards), and centrifugal force where the same object is flung out from a central point (spiralling outwards). Where the two forces momentarily interact there is a balance. If that central point is spinning like a top, anything drawn in is also flung back out at the moment of contact.

Nage tries to make the centrifugal force greater than the centripetal force in order to throw Uke away. If both forces are equal, inward and outward movement will become a circle and balance is achieved.

The moon orbiting the earth, the earth orbiting the sun are examples of this balance of opposing forces where escape velocity (centrifugal force) is balanced against gravity (centripetal force) so a more or less stable orbit is achieved. For us it is stable, as are the rest of the planets in the solar system and the stars in the galaxy and galaxies in the universe.

In Aikido Nage tries to balance Uke's force with redirection through the creation of a moment of stability which is a manifestation of **musubi** before deciding what direction and how much added force is needed to throw or take Uke down.

Most of our training is to develop this brief moment, to try and understand how it works, not by rationalising it but by feeling it deep inside.

This can only be done with practice and repetition so the body learns on a muscular and instinctive core level.

Musubi is movement, balance, and coordination. Without movement there can be no connection, or joining of opposites. Without the balance obtained by the joining of opposites there is only chaos.

Everything in the universe from the smallest particle to the largest object, from single cells to massive organisms demonstrates **musubi** in its broadest sense — life and order.

In Aikido musubi can only be experienced if the participants in the practice are relaxed and sensitive to each other's intent and subsequent movement, each allowing the other to adjust to any nuance in movement as a technique is being created.

Once the technique is over, there is a lingering mental contact, as each maintains awareness of the other, called **Zanshin**. It is particularly important that Nage maintains **Zanshin** so he can be prepared and aware of Uke's intent to get up and attack again.

Awase, and Zanshin are both a part of musubi, and are probably inseparable.

Part Five

NAGE WAZA — Throwing Techniques

There are literally thousands of techniques where Uke (*the person attacking – and consequently receiving Nage's response*) can be thrown or made to take a fall. The person who counters Uke's attack is called ***Tori, Shite, or Nage***. Most often the word **Nage** which means throw is used to describe the person doing the throw. **Nage waza** simply means throwing techniques.

Throwing techniques are loosely grouped together by the characteristic that most effectively describes them: **Irimi Nage** or ***entering throw***, **Kaiten Nage** or ***circular throw***, **Shiho Nage** or ***four corners throw***, **Koshi Nage** or ***hip throw***, **Kokyu Nage** or ***breath throw***, and so on. In all groupings we find techniques that are either organic or geometric, that is precise and angular, or fluid and circular, or a combination in varying degrees of the both.

Kokyu Nage are perhaps the most difficult throws to grasp which belies their apparent simplicity because the concept of **Kokyu**, meaning ***breath***, is intangible.

Perhaps the easiest of the throwing techniques for a beginning student to learn is **Tenchi Nage**, which means ***Heaven and Earth throw***.

This is a throw where half of Uke is being extended down towards the ground while the other half is being extended up towards the sky. As Uke moves forward his upper body will be destabilised and tipped backwards while his lower body will continue forward. This causes him to fall onto his back, taking a side breakfall (**Yoko Ukemi**) or **Ushiro ukemi** as a backwards roll.

Gyaku Hanmi Katatetori Tenchinage Omote

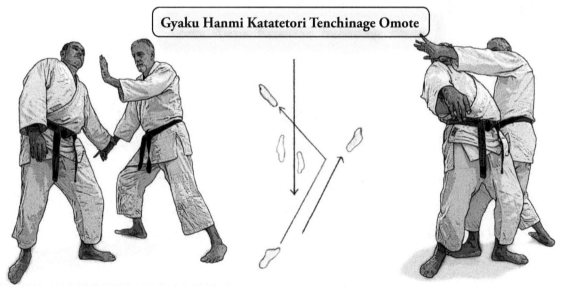

Seen here as a stretching exercise to help loosen the muscles and prepare the body for the throwing technique, Uke grasps Nage's hand (**Katatetori**) in **Gyaku Hanmi**. Immediately Nage steps with his outside leg to the rear of Uke extending his hand palm down towards his knee. Since Uke is holding on this will cause him to lean backwards towards the point behind his lead leg where he is weakest and most easily unbalanced.

This is the earth aspect of the technique...

Nage then repositions his centre so he is facing towards Uke's centre, brings his (inside) back leg together for a moment with his front leg then steps through behind Uke.

At the same time as he enters he extends his other arm up along Uke's centreline to tip over his head and opposite shoulder.

This is the Heaven aspect where part of Uke is extended upwards...

We pause at this point using the movement as a stretch and warm up.

To continue the technique into a throw, Nage would simply step through a little further extending Uke's head up and over while continuing to extend his arm towards the ground. Uke will have to take a breakfall around Nage's leg because there is no room to step back for a roll.

Ryotedori Tenchinage Omote

Usually **Tenchinage** is practiced from a two hand grip (**Ryotetori**). The position shown here is **gyaku hanmi**. (*Hidari hanmi for Nage and Migi Hanmi for Uke.*)

This begins in exactly the same way as the stretching exercise described with one hand grabbing. Nage extends Uke's leading arm behind his leading leg to the point where he begins to tip over backwards while at the same time brining his other hand up inside of Uke's grip to reach up and over Uke's shoulder. Finally Nage steps right through behind Uke to throw him down onto the mat.

Note that Uke has maintained his original **gyaku hanmi Katatori** grip on Nage's wrist so he can use it to help lesson the impact of the side breakfall. Once he has finished the fall he will let go.

There are other ways of receiving this technique but they depend on how fast Uke has attacked and how quickly and exactly in which way Nage responds.

The exercise shown above is from a static start and is done slow enough so each participant can study his side of the technique, that is the doing and the receiving.

Diagram of movement for Ryotedori Tenchinage Omote from a static start.

A static start with Uke neither pushing nor pulling, but simply grabbing both of Nage's wrists.

Nage will step in and do the **omote** form. **Nage's movement is triangular.** He steps out to go past Uke's lead leg, repositions his angle in relation to Uke, and then steps in behind Uke at the same angle with his other leg. This basic form can be considered geometric because of the fairly precise angles of entry to get in a position for the throw.

If Uke pushes Nage will yield rather than trying to stop him. Yielding or blending allows Uke to continue his forward pushing movement which will take him past Nage who will lead him around using **Tenkan** (*backwards turning movement*) to bring him into a position to be thrown. The throw will be the same as it is for **Omote**; it just takes a more circular route to get there. This is an Ura form.

If Uke pulls Nage's natural tendency is to step in to do the Omote form.

The Ura forms are more organic and amorphous. There are no precise angles, simply circles that bring Uke around into a position where he looses his balance allowing Nage a space to enter for the throw...

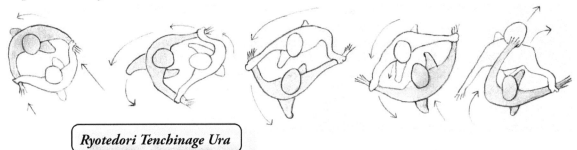

Ryotedori Tenchinage Ura

The arrows indicate that Uke initiates by pushing and extending towards Nage. Rather than fight this advance **Nage simply steps back into a Tenkan movement drawing Uke around** him. He allows Uke to continue his forward movement to a position where Uke's feet go out from underneath as he is led around by the circular backward step Nage has taken.

Uke has grabbed Nage and is pushing, or alternatively he has moved forward and grabbed both of Nage's wrists.

Nage takes a **Tenkan** step back and around so he is now facing the opposite direction while at the same time he continues to draw Uke forward. This will bring Uke around in a half circle so while still moving forward he is also facing the opposite direction to what he was when he started.

Nage, having completed this **Tenkan** step, continues to draw Uke forward until a point is reached where Uke's feet have started to go out from underneath while his upper body has stopped. Nage steps through to throw Uke backwards.

Ryotedori Tenchinage Ura — Irimi Kaiten form

If Uke grabs Nage, steps back and pulls, Nage takes advantage of this movement and steps forward (**Irimi**) to enter outside of Uke's front leg making a complete **Tenkan** step, which is in effect **Tai No Henka**.

If Uke maintains his two handed grip this move will twist his upper body to draw it around in a tight half circle. Nage immediately follows with **Kaiten**, *turning back 180 degrees,* while at the same time extending his inner arm down behind Uke's body position and striking towards Uke's face to tip over the head with his other hand as he steps through for the throw.

This is a close tight movement using small circles compared to the more standard Ura form which employs larger movements and bigger circles.

Nage could also make this entry Irimi Kaiten rather than Irimi Tenkan, *(see below)* with a second **Kaiten** turn to reverse his body position to topple Uke into the throw down. This is an even closer and tighter movement and is the way to do it from a strong static start rather than with movement initiated by Uke as described above.

Uke grabs Nage and attempts to pull him forward...

Nage takes advantage, steps forward outside of Uke's lead leg, makes kaiten...

dropping Uke's leading arm...

Without pausing Nage reverses the Kaiten move, turning to face towards Uke's rear, in the process dropping Uke's lead arm and extending it out behind.,,
The raised upper arm extends through as an elbow sstrike to Uke's face, or over Uke's head toppling him over backwards.

Nage does not have to step through for the finish as the turn is sufficient to throw Uke so far off balance he must take a backwards ukemi.

Training with weapons assits in the understanding of Maai — combative distance, and timing. It also helps us to understand the attacking line and where we should be if our attack and defense is to be accurate...

Taking a look at a more advanced concept using **Bokken** angainst **Tanto** attack we can see that we have what could be considered *Tenchinage*...

The entrance to cut down the attacking arm is the same as if doing **gyaku hanmi katatetori tenchinage**. (*The bokken is drawn and Nage moves in to cut down as Uke attacks with yokomen.*)

Nage could proceed from the top image directly to the bottom image without the backwards turn and it would be the same as **Tenchinage Omote**. However in this case Nage has made a backwards turn which assists in tipping Uke further back into an unbalanced position before he makes the final sstrike with the hilt of the **bokken**. *This then makes it more a kokyunage than tenchinage...*

Kaitenage — Circular Throw

Kaitenage is another technique taught as soon as the student is capable of taking a forward rolling ukemi. (**Mae yoko ukemi.**) Plenty of body movement by both Uke and Nage takes place in **Kaitenage** and forward rolling is what Uke needs to be comfortable doing. It is reccomended that forward rolling practioce becomes a regular part of training for beginners and early kyu graded students,.You should do literally thousands of these to be able to comfortably roll out of any situation.

As the name implies, **Kaitenage** also utilises **Kaiten Tai Sabaki** movement by Nage as he sets up Uke for the throw which is generally a forward or side roll.

Kaitenage uses large circles turning Uke completely over and throwing him with a kind of rolling over movement extending Uke's arm in a circular fashion across his upper back to project him into a forward roll.

The circular movements, **especially in the Ura form are parallel to the surface finishing with the final throw which uses circles that are more or less vertical.**

With the Omote form the initial entry is a straight line angled enough the take Nage off the line of Uke's forward movement before commencing the circular rotation of Uke's arm to position him for the throw.

Kaiten also refers to the body turn Uke makes while rolling out of the projection as well as the movement Nage makes while entering. The word Kaiten simply means body turn and is usually only referred to a stepping and turning movement which is basic Tai Sabaki.

Gyaku Hanmi Katatetori Uchi Kaitenage Omote.

At the moment Uke's fingers begin to tighten the grip on Nage's wrist, Nage steps forward at an oblique angle taking Uke's arm back past his centre. At the same time he strikes with an **atemi** to Uke's face. This **atemi** distracts Uke enough (*as he tries to deflect it*) to allow Nage to step under Uke's wrist.

As Nage passes under Uke's arm he immediately makes a **Kaiten** body turn (**180 degrees**) which alters his **hanmi** position and has him facing the same direction as Uke.

On completion of the **Kaiten** Nage cuts Uke's arm all the way down to the mat. He steps back as Uke's hand reaches the mat and completes the rotation of the arm having made a complete circle.

Half way through this circular movement Nage has placed his other hand on the back of Uke's head to hold it down, so that when the arm is rotated back up Uke's upper body will stay down and remain partly twisted. Uke will start to lose the grip as his arm is rotated up over behind and Nage takes this opportunity to firmly grasp Uke's wrist.

Finally Nage steps forward (*using his knee for **atemi** into Uke's face*) and extends Uke's arm over the top of his shoulders to complete the body twist that will project Uke into a forward roll. (*bottom image previous page*). (**Mae Kaiten Ukemi**)

As a precaution Nage could bring his free hand up to protect his face, so that when Nage steps forward he can push away from the knee coming into his face, and this will assist him in taking the forward roll.

> ## Gyaku Hanmi Katatetori Uchi Kaitenage Ura

This basic form is all circles in a parallel plane finishing with a slightly more diagonal rather than vertical circle of Uke's arm leading into the projection.

The moment Uke grabs Nage enters with **Irimi Tenkan Tai No Henka** then either leads Uke around in a circle, or as in the example above Nage steps back after the **Irimi Tenkan** to turn Uke right around. Note that Uke has been stretched forward and is unbalanced.

At this point the technique is the same as the **Omote** form. (*on the previous page.*) *Nage enters with an atemi to Uke's face and while Uke's attention is momentarily taken away slips under the arm and cuts it down towards the floor in a big circle to come up behind. With his other hand Nage holds down Uke's head to prevent him from rising up.*

From this point on however, the Ura form is different. Nage draws Uke's head in close to his hip and holds it firmly while entering with another **Irimi Tenkan** to the rear of Uke. In effect he walks around behind Uke who is forced to follow because he is literally stuck to Nage. There should be no gap between Uke and Nage with both moving as a whole unit.

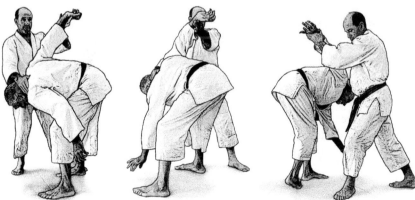

Coming far enough around Uke will probably lose balance and fall before he is thrown, but if not Nage will finish with a **Kaiten** body turn to extend Uke's arm over the shoulder to throw him.

Gyaku Hanmi Katatetori Soto Kaitenage Omote.

The other basic form is to enter not from the inside or Uchi to go under the arm, but to enter from outside of the arm, the Soto or Ura side. Apart from the entry to set up Uke's position for the throw the rest of the technique is the same.

Nage steps to the outside which begins to turn Uke's centre offline. He can also make **atemi** to Uke's face to help distract his attention. As he begins to make a half **Tenkan** he cuts with his **Tegatana** in towards Uke's face, further unbalancing him.

This enables him to come around the arm from outside to finish the **Tenkan** move ending parallel but slightly behind Uke's centreline.

Nage cuts Uke's arm down to the mat as he steps back. Simultaneously he holds Uke's head down to prevent Uke from standing back up. Nage rotrates Uke's arm back up and over to twist Uke's body forwards at an awkward angle. He then steps forward to project Uke away into a forward roll.

> **A few words about KAITEN...**

The word **Kaiten** appears in a variety of combinations. By itself it means rotation, revolution, or turning. **Kai** by itself means turn, or rotate. It can also be read as **mawaru** which means to turn and is written with the same kanji.

A forward roll is called **Zenpo** or **Mae Kaiten Ukemi,** meaning a forward fall with a body turn or rotation, shortened to *Mae Ukemi*. **Mae Ukemi or Zenpo Mae Ukemi is actually a forward breakfall** where Uke falls flat onto his front ending up in a position similar to that taken for push-up exercises. *See pages 51 - 52.*

Yoko Kaiten Ukemi means a side fall with a body rotation or a sideways roll, whereas **Yoko Ukemi** simply means a side breakfall. Similarly **Ushiro Kaiten Ukemi** means a back fall with a body rotation, a backwards roll. **Ushiro Ukemi only means a back breakfall.**

With **Sabaki**, or body movement, **Kaiten** just means a body turn, usually a 180 degree turn to face the opposite direction. **Tenkai** is also a body turn without any forward stepping and is a much closer and tighter turn than **Kaiten.**

Kaiten is sometimes substituted for **Tenshin** which is also a body turn, but one that is affected upon Uke by Nage as a part of his opening redirection of Uke's attacking energy.

> **Gyaku Hanmi Katatetori Soto Kaitenage ...**

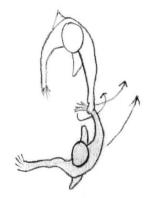  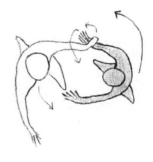 

These drawings represent a shortened form. Doing the basic forms of **Kaitenage** requires a fair amount of mat space since the movements of both Nage and Uke are quite expansive.

   It is essential that the basic forms be understood before moving on to look at some other ways that can have minimal movement on the part of Nage but which are equally as effective upon Uke as the basic forms.

   Here in all of these examples, the Kaiten refers not to the circular rotation of Uke's arm but to the rotation of Uke's body down (*with his arm*) **as well as the rolling ukemi used to escape**. *The Kaiten — rotation — is what happens to Uke's body.*

The moment Uke grabs Nage's wrist from **gyaku hanmi** Nage moves to the **Ura** side, off the line of attack, while at the same time he rotates his hand under Uke's grasp and over the top.

As he begins his entry to the side of Uke Nage cuts Uke's wrist down and back in a circular manner.

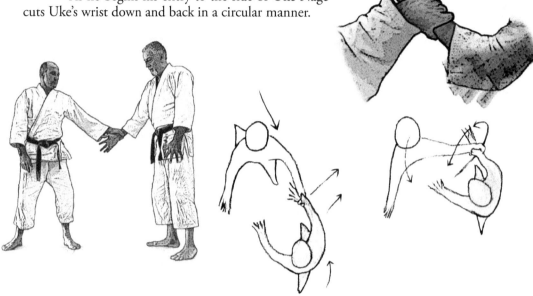

This cutting down will turn Uke over from the waist and allow Nage to place his other hand on Uke's head to hold it down. This rotating circular movement is continued until Uke is drawn in close to Nage. To assist in keeping Uke down and unable to rise up again, Nage holds Uke's head down.

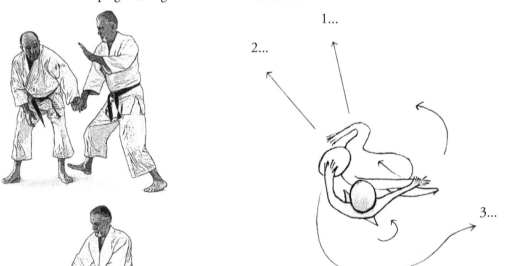

Once Nage has control of Uke's head he draws it in towards his hip, or he moves his body in close so Uke's head is held against his hip. From this point three different directions to throw or project Uke are obtained. They are directly sideways, forwards at an oblique angle of 30 to 45 degrees, and **Tenkan** which takes Uke around 180 to almost 360 degrees to project him back to the rear.

The first two throws involve hardly any movement from Nage after the initial small entry, but the **Ura** form requires a **Tenkan** followed by a **Kaiten** turn from Nage in order to lead Uke around in a circle to the rear before being thrown.

1...

With the rotation complete Uke's arm should finish parallel to his hip. His grip will have been broken and Nage will now have a firm grasp of Uke's wrist which he will hold against the hip as he draws Uke's head in close.

Nage's position is square on to Uke side.
(*See drawing at bottom of page 122.*)

From this finish position Uke can be thrown in various directions with hardly any effort other than a simple extension.

Firstly we will look at the two throws that are **omote**. Directly sideways is a simple extension from Nage once he has positioned himself in close and taken Uke's head down. Nage doesn't have to move anymore, he simply extends his arms forward

Uke will find himself falling directly to the side which may be difficult at first to receive, but with some practice he will soon learn to change his body position in the air so he can take the fall as a forward or semi circular forward roll as he would in rolling from an over-extended **Yokomen uch**i strike.

The extension is directly through the hip and the head. Nage doesn't turn or twist in any way, he simply extends both arms forward.

Remember, Nage is square on to Uke's sideways position before beginning the throw.

Nage simply extends his arms directly in front, which pushes Uke's hip and head forward at the same time.

No other movement is needed.

Because he is going sideways Uke will have to take **yoko Kaiten ukemi** or twist in the air so he can receive the fall as a forward or **mae Kaiten ukemi.**

In the second way, having entered exactly the same as before to bring Uke in close, instead of sending Uke sideways Nage twists his hip around so his centre is facing (*about 30 to 45 degrees*) towards Uke's head.

To throw Uke Nage extends diagonally from the hip towards the opposite shoulder. Uke's arm stays against his hip.

He will easily be able to take a forward roll from this extension.

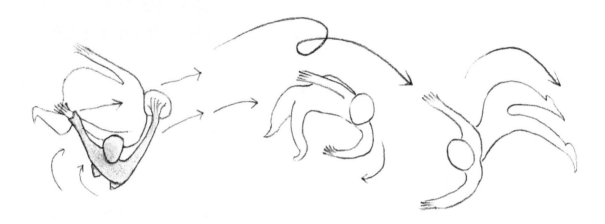

2...

In effect once Nage has drawn Uke in to lock him against his centre, Nage makes a **Kaiten** body movement which creates a **hanmi** position from which he extends forward. Uke will take mae kaiten ukemi without having to twist from a sideways position since he is being thrown forward in relation to his body position.

As shown in the drawings above **the angle of the throw is oblique**, somewhere between 30 and 45 degrees.

The third throw is an Ura form and involves Nage having to turn **Tenkan. Because Uke's head is held close to Nage's hip, when Nage turns to the rear Uke will have no choice but to follow.** At the end of the turning movement Nage makes a further **Kaiten** move with his hips and projects Uke forward in exactly the same way as in the second example.

To finish with **Ura**, Nage needs to make a small **Irimi Tenkan**, stepping a little to the rear of Uke and drawing Uke's head towards his hip as he commences the turning back part of the **Irimi Tenkan**. At the same time he extends Uke's arm in a slight circle across Uke's lower back.

As Uke is drawn around in a circle the arm Nage is holding appears to remain in the same relative position beside the hip because Uke's whole body is turning as a single unit. In fact both Uke and Nage are turning as a single unit so the relationship of one to another remains the same until Nage decides he has turned far enough to the rear.

The movement is finished with Nage making a **Kaiten** turn with his hips and projecting Uke forwards at an oblique angle. Sometimes a further step through follows the **Kaiten** but usually it is not needed because by this time Uke is committed to taking a forward roll.

The angle is much the same as that already described for the second variation (**Omote**), it is simply tacked on to the end of the **Irimi Tenkan** to complete the technique with the throw.

3···

From the first position Nage takes a small entry step behind Uke's nearest foot, and follows with a small **Tenkan**.

This turns Uke around so he is now facing the opposite direction. Without pausing Nage continues to enter behind Uke with a sliding step and allows his hips to turn towards Uke (*in the process of making a **Kaiten** body turn*).

Finally releasing Uke's head Nage extends along Uke's trapped arm locking it as he completes the **Kaiten** body turn. The extension along Uke's arm is slightly diagonal which will tip over Uke's shoulder and upper body to the side away from Nage and is more than enough to throw Uke into a forward roll. **If the turn is a full 360 degrees** then Uke will be going forward in the same direction he was facing at the moment of being drawn in before the turn commenced.

Gyaku Hanmi Katatetori Uchi Kaitenage ...

Starting from **Gyaku Hanmi katatetori** Nage moves to the inside (**Uchi or omote**) and drops his centre while reaching down towards the mat. If one thinks of reaching down as if to pick up a coin that is directly in front of Uke the movement should be relaxed and almost without any strength involved. After all, bending down to pick up something is a perfectly natural movement. This naturally draws Uke forward and down as well.

As Uke involuntarily bends over Nage reaches forward with his free hand and holds Uke's head firmly down.

Nage can now step up and in close to Uke while continuing to hold the head down.

The finish position is again exactly as described for the previous **Soto** movement from which the same three directions throws can be executed with little effort.

> ## Yokomen Uchi Kaitenage ...

Yokomen Uchi Kaitenage:

Nage enters with a direct **Irimi** to tip Uke over backwards before he has the chance to get fully into the strike. **The important principle here is to enter deep enough so that Uke can not turn and swing back with his other arm to strike Nage in the face with an elbow.**

Maintaining the extension that keeps Uke tipped backwards Nage Swings Uke's arm around in a wide arc to tip Uke's head and other arm forwards and downwards. At the same time Nage reaches out to hold Uke's head down while he makes a **kaiten** body turn. At the culmination of the **kaiten** turn Nage extends Uke's rear arm diagonally across his back to project him forwards into a rolling **ukemi**.

It should be noted that **the hand holding Uke's arm is in the gyakute position** (*thumb pointing down with palm facing to the rear rather than the other way as used for the standard forms already described. With those the thumb is up and the palm is facing towards the front.*)

This is more difficvult to do as it requires more precise timing and a deep entry.

As a consequence it is only attempted at a higher level of training. Perhaps from 2nd or 1st kyu and above...

*The movement shown here is exactly the same when doing **Kaitenage** from **mawashi ge**ri or turning kick ... See next page.*

Mawashi Geri Kaitenage ...

Before the turning kick arrives,
Nage is already entering...

Nage continues to enter, capturing
the leg and cutting down the head.

Having entered behind Uke's centreline Nage
makes a **kaiten** turn of the hips so he is facing towards
Uke's exact centre. All Uke's weight is on the one leg
and as Nage continues to raise the captured leg it tips
Uke over forwards.

Uke reaches down to place his body in a position to make a forward rolling **ukemi** to escape landing
on his head.

*Note that this body movement by Nage is exactly
the same as for the previous* **yokomen uchi kaitenage**,
*except in this case he has captured the leg instead of the
arm. It would also be the same if Uke grabbed Nage's collar
(**Munedori**) and attempted to knee Nage in the stomach.*

Kotegaeshi — Outward Wrist Turn

Kotegaeshi comes from two words: **Kote**, meaning wrist, and **Gaeshi** (or *Kaeshi*) which means outward turn. To develop strength and flexibility in the wrist it is often practiced alone as part of the joint warming exercises at the beginning of a class.

(See page 19 wrist exercises...)

Kotegaeshi can also be grouped with techniques that are referred to as **Sutemi Waza** (*Sacrifice Throws*). **Suteru** means to throw away or to discard, and as a secondary meaning it is to give up or to abandon. **Sute** by itself simply means throw down. Uke, in effect, throws his body down sacrificing himself in order to protect his wrist from damage.

Depending on how his wrist is being turned, at what height above the ground, at what angle and which direction Uke will decide in an instant which way to throw himself. The **ukemi** could therefore be forward, sideways, or backwards.

Although **Kotegaeshi** means outward wrist turn, Nage should remember that it is not simply a throw which twists Uke's wrist outwards. It is a means of shifting Uke's centre to make him unstable, to make Uke realise that if he doesn't take control of the **ukemi** needed to protect himself, his wrist could be broken or the tendons and ligaments stretched far enough to separate them from the bones in the joint.

Either way it is a painful result which needs to be avoided.

If the wrist is twisted outwards in the correct manner *the extension of the twist should be more along the arm towards the elbow which will naturally turn over as the wrist is turned outwards.* If Nage points Uke's elbow towards Uke's centre-line in an attempt to extend through this point and downwards beyond it to the weak point in Uke's stance it will turn over his upper body making him completely unstable.

Uke will throw himself to escape the wrist twist.

The height at which the wrist is twisted outward will determine the **ukemi** Uke takes. If the wrist is kept above the **obi** near the mid chest level the **ukemi** will most likely be underneath and backwards.

If it is below the **obi** most likely the **ukemi** will be forward, in between these two positions the **ukemi** is often sideways. **Uke should take whatever ukemi is the most comfortable for him at that moment.**

If the technique is being practiced without an arm pin, Nage will let go and allow Uke to take a rolling ukemi. (***Mae Kaiten Ukemi***).

If **Katame waza** is to be applied Nage will not let go of the wrist and will follow Uke and turn him over so he is facing down if the fall is backwards, or if it is over the top into a breakfall Nage will still follow Uke without losing his grip so Uke can be positioned to be locked and pinned so he can't escape. Almost evey hold down or pin (*Katame Waza*) will have Uke face down to the mat making it more difficult for Uke to counter attack or attempt to escape.

The pin for Kotegaeshi is the same as that used for Nikyo.
See pages 90 , 91 for a description of this pin.

Ai Hanmi Katatetori Kotegaeshi

The moment Uke touches Nage's wrist to take hold Nage immediately steps off line and extends his arm forward (Irimi Kaiten) which induces Uke to reach further and become slightly unbalanced.

Nage takes Uke's wrist with his free hand. It slides down along his arm until he can grasp Uke's wrist. Having taken Uke's wrist Nage now extends forward and down to break Uke's original grip and to make him come further forward and more unbalanced.

As he leads Uke forward Nage steps back, or out and back, in effect turning his original **Kaiten** into a full **Tenkan**. By sweeping Uke's arm back as he steps back he causes Uke to spin around in a wide circle. Nage enters before Uke can complete this circle and tips Uke's wrist over which automatically tips Uke's upper boddy over.

Uke is now in a position to take a forward or a sideways **ukemi**.

If he finishes on his back, Nage who still has hold of the wrist grip will turn Uke over to position him for the pin. Nage could also extend further out allowing Uke to take a forward roll... In the example here however he will turn Uke over and pin him to the floor.

To turn Uke over for the final pin, in this particular case, Nage makes use of the momentum in Uke's **ukemi**, and without losing the grip on Uke's wrist he continues to twist so Uke is forced to avoid damge to his wrist by turning himself over.

This puts him face down at which point Nage can apply the hold down pin.

(*The same pin as for Nikyo...*)

Ushiro Riotedori Kotegaeshi

This is more difficult because Nage needs to get Uke to come around to the front before applying **Kotegaeshi** (*outwards wrist twist*). He does this by leading him forward as he comes around to grasp the other wrist. He needs to extend Uke forward enough so he can be turned around in such a way that that Uke is stretched out and unbalanced which will allow Nage to apply the **kotegaeshi** to Uke's wirst.

In this example Uke fell sideways onto his back so Nage will take Uke's elbow and rotate it across his face to turn him over for the final pin.

To turn Uke over Nage will take hold of Uke's elbow without lessening his grip on Uke's hand which maintains the **kotegaeshi** twist. By rotating the elbow down over the back of the forehead rather than around across the face, Uke's arm, shoulder and upper body are locked together and he will be unable to prevent being turned over onto his face. *(next page.)*

Turning Uke over for application of Katame Waza

Turning Uke over if he falls onto his back can sometimes be difficult.

If the technique is done fast this is not a problem as Nage can utilise Uke's movement to assist with the turn over even if the receiving is backwards **ukemi**. Commonly, at fast speeds the **ukemi** is mostly over the top. But if the technique is practiced slowly almost always the receiving will be backwards with Uke finishing flat on his back and fairly solid against the floor.

While Uke is on his back Nage should point the fingers of the hand he still has grasped towards Uke's centre. Taking the elbow with his free hand Nage will rotate Uke's elbow across his forehead as if brushing the back of his head. This movement locks the upper arm at the shoulder joint and the rotation will always turn Uke over onto his face.

As soon as Uke is turned over Nage still maintaining a strong grip on Uke's hand drops one knee in front of Uke's shoulder to prevent any attempt to escape forward, and by keeping Uke's arm extended across his other knee it prevents Uke rolling back in an attempt to elbow strike Nage's face. If Uke makes any movement that might suggest an attempt to escape Nage simply uses his knee to extend Uke's arm into the shoulder joint which pushes Uke's face firmly into the mat.

To finish Nage drops his other knee while drawing Uke's elbow in tight against his centre. Uke's shoulder is held tightly with both knees locking it in position. Nage also cradles Uke's hand with his elbow locking it with his forearm.

A gentle rotation towards the back of Uke's head or the other shoulder will have Uke tapping the mat in submission.

Always apply the final pin with caution as a sudden turn or twist will damage Uke's shoulder joint, possibly tearing the rotator cuff and attached muscles. It could also hyper extend the elbow joint. Always release Uke as soon as he taps indicating submission.

A closer look at Kotegaeshi grip...

...this time from **Chudan Tsuki** which is the most common attack practiced with **Kotegaeshi**.

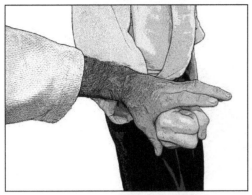 

After redirecting the striking punch Nage allows his hand to slide down along Uke's arm until it rests on top of the fist.

The thumb sits over the back of the knuckle joint between the ring finger and the little finger. The other fingers close over Uke's fist to lock Uke's thumb.

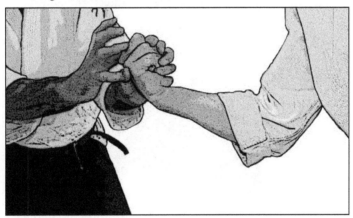

As Nage turns over Uke's hand with an outward twist he brings his other hand to rest over Uke's fist. This adds power to the outward movement and also extends energy down along Uke's arm in towards his centre.

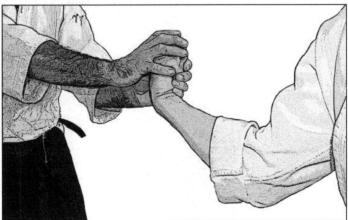

Extending into Uke's centre while turning the wrist outwards turns Uke's upper body over and positions him to take a fall. He will take the fall to protect his wrist.

Chudan Tsuki Kotegaeshi Ura

When Uke attacks with a punch to mid level (**Chudan Tsuki**) Nage enters to the **Ura** side at an oblique angle. The angle should be just enough to avoid the punch. As he enters into Uke's space Nage rests his leading hand against Uke's forearm and redirects the punch.

Nage finishes his entry with a **Tenkan** movement while allowing his hand to slide down Uke's forearm to grasp the wrist.

At the finish of this first **Tenkan** move Nage should now be parallel to Uke and holding Uke's wrist in a firm grasp

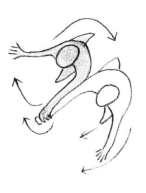

This grasp should be done so that Uke's thumb is trapped by Nage's fingers and Nage's thumb is resting on top of Uke's two smaller knuckles (*Page 133*)

Nage makes sure that he positions Uke's wrist so it is in line with his centre. This way when he moves Uke will be compelled to move as well.

Nage extends slightly forward to break Uke's balance while at the same time he also turns his hips back beginning another **Tenkan** move which will swing Uke around in a circle.

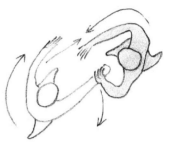

At the finish of the circle which has Uke revolving right around Nage's centre point Nage opens Uke by entering (*with **atemi** to Uke's face*) and by starting to turn Uke's wrist over towards the outside.

The **atemi** to Uke's face prevents Uke from counter striking with his free hand. He will most likely use it to deflect the **atemi** which has the effect of distracting him momentarily as well as turning his body towards the direction his wrist is being turned.

Nage can now finish the outward wrist turn taking Uke's wrist over and down at an oblique angle towards the mat.

Uke will roll over his trapped wrist, or roll away to the side of it in order to unwind the twist and save his wrist.

As Uke completes his breakfall Nage still holding the wrist will follow Uke's movement to keep up with him to make sure he is turned over onto his face so an appropriate pin can be applied.

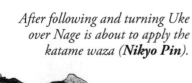

*After following and turning Uke over Nage is about to apply the katame waza (**Nikyo Pin**).*

Chudan Tsuki Kotegaeshi Omote

Chudan Tsuki Kotegaeshi Omote is exactly the same as the beginning of the **Ura** form with Nage entering to the outside (**soto or ura side of the strike**), **but instead of an Irimi Tenkan movement, the movement is Irimi Hantai Tenkan.** *Nage finishes at a 90 degree angle to Uke* instead of parrallel as he would for the Ura form.

The redirection of the striking arm is the same, but from this point on it is different.

Instead of turning **Tenkan** to bring Uke around in a circle as he would for the Ura form, **Nage steps forward and turns around Uke's grasped fist with a small Irimi Tenkan in front of Uke while striking Uke's face...**

The **atemi** to Uke's face will momentarily distract Uke from the fact that his grasped wrist is being turned over to the outside.

This leads Uke forward and Nage can now throw Uke who will travel more or less in the same direction forward as he was when attacking with the punch.

Keeping hold of Uke's hand, Nage follows Uke to turn him over in preparation for the pin which can be done standing or in a seated position.

This is obviously different from the Ura form where Uke is turned right around thrown back towards the direction he came from. In fact Uke can be made to fall in any direction from continuing his movement straight forward as explained for **Omote**, or turning and throwing him to either side approximately 90 degrees to his initial direction of travel, or completely around to throw him back towards the direction from which he initially attacked.`

In this example the pin is the seated. Nage drops to his knees while

maintaining the **kotegaeshi** extension down through Uke's arm to hold him onto the floor.

Trapping the shoulder with his knees, Nage places Uke's wrist in the crook of his elbow, draws Uke's elbow in towards his stomach and slowly rotates the trapped arm towards Uke's head to apply the pin.

curved line arrows indicate direction Nage will take Uke's fist and entry through Uke's centre... Straight line indicates Uke's line of attack...

As nage enters curved lines indicate how Uke will be turned around...

For any of the **Kotegaeshi** forms the principle of entering directly behind Uke's shoulder into his blind spot as he comes forward is going to spin him around into a throw.

Rather than trying to make Uke come around as one would traditionally do for **Kotegaeshsi Ura** — which often results in both partners back where they started from, facing each other and giving Uke the opportunity to counter Nage's attempt to apply **Kotegaeshi** because both Uke's large forward circle is the same as Nage's backwards circle — Nage either cuts his circle small so he enters behind Uke before Uke can complete the larger circle, or, and more importantly, Nage steps off line as the punch reaches his stomach. Instead of defecting it, he allows Uke to continue forward (*in fact he encourages this forward movement by extending the grabbed wrist forward to help unbalance Uke*). He then enters in a straight line at an oblique 25 to 30 degree angle right through Uke's shoulder to finish behind. But because he is holding Uke's wrist and turning it outwards as he does this it spins Uke right around into an unbalanced position from which he must take ukemi (**sutemi waza**) to protect his wrist.

The image above shows Nage about to enter exactly into the spot occupied by Uke's shoulder. Because he is holding Uke's wrist and hand this will spin Uke around into a mae kaiten ukemi.

Pinning while standing...

The standing pin is slightly different in application but it does require that Uke's arm be bent in the same manner as for the seated pin, and turned towards Uke's head in the similar way to apply the locking pressure to hold Uke onto the mat.

The standing pin is generally applied when dealing with an attack with a **tanto** (*A knife for practice purposes usually made of wood*) or a **bokken**. (*The bokken is a wooden replica of a sword or* **Katana**.) Holding the hand in the **Kotegaeshi** grip, instead of dropping to the knees and pinning the shoulder Nage remains standing and rests the Uke's hand against his knee. Note that Uke's arm should have the same bend in it as it would if seated. Nage uses his knee to apply presseure to twist Uke's arm towards his head.

As the pin is applied and pressure increases Uke's grip will loosen and Nage can safely take the knife away.

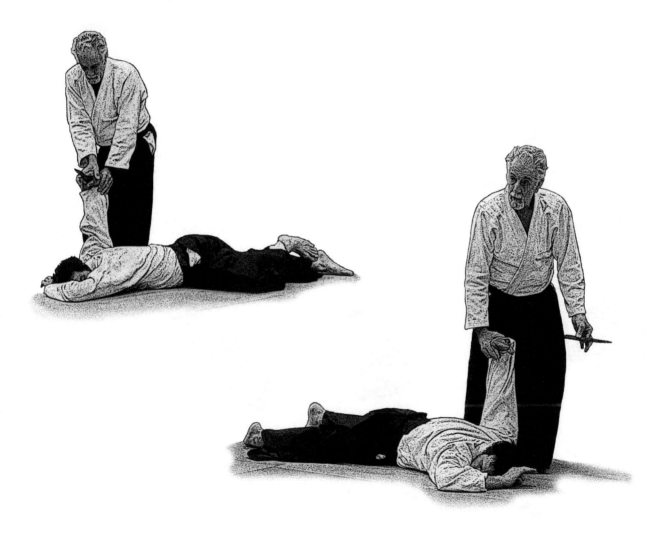

Hanmi Handachi Tsuki Kotegaeshi...

This is the same as the standing form except that Nage is seated while Uke is standing, which of course gives Uke an advantage and puts Nage at a disadvantage since it is much more difficult to move on the knees than it is while standing.

Techniques in **hanmi handachi** are not usually practiced until the student has some ability to perform **shikko** comfortably. (*See page 36 to 39 for a description of shikko.*)

Because Nage is seated rather than standing, the punch (*normally **chudan tsuki***) will come towards his face instead of mid level.

The response however is virtually the same as for **Chudan Tsuki Kotegaeshi Ura**. Nage enters —this time very slightly since movement is restricted— and makes a **Tenkan** turn around the incoming punch. At the same time he redirects the punch downward. He allows his hand to slide down Uke's arm until he can grasp the fist in a firm grip.

As he continues to turn he extends Uke's attacking arm in an arc spiralling down and around in front which forces Uke to follow around the periphery of this wide circle. As Uke follows this arc he will become more and more unbalanced.

Once Uke has passed Nage's centreline his balance should have reached a point where he is ready to fall over. At this point Nage turns Uke's wrist over and outward and at the same time extends Uke's forearm so his elbow points and moves down to a spot behind Uke's unbalanced centre.

Nage leads Uke into an unstable position where he can be easily toppled into a fall because his legs have gone much further around than his upper body.

As Nage applies the outward wrist turn (**Kotegaeshi**) and Uke begins to feel that he has no choice but to fall, he positions himself ready to either roll over his own wrist or in the example shown below, to roll away sideways into a break-fall to alleviate the pressure of the twist on his wrist.

From this point Nage will take Uke's elbow and moving across behind Uke's head, will turn him over, exactly the same as for the **Tachi Waza** version already described (*page 132 and 143*), so he can apply the pin, which is the same as for **Nikyo**.

Ushiro Ryokatatori Kotegaeshi...

Kotegaeshi from this attack where Uke has come from behind and grabbed both shoulders is often seen as extremely difficult. *In reality it is not all that hard to do.*

As Uke begins to come around behind, Nage waits until the second hand has started to grip then steps forward on that side. This small step forward opens a space between Uke and Nage which Nage can use to step into backwards. It also assists in disturbing Uke's balance. As he steps under the arm Nage begins a **Kaiten** body turn and uses his outside arm to swing around to grasp Uke's hand and wrist. **Atemi** to Uke's face with hand or elbow could be applied at this point if Nage wishes.

The **Kotegaeshi** grip should already be on though the outward twist is not applied until Uke's hand has come away from Nage's shoulder. Completing the **Kaiten** body turn both Nage and Uke are facing the same direction.

Nage continues to turn and step forward putting pressure against Uke's arm. Uke's grip breaks and Nage can now take his hand away from h the shoulder and lead him around into position for the outward wrist turn. (*Kotegaeshi*).

Note that once the hand grip has been taken, both Uke and Nage are moving in virtually the same manner as previously shown for the **hanmi handachi** form.

When Uke has come sufficiently far around in wide circle and is still moving but not stable, Nage begins to enter and turn Uke's wrist to the outside, cutting it down towards the mat. Immediately Uke's upper body will begin to turn around and over, (*basically pivoting around his elbow*) so he becomes more unstable and must take forward or sideways ukemi to protect his wrist.

Keeping hold of Uke's wrist Nage continues to move in following Uke's downward fall so he can apply the required pin to restrain Uke. Sometimes he will have to turn Uke over before being able to apply a seated pin, especially if Uke has taken a breakfall sideways instead of rolling over the top...

Nage drops to his knees as Uke is turned over in preparation to apply the pin...

Close up view of Nage taking Uke's hand in preparation to apply Kotegaeshi from Ushiro Ryokatatori.

These closer views show at the completion of the turn after Nage has stepped under Uke's arms, his hands and arms grasping Nage's shoulders are now crossed over in front and Uke's fingers are partially trapped by the twisted Gi.

As Nage finishes the turn he reaches for Uke's lower hand which is still trapped grasping the shoulder. He may apply at this moment an elbow strike to Uke's face as he reaches across to take the trapped hand.

Once the hand is taken, Nage turns slighttly towards Uke, which applies strong pressure against his elbow. This pressure against Uke's elbow shifts Uke's body forward into an unstable position. (*Clearly seen in the middle image.*)

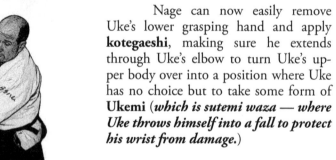

Nage can now easily remove Uke's lower grasping hand and apply **kotegaeshi**, making sure he extends through Uke's elbow to turn Uke's upper body over into a position where Uke has no choice but to take some form of **Ukemi** (*which is sutemi waza — where Uke throws himself into a fall to protect his wrist from damage.*)

Falling over the top unwinds the twist on the wrist.

Thinking about advanced techniques and difficult forms...

With any advanced forms the core or basis of the technique is the same as that studied and practiced for the fundamental or basic form (Kihon Waza).

Getting to the point where the technique can be applied is often the difficult part, and sometimes, as in the case of dealing with a **Yokomen** attack to which is expected a **Kotegaeshi** response, much confusion can arise simply because we have an **omote** and an **ura** entry (*uchi or soto*) to which we can do in either case an **omote** or **ura** finish. **Omote entry is sometimes called Tenshin entry because it twists Uke around while the Ura entry is sometimes called Irimi entry because it is a direct entry to tip Uke over backwards.**

In fact **this applies to any basic or fundamental technique in that there is an omote or an ura entry which normally leads on to omote finish for omote entry or an ura finish for an ura entry.**

The first technique studied with **omote** and **ura** forms is usually **shomen uchi Ikkyo,** where there are various reasons why we do the **omote** or the **ura** form, most of which have to do with timing of the entry and the **maai** of the two partners, But sometimes the **ura** is chosen over the **omote** in the case of multiple attacks to prevent another from attacking by placing Uke in the way.

But matters become complicated when **Ikkyo** is attempted from the **Morotedori** (*two hands on one*) grip where we find an **omote** entry can be finished either **omote** or **ura**, and the **ura** entry can also be finished with an **omote** or **ura** finish.

Logically the omote entry leads more naturally to an omote finish and likewise the ura entry positions Nage behind Uke so an ura finish is the most natural outcome, but since in both cases either finish can be performed it becomes a matter for Nage to decide which way to go depending on how Uke is responding and moving, or alternatively how Nage is positioned so there is a choice of either entry.

This means there is not a clear-cut delineation but rather an *amorphous and fluid interaction* which leads into various combinations.

It all depends on Nage's and Uke's sensitivity to each other's movements and efforts to find holes in each other's technique where a **kaeshi waza** (*counter technique*) may prevent the other from achieving the initial goal.

Basic forms need to be practiced and studied first before moving beyond the form and modifying it to suit your particular body shape and inclinations.

It will be noted that in all advanced forms the core principle and technique is the same as the most basic — the only real complication is in the attack and how you get from that back into a basic form that is already understood...

Yokomen Uchi Kotegaeshi Ura

With **Kotegaeshi** from **Yokomen Uchi** Nage can enter **omote** or **ura**.

Whichever entry is chosen Nage will aim for a common point in the interaction with Uke which is the same for all the forms of **Kotegaeshi** discussed so far. **This is the point where Nage takes hold of Uke's wrist (*and hand*) in preparation to apply the takedown or to create the throw.** At this point, any movement from Nage whether turning back or turning forward, will create a specific response from Uke who will have no choice but to move because he is connected to Nage. *From this point on the finish is almost always the same.*

Entering Omote employs the Tenshin body movement to continue Uke's attack past Nage's centreline which opens Uke's body to a number of responses. This movement doesn't stop Uke's movement but allows and encourages it to pass by in a circular fashion to a point where Uke's balance is disturbed just before the moment that Nage takes hold of Uke's wrist.

see pages 71 to 73 for information about dealing with and responding to Yokomen Uchi attack,,,

Nage enters to the Uchi side of the attack with a small **Irimi Ashi,** and **atemi** to Uke's face before using that arm to sweep across to Uke's elbow or just below it. Taking a small step back Nage continues to sweep Uke's Arm in a circle until it just passes Nage's centreline and there is space for him to enter and grasp the wrist. Entry is made by using a small **Tenkan** movement around the end of Uke's extended arm so Nage finishes on the outside of Uke's arm with the wrist firmly grasped in preparation to apply **Kotegaeshi**.

*Nage is in position now for the **ura** finish described on pages 135-137.*

Yokomen Uchi Kotegaeshi Ura

If using the **direct Irimi entry (Ura)** Nage slides across diagonally to contact Uke's striking arm as the strike is about to commence. This is an **Irimi Ashi** at an oblique angle from the side to attack both Uke's striking arm as well as the face. **The movement is still inside of Uke's arm and is attacking Uke's centre.** The result is Uke will have his movement interrupted and will find himself stretched over slightly to the rear with his balance disturbed. Nage reaches across when Uke deflects the **atemi** and allows his hand to slide down along Uke's arm to sweep it around in front.

The moment the hand is lined up with Nage's centre, Nage steps around to Uke's rear grasping the hand and wrist and extending Uke forwards. to make sure he remains off balance. This **Tenkan** movement places Nage in a position to lead Uke into **Kotegaeshi Ura**.

This is the same irimi entry as above seen from the opposite side...

The **Ura** finish means Nage stays outside of Uke's arm, makes **Tenkan** to bring Uke forward and around exactly as described for the response to *Chudan Tsuki Kotegaeshi Ura (pages 134 – 137).*

The **Omote** finish means Nage must come around in front of the trapped arm with an **Irimi Kaiten** movement before turning the wrist over for the **Kotegaeshi** application. *This is exactly the same as described for Chudan Tsuki Kotegaeshi Omote (pages 136– 138)*

Depending Uke's **ukemi**, Nage may have to turn him over to a face down position to apply **Katame Waza**. (*See page 132.*) The **Katame waza** (*pinning technique*) is either the standing or seated form. Usually the seated form is used unless Nage is disarming and taking a weapon from Uke in which case the standing form of pin is used. (*See page 139.*)

Kotegaeshi from Chudantsuki with Tanto...

Uke is about to attack Nage with a strike to the stomach using a **tanto**. Training with replica weapons such as a wooden knife allows both Uke and Nage to study timing and **maai** or *combative distance*. It becomes very clear when using a weapon that Nage needs to position correctly as well as to have some precision with movement otherwise the technique will not work. It also becomes clear how much Nage needs to harmonize and blend with Uke's movement so all the elements work together. **Maai, Musubi, Ki no Nagare, Kuzushi,** and finally control to hold Uke down while disarming him...

Nage blends with the attack, drops his centre to disturb Uke's balnce while still leading him forward, and takes contol of the wrist.

  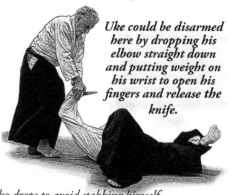

Uke could be disarmed here by dropping his elbow straight down and putting weight on his wrist to open his fingers and release the knife.

Nage turns the tanto back towards Uke who drops to avoid stabbing himself.

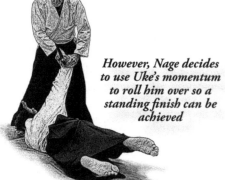 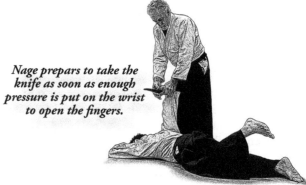

However, Nage decides to use Uke's momentum to roll him over so a standing finish can be achieved

Nage prepars to take the knife as soon as enough pressure is put on the wrist to open the fingers.

Shiho Nage
Four Directions Throw.

The body movement for Shiho Nage is based upon the four directions Shiho Giri (*or eight directions Happo Giri*) **cutting exercise with a sword or bokken.**

The four directions cutting exercise (**Shiho Shi Shomen**) is a fundamental exercise that teaches good posture and correct **Irimi** when doing the cut.

Shiho Giri (*see page 16*) teaches entering and turning from a practical viewpoint when practiced with a partner, and in its simplest form with Uke holding Nage's wrist in **Gyaku Hanmi** it is a fundamental technique that provides a solid base to expand into many variations.

Gyaku Hanmi Katatetori Shihonage Omote

The moment Nage's wrist is grasped he makes a small **Irimi** step behind the line on which Uke's front foot is situated, and turns his body with **Kaiten** to change stance. In the process of doing this he will have drawn Uke forward so his upper body is beginning to twist off balance.

With Uke's grasping hand now beginning to loosen Nage can grip Uke's wrist which is right in front of his centre. **Raising both hands as if holding a bokken** further extends Uke off balance and raises his centre making him weaker. This raising movement also extends Uke's elbow upwards.

To finish, Nage steps forward with his rear foot to a point just in front of the line along which Uke is being extended. At the same time he continues to raise his hands as if going to make a sword cut. A quick body turn will have Nage changing stance again so that he is now facing towards the rear of Uke. This turn also causes Nage to lean over backwards into an even more unbalanced position.

Nage should find his centre facing almost diagonally into Uke's kidney area before cutting down (*as if making a shomen cut with a bokken*).

Uke will come down onto his back, and if Nage maintains the grip he will pin Uke to the mat and finish with an **atemi** to the face..

If he lets go Uke will take a backwards rolling ukemi. (**Ushiro Kaiten ukemi.**)

Gyaku Hanmi Katatetori Shihonage Ura

With the Ura form the entry has to be to the rear of Uke. At all times Nage stays behind the imaginary line that Uke is standing on.

Nage slides his front foot to a position just behind Uke's front foot, at the same time bringing his grasped wrist in line with his centre.

Nage takes a large **Tenkan** step so that his back foot ends up completely behind Uke and roughly in between Uke's legs. Grasping Uke's opened wrist Nage raises his hands up along his centreline as if preparing to cut with a **bokken**. As his hands pass in front of his forehead, Nage turns completely to the rear, readjusts his position so he is looking at Uke's back and cuts down as if finishing the **shomen** cut with a **bokken**. If he hangs on he finishes with Uke pinned as shown here; if he lets go Uke will most likely take a back rolling **ukemi**.

Note, in both Omote and Ura when Nage has pinned Uke to the mat he can finish the technique with a strike to Uke's face using his other hand, or in more advanced practice if the shihonage was done in response to a weapons attack (with tanto or bokken) he can disarm Uke using his free hand to take the weapon away while keeping Uke pinned.

Both the Omote and Ura forms of Shiho Nage from gyaku hanmi katatetori are basic forms and should be studied carefully before moving on to other more complex ways.

Hanmi Handachi Katatetori Shihonage Omote

Techniques where Nage is seated and Uke is standing are referred to as Hanmi Handachi. These add a level of difficulty to the practice which makes it more advanced practice than the same technique practiced as **Tachi Waza** (*Standing technique*) although essentially the body movements of both Uke and Nage are the same as they would be if both were standing.

For **Hanmi Handachi Katatetori Shihonage Omote**, the moment Uke takes hold of Nage's wrist, Nage must immediately extend his arm forward as he grasps Uke's wrist. **Again he is raising his hands as if going to cut shomen with a bokken**. He must also take a step forward commencing a large **shikko** movement.

As can be seen in the picture above, this movement twists Uke's upper body down and around towards the front taking away enough of his balance to prevent him from following through with a kick, or a strike with his free hand to his seated partner after his initial grabbing attack.

This position also allows Nage space to swing his back foot forward and turn to face towards Uke's rear while not giving Uke back any of his balance. If anything Uke has become even more unbalanced as Nage finishes the turn.

The technique is finished in the same manner as for the standing form.

Nage cuts down as if wielding a bokken and Uke comes crashing down to the mat utilising a side breakfall to lessen the impact.

For receiving, Uke could opt to turn his body a little more to the front to roll over the top of his trapped wrist as Nage cuts down, or as in the case shown below he takes a backwards fall to finish on the side away from Nage. To facilitate the backwards fall Uke brings his head to his trapped wrist so the whole upper body can fall as a single unit making it easier to take the fall.

It is advisable to practice receiving both ways as this makes for a more flexible Uke who has more than one option when it comes to receiving **Shihonage**.

From **Hanmi Handachi**, because Nage is seated, the finish is almost always with a pin to hold Uke in place while Nage makes a final **atemi** to his face.

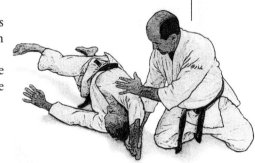

Yokomen Uchi Shihonage Omote

When Uke strikes to the side of Nage's head, Nage moves with a slight **Irimi Tenkan** to the inside of the strike so he can reach towards Uke's face with an **atemi**. This movement is small and should only be sufficient to guarantee that Uke's Yokomen strike will miss its target. The Tenkan part of the movement is only allowing the leg to drift across enough to maintain hanmi and is not a big step.

The entering movement is accompanied by a downwards sweep of Uke's attacking arm. Nage sweeps the arm so he can catch Uke's wrist with the hand he previously used to strike at Uke's face. With both hands grasping Uke's wrist Nage steps forward, **raising his hands up as if going to cut shomen with a bokken.** At the apex of the rise he turns (**Kaiten**) and begins to extend Uke's arm back behind Uke's shoulder.

The final move is to cut down so Uke finishes on his back and Nage can apply a pin.

If Nage lets go when Uke is half way down to the mat he will simply roll backwards to escape.

For continuous practice as in Jiyuwaza with multiple attackers Nage will simply let go, allowing Uke to roll back up to be ready to attack again, while he deals with another partner already coming in to attack.

Yokomen Uchi Shihonage Ura

When Uke strikes **Yokomen** to the side of Nage's head, Nage moves to the outside with and enters (*Irimi*) to capture the striking arm before it really commences the strike proper., at the same time with **atemi** to Uke's face. This entry which takes Uke's arm to the rear also tips Uke over backwards making him unstable.

Nage sweeps Uke's arm down and around. As soon as it reaches his centre, he instantly moves around it and enters behind Uke's shoulder. He continues to extend and lead Uke's arm out and around as he begins a full turn to the rear. At the same time as he commences the turn he raises his hands as if he is going to make a **shomen** cut with a **bokken** while allowing Uke's arm to slide over his head to finish in front ready for the downwards cut.

Nage continues to slide in behind Uke cutting his arm down at the same time. Uke positions himself for the fall as he feels his arm being cut down by stepping back and bringing his head close to his trapped wrist. Once Uke is on the mat Nage moves in to apply the pin.

> ## Morotedori Shihonage

Three approaches to dealing with Morotedori when wanting to do Shihnage...

Having described the complete technique for **Shihonage** from **katatetori gyaku hanmi** and from **Yokomen uchi** it should be sufficient to say that, when we do **Shihonage** from **Morotedori** or **Riotetori**, once the technique has been commenced it is the same as those basic forms of **Shihonage**. What makes the difficulty here is dealing with a two handed attack. *In fact most of what appears to be complicated is only because the attacks are less straightforward.* Once Nage has dealt with the attack the rest of what follows is invariably the same as the very basic forms first studied.

> *In all cases of two handed grabs Nage has a choice of dealing with either of the two hands. Having chosen one he then ignores the other and treats the hand chosen as if it is the only hand grabbing. That way the second hand doesn't confuse the situation.*

Example One...

In this first example Nage's palm is facing down so Uke's grip is on top.

Nage reaches across and grasps the open wrist. He then proceeds to treat that wrist as if Uke was grasping only with that hand. Nage repositions himself by changing hanmi and swings Uke's hands across his centre making it easier to break the grip. He needs to draw Uke forward to disturb his balance, and from that point on the form of shihonage that follows is then exactly the same as from **gyaku hanmi katatetori.**

Uke will naturally let go with his other hand as his body is twisted around into the throwing position, because he will need that hand to make a break fall in order to receive the throw.

Example Two...

In this second example Nage's palm is facing up so Uke is in effect gripping the underside of Nage's wrist.

Nage simply reaches up and grasps Uke's wrist from underneath while reaching for Uke's hand at the same time. Nage also realigns his centre so it is facing directly towards the two handed grip he now has on Uke's hand

As Nage turns his body to commence the technique Uke's body is naturally twisted into a stretched out and slightly unbalanced position. ***Note this example is the opposite of example one, and is in effect the same as doing Shihonage from Ai Hanmi Katatetori if the second grabbing hand is ignored.***

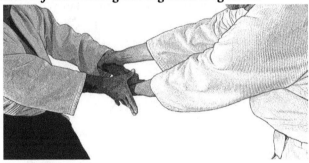

In this third example Nage's hand is once again facing palm down.

The moment Uke grabs Nage twists his hand slightly tot the outside so his hand enters between Uke's two hands and he can use his **Tegatana** (*outside edge of the hand*) to sweep Uke's arm down. At the same time Nage enters across slightly in front of Uke which creates a downward circling movement of Uke's outer arm and stretches Uke over with a twist to his upper body.

Nage catches Uke's wrist with his free hand and continues the circular sweep.

Once again as the hands pass Nage's centre the technique is finished the same as it would be from **gyaku hanmi Katatetori.**

Example Three...

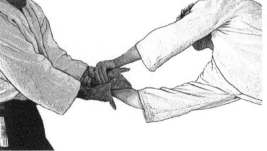

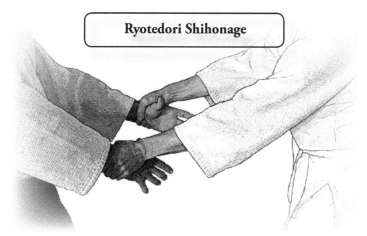

Ryotedori Shihonage

Once again Nage can select either wrist to use for applying the shihonage.
The first and simplest way is to treat either grasping hand as gyaku hanmi kata-
tetori attack and respond accordingly while ignoring the other hand.

In this example Nage has chosen **Hidari** (*the left side*) and proceeds to enter, to turn and prepare to cut down to finish the technique. Note in the picture below Uke has yet to let go with his other hand so he can use it to receive with a break fall.

Example Two...

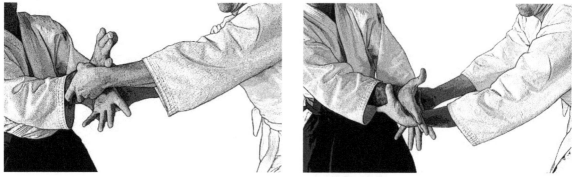

This second example is the logical outcome when movement is involved, with
Uke running forward and grabbing both of Nage's wrists.

As Uke comes on with a strong forward movement Nage circles back and around to one side, leading Uke forward sweeping him around with **Tegatana** in a circle until Uke begins to lose balance as his upper body is twisted.

Continuing the circular sweep Nage (*with control of Uke's wrist as in **Ai Hanmi Katatetori***) enters in preparation to finish the technique.

Having kept Uke off balance Nage enters and turns ready to cut Uke down and finish the shihonage.

*Note: the initial move to cut the wrist in a circular fashion is similar to Nage's response to a **Yokomen Uchi** attack if focus is only on the hand you are taking if you ignore the other one grabbing at the same time.*

We are often told that there are many different ways of doing any one technique, and every instructor and teacher will prefer one way rather than another. It doesn't mean that any particular way is correct and the others are not, it simply means that one particular teacher prefers a certain way because it is easier based on his physiology or body shape and ability to move, or perhaps he finds it more comfortable because that way was the way he first learned it.

The reality is there really is only one way to do any particular thing and this is based on correct application of principles, which must be the same in all cases. Diverging from these principles opens Nage to counter-attck or **Kaeshiwaza**.

Unfortunately, to find that one particular way is a lifetime's endeavour...

However, we do the best we can...and continue to study...

Ushiro Ryokatatori Shihonage

The drawings represent Uke coming around behind Nage and grasping both shoulders.

Ushiro Ryokatatori Shihonage

Example One...

The moment Uke finishes with the second grab Nage steps forward on that side. This opens a space between him and Uke and also stretches Uke forward just enough to disturb his balance. Without pausing Nage continues that forward movement into a 360 degree turn taking the elbow of the arm Uke first grabbed with and extending it forward as the turn is completed. Nage drops his centre so he can move forward through the space between them under Uke's other arm.

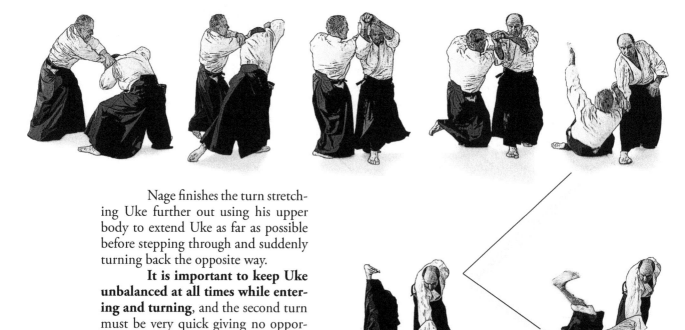

Nage finishes the turn stretching Uke further out using his upper body to extend Uke as far as possible before stepping through and suddenly turning back the opposite way.

It is important to keep Uke unbalanced at all times while entering and turning, and the second turn must be very quick giving no opportunity for Uke to counter the application.

The final stage is to step forward and cut down as if cutting with a **bokken** to take Uke down where he can be finished with a pin (*possibly followed with **atemi** to the face*).

Nage has held Uke's wrist all the way down and as Uke finishes the breakfall Nage appies a pin to Uke's wrist and elbow.

Example Two...

In this second example of commencing **shihonage**, Nage doesn't continue the circular movement of the previous example but after stepping forward to encourage Uke to reach with that second hand far enough to disturb his balance, Nage immediately steps back under the arm that first grabbed his shoulder.

In order to properly step back, Nage must drop his centre quite a lot lower than he would have for the previous first example. Stepping under that arm Nage commences a **Kaiten** body turn which will stretch Uke out and twist his upper body, while at the same time grasping Uke's wrist with one hand and reaching for the elbow with the other hand.

Note: In this example Nage grasps the second arm used to grab with, rather than the first as was the case for the previous example.

As the turn is completed Uke's hands will break free of his grasp on Nage's shoulders but because Nage a has a firm grasp on the second arm at the wrist and elbow the completion of the **Kaiten** turn will stretch Uke out into an unbalanced position.

Continuing to extend forward to maintain Uke in an unbalanced position Nage will suddenly turn back, and as in the previous example, will step forward and cut Uke's arm down as if it were a **bokken**.

Uke of course will adjust his receiving in accordance to the way he senses the technique being done.

To reiterate the differences: we find **in the first example** the first movement Nage makes is circular, continuing forward into the turn, and the movement is almost parallel to the surface with very little up or down movement. The first arm that grabs Nage's shoulder is the arm Nage applies the technique to.

In the second example the first movement Nage makes is to reverse the forward momentum by stepping back and dropping his centre so he can go underneath Uke's grabbing arm. This version contains a deep up and down movement rather than a parallel movement.

The second arm that grabs Nage's shoulder is the arm Nage applies the technique to. The two methods shown here are relatively uncomplicated and therefore easy to study.

In the finish below Nage has let go of Uke and he will roll away sideways.

Hanmi Handachi Katatetori Shihonage Ura

The omote form *(see page 151)* **is the way expected during Kyu grade tests.**

The **Ura** form is a little more complicated because if Nage attempts to do it in a similar manner to which he would do the **tachi waza ura** form then his legs will be trapped against Uke's front leg leaving him unable to complete the technique.

One way to get around this problem is to use an advanced form where Nage, using small movements, adds tremendous torque to Uke's upper body which compels Uke do all the work.

Nage immediately locks Uke's wrist, elbow and shoulder The moment Uke takes hold of Nage's wrist. Any extended energy or slight movement from Nage will be magnified and sent up along Uke's arm, through the shoulder and into his upper body.

By raising his hands as if preparing to cut shomen with a bokken Nage adds a twist to Uke's arm that make Uke run around behind Nage to relieve the intense pressure and pain in his wrist and elbow.

Having raised his hands to be level with his forehead Nage now only has to turn his body slightly to the other side and that small twist will send Uke flying around behind. Nage then finishes the **shomen** cut by cutting back down again.

All Nage has done is to raise his hands, turn his body slightly and lower his hands. The transference of energy and torque into Uke has makes Uke respond rapidly in order to protect his wrist and elbow from being damaged. By trying to keep up with the magnified extended movement he makes a large circle around behind Nage and never quite catches up. To save himself he will have to take **ukemi** by flipping over his twisted arm and wrist.

Throughout the technique Nage has not moved his knees or shifted his lower body; the only movement is from the waist up.

This method of doing the **Ura** form is only practiced at advanced levels because it requires a very responsive Uke. If Uke doesn't respond quick enough he could easily find himself with a broken wrist and damaged elbow. And like any other dangerous technique it should only be practiced in class with a qualified instructor or teacher supervising.

Hanmi Handachi Ryotetori Shihonage Omote

With Ryotetori all of Uke's weight and energy is bearing down upon Nage.
Attempting to do **shihonage** as he would from **Hanmi Handachi Gyaku Hanmi Katatetori** will not work with **Ryotetori**. To be successful Nage must use his legs and stand up in order to counter the downwards pressure from Uke's two handed grab.

The moment Uke grabs both wrists Nage drops his arms slightly which causes Uke to momentarily fall forwards, at which instant Nage will redirect the downward energy up at an angle which twists Uke's upper body and creates a space for Nage to stand up in. Alternatively if there is not too much weight bearing down Nage simply redirects Uke's energy around in a semi-circle towards the direction where he is proposing to stand up. Both ways to initiate the unbalancing of Uke and creating of space to stand up in depend on timing and sensitivity to Uke's energy flow, and this only comes with practice.

A thorough understanding of basic Tachi Waza Gyaku Hanmi Katatetori Shihonage is essential before moving on to more complex ways of doing this technique.

Once Nage has finished standing and stretched Uke up while keeping him unbalanced, Nage makes a sudden turn and cuts down exactly as he would for all the basic omote forms already described.

It is unlikely an Ura form would be attempted from this attack since the only way Nage can respond is by standing up as shown above, which is Omote. It doesn't matter which way Nage turns Uke (to the Left or the Right) the act of standing up to finish the technique will make it an Omote form.

Yokomen Uchi Shihonage taking Bokken

Practicing Shihonage while taking the bokken from Uke is most often practiced from Yokomen Uchi, perhaps because it is easier to do the technique this way. There is ample time for Nage to enter inside of the **Yokomen** strike, to position his hands to grasp the hilt of the **bokken** and also Uke's right hand.

Remembering that the **bokken** represents a live blade (*Katana*) and is not simply a piece of wood, Nage must allow enough room for the **bokken** to pass between them (*theoretically so he won't be cut*) as he stretches Uke out to unbalance his upper body. As the **bokken** passes between them Nage follows the **bokken**, stepping forward...

The close ups of the hands show how Nage's hands must be positioned to take control of the cutting movement as well as the bokken so it can be directed between them while taking balance and control away from Uke.

There are other ways of doing this; from Gyaku Yokomen Uchi (page 278) as well as from Shomen Uchi, but the one shown here is perhaps the easiest to learn and should be studied first before moving on to other more difficult forms.

…and turning suddenly Nage cuts the bokken down in a diagonal arc towards the mat taking Uke down at the same time. If the bokken is cut straight down the **kisaki** would probably stick into the mat making an unwanted hole, so it is cut down in an arc to avoid this damage. As Uke releases the bokken to take ukemi Nage will finish by stepping away, holding the bokken ready to strike. Sometimes Nage maintains a hold equivalent to kotegaeshi (outwards wrist twist) with one hand while holding the bokken with the other.

With all weapons practice it is very important to maintain **Zanshin**. Uke should not bounce up right away but wait just in case (*as in some dojos*) Nage will step forward to cut or strike with the captured **bokken** as the proper finish to the technique. If Uke jumps up too quickly he will get hit. Nage will indicate the finish by lowering the **bokken**, moving away, and as Uke gets up will offer it hilt first so Uke can take it back for the next repetition.

One can also see in the sequence of the technique that the movement Nage makes is exactly the same as previously explained for **Yokomen Uchi Shihonage Omote,** the only difference being the presence of the **bokken** which must be allowed for in the **maai**, and perhaps the timing of when you move.

IRIMINAGE
Entering Throw

Irimi means entering and **nage** means throw. This implies that **Nage** the thrower or person doing the technique **must enter deep into Uke's space and attack his centre.** This is the main difference between **Iriminage** and many other throws that require Nage to enter before doing the technique.

With many other throws Uke's centre is not necessarily attacked, any part of his body can be used to create a throw, but **with Iriminage Uke's centre must be destabilised,** and this is often accompanied by the use of Uke's head being turned, twisted or tipped over in some fashion during the process that finishes with a throw.

Since **Iriminage evolved from techniques used to break necks** as a means of defence against sword or spear attacks, it is still a dangerous technique and should be practiced with caution. It is cooperation that allows each partner to learn, with one lending his body to the other to study the technique, and both taking turns to be Uke and Nage.

Iriminage has as many variations as one can imagine, but they all have the one concept at the core, and that is to attack the attacker's centre immediately and directly, to take control of it the moment Uke begins his attack.

Nage must enter deep enough to finish behind Uke (*having gone right through him*) **to the point known as his blind spot** (*Shikaku*) where Uke is completely unbalanced, can't counter from either side and thus can easily be thrown.

Getting to this point can be a direct line in, or a circle around, or a half circle and a direct line, or any combination of moves that gets Nage to the right position to do the throw. (***And there really is only one position to execute this throw.***) In the process Nage and Uke learn about the relationship between straight lines, circles and spirals, and how a straight line is only a small part of a huge circle, and that spirals are continuous circles that are rising or falling.

The 2nd Doshu, Kisshomaru Ueshiba, the son of the Founder said in an article published in The Aikido, the official newspaper of Hombu Dojo: *I place the flow of sperical rotation at the very foundation — as a form without corners, a circle is without interruptions or breaks, each ending connected to another beginning.*

Follow a straight line for long enough and you will go all around the world to finish exactly where you started.

Iriminage gives us the opportunity to study this relationship and the means to internalise it, and because learning it is a long and slow process it also teaches us patience and perhaps a little humility.

For most of us, to really undersdtand Iriminage, will take a lifetime.

This applies to not only Iriminage, but to basically every technique that is an application to an attack.

Every training session will, or should, include Iriminage, because one can always improve understanding of its underlying principles. ***It is a fundamental technique and you never really finish learning it.***

There are many places within the following examples where strikes can be made to the opponent's head or upper body with elbows, fists, etc. In most Aikido techniques there are a multiplicity of strikes that can be done with various parts of the body but for safety reasons these are not gone into in much detail until students are advanced enough to be in complete control of their own body movements and ability to strike and to stop in time if a suitable response is not happening.

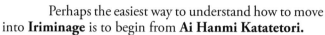

Ai Hanmi Katatetori Iriminage Ura

Perhaps the easiest way to understand how to move into **Iriminage** is to begin from **Ai Hanmi Katatetori.**

As contact is made between Nage and Uke Nage must resist trying to drag Uke around and instead he leaves his hand as gripped by Uke where it is and moves behind Uke with a large **Irimi, (Issoku Irimi Kaiten.)** while at the same time reaching for the back of Uke's neck. He makes a **Kaiten** move the moment he grasps the neck, turns back so his centre is lined up with his extended gripped arm.

Once his arm is lined up Nage steps back with his outside leg and extended arm in unison to make a large **Tenkan** to the rear of Uke. Since his whole body is turning and Uke is connected to it Uke has no option but to follow the movement around in a circle.

As he finishes turning Nage continues to draw Uke around. Uke will now find his upper body is out of synchronisation with his legs which are getting left behind. The further around he comes the more unbalanced he will get with Nage completely behind him and tipping him over.

Nage now simply takes one step further behind Uke who will come crashing down to the mat.

This is an Ura form because Nage enters behind Uke and turns Uke around to the rear before attacking his centre for the final throw.

Uke has taken a side breakfall rather than a back roll because his leg was trapped by Nage's entry behind.

Shomen Uchi Iriminage Ura

The most common basic form of **Iriminage** is practiced from **shomen uchi** attack. The moment Uke steps in and commences the **shomen** strike Nage also steps in and raises his arm to meet the **shomen** at the midway point. *This is not a block.* With his forearm just touching Uke's elbow Nage doesn't try to stop the downward strike but moves around it with a **Irimi Tenkan** while at the same time reaching for the back of Uke's neck.

If he is caught wrong footed he can alternatively make a sliding step forward to enter with a **Kaiten** body turn to position himself for the **Tenkan** step behind Uke. (*See pages 67 for Irimi Tenkan and Issoku Irimi Kaiten Tai Sabaki.*)

Once positioned behind Uke, Nage will cut Uke's elbow down with his **Tegatana** while making a further slight entry behind. This will turn Uke around allowing Nage to step through and attack Uke's centre to throw him.

Of course Nage could enter directly attacking Uke's centre but **this Ura form is always practiced because it helps beginners understand the principle of turning around a strong incoming attack to defuse it, making it weaker so it can be controlled.**

In this case Uke takes a back roll having set himself up by stepping back as Nage entered.

Ai Hanmi Katatetori Iriminage Omote

In the **Ai Hanmi Katatetori Omote** form Nage simply takes a step into Uke's blind corner or weak spot (**Shikaku**). At the same time he spirals his gripped hand in towards Uke's centre moving it up along the centerline into Uke's face. Once Uke's head is tipped over he has no option but to fall backwards taking ukemi to the side away from Nage. Nage does not need to grasp Uke's neck as the strong angular entry straight into his centre will unbalance him backwards.

The same principle applies for **Shomen Uchi Omote** (*not shown here*). Nage meets the **shomen** with his forearm against Uke's elbow (*exactly the same start as for the Ura form*) but instead of stepping around it he steps a fraction off line and allows it to continue on down past him. The moment it has gone past the midway point Nage shoots his arm over the top of Uke's descending arm straight into Uke's face to turn his head to the side. As his arm reaches towards Uke's face Nage enters into Uke's centre completely destroying his balance throwing him into a side breakfall. The angle of entry is the same as that already discussed for **Ryotetori Tenchinage Omote.**

Chudantsuki Iriminage Omote

This is essentially the same movement as that above for Ai Hanmi Iriminage Omote.
As Uke steps forward with the mid level punch, Nage moves off line by sliding forward just outside of Uke's striking fist. He finishes the entry with his centre directly in line with Uke's centerline. With his leading arm he strikes **atemi** to Uke's lower back or kidney area to help move Uke's centre forward while at the same time with his other arm he strikes towards Uke's face to make Uke fall backwards. The strike to Uke's face is accompanied by a slight turning of Nage's hips to emphasize the forward movement of the strike to the face. In this example Nage doesn't have to step forward to finish.

Chudantsuki Iriminage Omote ...

Nage enters deep behind Uke. (*This is a sliding forward step so hanmi doesn't change.*)

As Nage enters he allows the back leg to slide a little further offline in a partially circular manner which allows him to attack Uke's centre by striking an **atemi** into Uke's lower back or Kidney area as he angles his body to face directly at Uke's centerline.

The **atemi** to the lower back forces Uke's Centre forward while Nage's other arm makes a circular **atemi** around into Uke's face which stops Uke's Upper body moving while the lower part continues forward. Uke will very quickly fall backwards.

If the reader examines the movement for **Tenchinage Omote** *on page 114* it will be clear that this entry has exactly the same body movement and angles off to the side and back in behind Uke. The only difference for **Iriminage** here is that Nage's movement is closer to Uke.

Nage steps off line as Uke commences the attack.
He then makes irimi directly towards Uke's centre, with an atemi to Uke's face that travels over the atemi Uke attempts with his original attack. Basically Nage's atemi travels up along the line of Uke's atemi until it reaches his face and knocks him over backwards.

In the middle drawing Nage has repositioned himself by bringing his back leg together with his other leg and by turning his hips slightly he lines himself up with Uke's centre.

The third drawing shows Nage stepping directly behind Uke's lead leg to prevent Uke from stepping back to escape the atemi directed at his face. As Uke perhaps leans back a little to avoid the atemi he unbalances himself which allows Nage's further entry to throw him down.

Although depicted as 3 separate movements and initially practiced like that for the first few times, it should be remembered that it is in fact one continuous movement that begins when Uke steps forward to attack and finishes with Uke on the mat having taken **Ushiro Ukemi***.*

This response is direct with no circular movement. There is only a slight dropping of the centre by Nage at the finish to add acceleration to Uke's fall.

Chudantsuki Iriminage Omote ...

Too often we forget that to make Aikido effective we need to have a strong attack. We need an attack that makes us feel that there is a threat, that if we don't move at the right moment we will be hit. Often the training is too '*laid back*' with Uke not wanting to hurt Nage by actually hitting... but if there is no real feeling that we could be hit if we don't move, then there is no point in practicing any technique.

Uke needs to attack with vigour and with a genuine committment to hit the target. He may choose at the last instant not to strike hard, but the intention should be real to begin with, or there is no energy for Nage to utilize in countering the attack.

And equally, Nage should be prepared to strike Uke with strong **atemi** should it be neccessary, because Uke also needs to feel the liklihood of being hit in order to refine the ability to recieve properly to escape recieving an injury.

In other words both Uke and Nage need to make what they practice have some semblance of reality... but of course, with control because we are in a dojo and not out there in the street.

The **atemi** slides in along Uke's attacking arm so he doesn't see it until it is almost in his face. Naturally he pulls his head back to avoid the strike thus contributing to unbalancing himself. Hidden from view here is the other strike which Nage makes to Uke's kidney or lower back area simultaneously to the strike to the face. Uke's legs will fly out forwards as his lower back is pushed forwards while his head is knocked back. The fall is **ushiro ukemi**. (***back breakfall***)

A softer alternatiave is to use open hand to roll Uke's head over backwards while the other open hand pushes Uke's lower back gently forwards. As soon as Uke is unbalanced and falling Nages walks past letting gravity do the work... ***Note that the movement of Nage is exactly the same here as well as above; the only difference is in choosing not to strike hard.***

Sokumen Iriminage

This is a **side entry Iriminage** which is often called **Kokyunage** because there are **kokyunage** that look very similar, especially if done from a hand grab, either **Ai Hanmi Katatetori** or **Gyaku Hanmi Katatetori**.

It can be classified as **Ura** since the entry by Nage is to the **Ura** (*soto*) side and the fall is to the rear, but it closely resembles the **iriminage** already depicted as **Chudantsuki Iriminage Omote** as far as Nage's body movement is concerned. (*The sketches show a chudantsuki attack.*)

Nage moves to the Ura side as the attack comes in and enters directly into Uke's centre.

Nage uses his whole body to shift Uke's centre. In effect **this is an atemi with the whole body** rather than a discrete part such as a fist or elbow or knee etc. The fact that Nage's extended arm will turn Uke's head over at the same instant is not so important. It is the attack to Uke's centre which counts. Nage places his centre in the place where Uke's centre was and because Uke can not step back to escape (since Nage's leg is behind him) he has leittle choice but to fall backwards.

This is a powerful **iriminage** *and unless timing and blending are done well there will be a clash as one body encounters the other.* The end result is the same but Uke will have the wind knocked out of him if the clash is too hard. If the blending and harmonising is right then Uke feels hardly anything until he falls and hits the mat.

The side entry refers to the fact that the throw is the result of Nage either using **Hantai Tenkan** (*a half tenkan movement*) to obtain the 45 to 90 degree angle for entry from the side. Nage uses the lead hand here rather than the trailing hand to cut Uke down.

Shomen Uchi Sokumen Iriminage

Uchi Waza...

The instant Uke raises his arm and starts to strike Nage enters at an oblique angle. **The whole body moves as a single unit attacking Uke's centre at both the Jodan and Chudan level.** Nage enters deep enough to so his centre is directly facing Uke's centre from the side while his arms simultaneously attack Uke's centre from the front.
If Nage enters deep enough he will force Uke to lean back to such an extent he has no option but to take ukemi.

Precise timing is essential for this technique to be effective otherwise there is a clash..

Nage should drop his centre slightly as Uke raises his arm for the strike, but should not enter until Uke has committed himself to the strike. Entering too soon will simply cause Uke to change his attack to something else.

As Nage enters he begins from the lowered position (*having dropped his centre slightly*) gradually rising until contact where the proper height is then maintained. If he has the correct angle Uke's **shomen uchi** will slide down across Nage's back. A slight change of angle or a continuation of the direct oblique entry will make Uke's upper body unstable. (*This can be assisted by* **atemi** *to the back of Uke's knee — Nage uses his own knee for this if he has positioned himself properly.*) Continuing to move through will topple Uke into a fall.

Note that the same technique can be applied to a punch to the head (**Men Tsuki**). Nage's movement and timing are virtually the same.

This is indistinguishable with Kokyunage done from the same attack.

Soto Waza — Ura

Nage steps to the outside of the striking arm using **Hantai Tenkan**. (*See page 33*) This is a half Irimi Tenkan turn to position the body at 90 degrees to Uke or directly to the side. At the same time Nage raises his arms and blends with Uke's downward striking movement, with one arm resting over the elbow and the other somewhere nearer to the shoulder.

Nage's hand on Uke's elbow assists with the downward movement and draws Uke's elbow in towards his centre as he enters sideways behind Uke's leading leg. This tends to draw Uke's balance to the side against Nage. Nage now allows his arm to extend across Uke's upper centerline, in the process turning Uke's head to the side away from Nage.

To finish Nage simply drops his centre, which lowers his whole body. This is not a big movement, but since Uke is totally unbalanced any slight downward movement will cause him to drop to the floor with a fair amount of force.

There is no need for Nage to turn and use his arm to throw Uke backwards, just dropping the arm slightly, or leaving the arm where it is and dropping the whole body from the centre is sufficient impetus to create the fall.

In the street this technique contains at least two powerful atemi. The first is an elbow strike to the side of Uke's head to stun and take away his balance. The second is to finish the throw down by making a downwards strike with the elbow impacting Uke's sternum and possibly cracking it as nage drops his centre. Needless to say, we do not practice in this way in the dojo as it goes against the basic Aikido concept of controlling the opponent with as little damage as possible. However there are places where these more violent forms are practiced and the student should be aware of those possibilities, especially at a more senior level.

A more advanced form is if Nage cuts through Uke's head and neck with his **tegatana as if cutting with a bokken or katana**. *This powerful cut (***kesa giri***) drops Uke to the mat instantly and is called* **Kiri Otoshi** *(Cutting Drop) and is similar in concept to* **sumi otoshi** *or corner drop.*

Shomen Uchi Iriminage with submission hold...

Preparing to enter around the **shomen uchi** strike, Nage has met Uke's striking arm and followed the wrist down to the point where he is prepared to make a large step to enter behind Uke. This is the same start as the standard **Iriminage** from **shomen uchi** that is practiced everywhere.

Entering directly behind Uke, Nage draws Uke's arm close against his chest and holds it there with a firm grip while reaching around to grasp Uke's chin from behind.

Twisting Uke's head back and around to the side away from him Nage drops to one knee takes Uke down to the mat. The inside knee is the one that drops to the floor, the outside knee stays up so Uke's arm can now be stretched across it with the elbow down so the arm is locked.

Finally Nage rotates his hand over the top of Uke's head so he can push the face away and stretch the arm against the elbow joint at the same time.

Nage needs to be careful when doing this so Uke's neckc is not damaged by a sudden drop to the floor. He needs to be lowered slowly and with control.

Similarly the pressure exerted against Uke's elbow when he is stretched out should be applied slowly to give Uke time to tap out. Too sharp or sudden a movement can damage the elbow irreparably.

It is up to the instructor to be aware of each student's capabilities when attempting this hold down and not to allow anyone to do this without supervision.

Chudantsuki Iriminage

Uke attacks with a mid level punch (**Chudan Tsuki**) or with **Shomen Uchi**. Once the attack is committed Nage enters with a large **Issoku Irimi** (*See page 28*) to get as far behind Uke as possible.

Entering behind Uke, Nage rests his hands on Uke's shoulders. Finishing his entry with a **Tenkan** step (*which makes this Issoku Irimi Tenkan*) Nage drops his centre as he passes behind Uke.

The weight of his arms and hands on Uke's shoulders combined with this sudden drop will cause Uke's centre and balance to collapse down into the empty space behind the leg he used to step forward when attacking with **Chudan Tsuki** or **Shomen Uchi**.

Even more effective is to rest one hand on Uke's forehead as the same movement is completed; gently pulling the head back while suddenly dropping the centre will send Uke pounding into the mat.

Morotedori Iriminage Ura

In this example of **Morotedori Iriminage,** Nage steps around the grip with **Irimi Tenkan** to Uke's rear. He extends Uke forward in much the same way as he would for **Ai Hanmi Katatetori Iriminage** to destabilise him.

Nage then leads Uke down and around in a semicircle as he steps further behind.

He continues to draw Uke forward in a circular fashion. As Uke comes around Nage raises his gripped arm and extending towards Uke's face he steps through behind to tip Uke over backwards..

As Uke continues to be drawn around in a circle he passes Nage's front leg. His upper body encounters the immobility of Nage's extended arm while his legs continue to move forward.

Nage slides a little further in behind Uke who has now completely lost his centre and is beginning to fall backwards.

One more final step and extension of the arm will add impetus to the fall.

Uke will have to let go as he falls so he can break the impact on the mat.

Hanmi Handachi Shomen Uchi Iriminage

With Uke standing and Nage seated a significant degree of difficulty is added to the practice. Nage is restricted in how he can move by being in seiza and remaining on his knees. This is a more advanced form of practice.

If damage to Uke's lower back is to be prevented then receiving also needs special practice. (*See pages 54, 55, and 56; receiving in Hanmi Handachi.*) Uke should try not to lean forward but to drop vertically down onto the inside knee.

As can be seen the basic movement Nage makes to enter behind Uke and to cut down the striking arm is exactly the same as the standing **Shomen Uchi Iriminage Ura** *but tighter or smaller because he is on his knees.*

For Uke however the added difficulty of coming down onto one knee and spiralling around a central point to position himself for the backwards *ukemi* adds a vertical spiralling dimension to an otherwise parallel circular movement, making receiving an interesting challenge and definitely something worth practicing.

Yokomen Uchi Iriminage Ura

Iriminage from a Yokomen Uchi is more difficult than Iriminage from Shomen Uchi, especially if the Ura form is what we wish to do. It is not as easy to get to the outside of the striking arm because of the angle of the strike.

With **Shomen Uchi,** a slight movement off line is sufficient to allow the descending strike to bypass, but to do that with **Yokomen Uchi** Nage would have to go too far to the side to bypass the strike, consequently it is easier to step inside or to step back and slightly in front of Uke, to assist the movement of Uke's attack by sweeping the striking arm in a semi-circle across the front of Uke. (*See pages 71-72 -73*)

However, if Nage enters (**Irimi**) at an oblique angle as Uke is preparing to strike **Yokomen** he can encounter the strike before it begins to deliver any power. The entering movement must be deep enough to tip Uke over backwards. At the same time Nage delivers an **atemi** to Uke's face.

The moment Uke's attention is focussed on the **atemi** coming to his face; Nage shifts his striking arm sliding it through underneath Uke's elbow. Raising Uke's elbow slightly allows Nage to pass through to the rear where he can take control of Uke.

Maintaining pressure against Uke's elbow to prevent him from turning back, Nage enters further behind Uke and takes hold of his neck. Nage drops Uke's elbow and draws Uke's head in towards his centre at the same time. With Uke now connected Nage continues entering behind Uke with an **Irimi Tenkan** to bring Uke around in a circle to the rear.

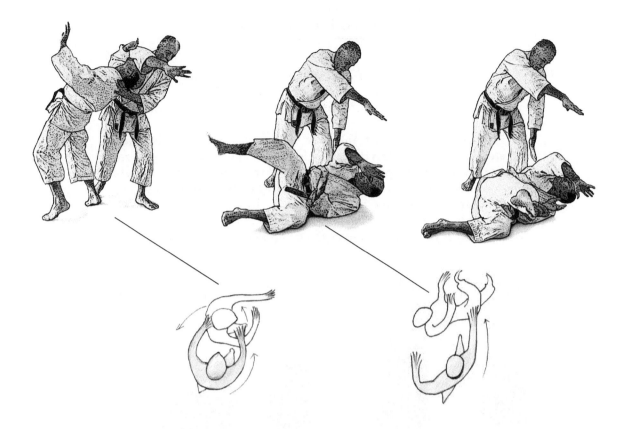

This entry is different from the standard way. Nage's arms are not crossed since he is going for the elbow rather than the wrist. If Nage cuts under Uke's wrist to go behind he will most likely run into a backwards elbow strike from Uke so to prevent this Nage cuts under Uke's elbow thus preventing a strike and allowing better control of Uke's body as he enters behind. Also, raising Uke's elbow will turn Uke right around making it easy for Nage to finish the technique.

Allowing Uke to rise as he comes past, Uke will find his legs going out from underneath while his head is still trapped against Nage's shoulder or upper chest area.

At this point Nage extends his arm past Uke's face (*in reality a palm heel strike or **Shotei** to the face*) which turns Uke's head over further destabilising him.

Uke has no option now but to fall backwards. Gravity with a slight dropping of Nage's centre will make falling inevitable.

In these pictures Nage has not stepped through because he has drawn Uke forward far enough to unbalance him. The common way to finish is with a step through as Uke's head is turned over with Nage finishing in **Gyaku hanmi** rather than **Ai hanmi** as shown here.

For those attempting higher **kyu** grade tests it is expected that from **yokomen** attack **three different ways of doing Iriminage are to be demonstrated**.

These would include the direct **Irimi Ura** version shown here as well as an **Ura** form after leading Uke around in a wide circcle, and one **Omote** form usually from leading Uke around in a circle but continuing the circle with Nage stepping around in front of Uke (*instead of behind as he would for Ura forms*) as he winds him up in an ever tightening circle until Uke's feet go out from under him.

Yokomen Uchi Iriminage Omote

This more advanced dynamic form requires Uke to be able to respond very quickly. It is not circular but rather a direct entry is made as ssoon as Uke has been twisted off line and is partially unbalanced.

As Uke attacks with **Yokomen Uchi** Nage enters and strikes with an **atemi** to Uke's face. This movement is **Irimi Tenkan even though it appears that Nage is stepping back. The initial Irimi movement is a slight movement across towards Uke's centreline while the Tenkan step gives the appearance that Nage is stepping back.** This movement is in fact a small part of a circle around the perimeter of Uke's reach.

(See pages 71 -72 for angles of entry against Yokomen Uchi...)

Nage does not sweep Uke's arm past his centreline, but enters immediately to the **soto** side of the arm to deliver a direct **tsuki** or a **Shotei** to Uke's face and a simultaneous **atemi** to Uke's Kidney area or lower back

The line of the strike is directly up along Uke's arm and straight into his face. The other strike to Uke's lower back forces Uke's hips (and centre) to move forward while the simultaneous strike to the face tips him over backwards

Uke needs to respond with an appropriate **ukemi** very quickly because he doesn't see the strike coming to his face until the moment it is about to impact. In fact, the action of pulling the head back to avoid danger is involuntary. We can't help it, and Nage uses that response.

Because the strike comes so fast up along Uke's arm his only option is to pull his head back, which of course will tip him over backwards. Nage ccould apply a strangle hold here but usually the impact of the strike to the face will make Uke pull his head back so quickly he will find himself falling into a back breakfall.

In these pictures Nage is using a palm strike rather than a closed fist. It is equally effective but less likely to cause any damage if Uke is slow to respond.

With practice in a controlled area such as a dojo, Nage will always allow Uke time to respond by adjusting the speed of his response to Uke's attack or perhaps by pulling the strike back at the last moment.

To finish, Nage follows Uke's downward fall by cutting down with his striking arm as he enters slightly towards the rear of Uke's centre. Once Uke has hit the mat Nage moves away with **Zanshin**, *that is not relaxing or taking attention away but being ready to respond if Uke tries something while on the floor.* Finally Nage moves away allowing Uke space to get up again.

Yokomen Uchi Iriminage Ura

This particular form also begins with an Irimi Tenkan movement that appears as if Nage is stepping back when he is in fact stepping forward before making the Tenkan movement.

This part of the form is exactly the same as for the direct entry already described on page 178.

There is an **atemi** to Uke's face which Nage uses to momentarily distract Uke. Normally Uke reacts to this **atemi** by pushing it aside so Nage continues that movement into a sweep across Uke's shoulder and down to his elbow which he directs in an arc to create the **Tenshin** body movement that disrupts Uke's balance (*see page 71*) and opens a space for Nage to enter behind Uke.

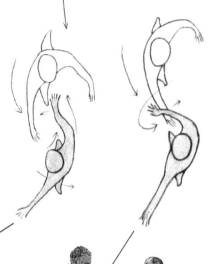

Above: Nage can be seen making the first **Irimi** movement to the side as he begins to take control of Uke's elbow. By sweeping the elbow across as he continues with the **Tenkan** step Nage easily controls the whole of Uke's upper body, shifting his balance and redirecting his forward momentum into an arc which takes Uke in a partial circle across Nage's centreline.

When Nage Has shifted Uke far enough to open a space behind, Nage immediately enters, again with an Irimi Tenkan movement which this time is a larger initial Irimi than the first movement used while dealing with the initial Yokomen strike.

As he begins to enter behind, Nage Takes Uke's neck while holding Uke's elbow in front of his centre point.

Rather than pulling Uke over Nage should focus on maintaining Uke's instability while he moves closer in behind

Nage needs to move very close behind Uke so there is no gap left between them, then when he makes the Tenkan step Uke will have no option but to follow.

Once Nage has drawn Uke around past him Uke will find his legs going out from underneath further unbalancing him. Nage tips over Uke's head and Uke will find himself falling backwards. As Uke falls Nage moves away while maintaining **Zanshin**.

Morotedori Iriminage Omote

Three variations.

The Ura form *(shown on pages 174 – 175)* is the method most often taught as the first way of showing how to do **Iriminage** from **Morotedori. Because Morotedori is a strong grip it is easier to go around it rather than straight into it.** Uke is much stronger simply because he has two hands grabbing on one which gives him a psychological if not practical advantage.

Variation One...

Nage usually enters to the rear on the **Uchi** side, or the side where Uke's lower arm is gripping, which if one looks closely is very similar to the method of entering for **Ai Hanmi Katatetori Iriminage Ura** *(page166)*.

As Nage enters to the rear he raises Uke's arms in an arc over his head.

When Nage is directly behind he strikes Uke's lower back with an **atemi** to push his hips forward. *In practice in the dojo this is a gentle push rather than a hard strike.*

Uke's lower body is shifted forward while at the same time his upper body is shifted backwards. He becomes unstable and falls backwards. This is helpd by Nage cutting down into Uke's face and centre with a strong **tegatana**. Uke lets go so he can take a break fall.

Nage moves away to the rear allowing a space for Uke to fall into. This makes certain Uke won't bang his head against Nage's knee and Nage is far enough away so that he can't be kicked in the face if Uke's legs fly up as he falls back.

Variation Two...

An upward circular movement across the front of Uke as Nage initially enters with a sliding step to maintain the **Ai Hanmi** stance will twist Uke over and back into a position where he is ready to fall. Nage now steps through at an angle behind Uke's rear leg while extending through over Uke's head.

Variation Three...

The previous two variations hand Nage entering around Uke's centreline. **This third variation attacks the centreline directly**.

Nage enters with an elbow strike into Uke's sternum. This is a whole body movement, not simply a strike with the arm. To achieve this Nage drops his centre slightly and aligns his arm and elbow with Uke's centreline. Nage then uses his legs to raise his whole body and as he moves directly forward his elbow strikes Uke's sternum.

Nage then steps through while his arm slides up Uke's centreline to become a palm strike to Uke's chin, tipping the head back.

Entering deep behind Uke as he makes the palm strike will take Uke down. Note in the above example Uke has grabbed Nage's arm (*after releasing his* **Morotedori** *grip*) in order to take a breakfall with less impact.

Gyaku Hanmi Katatetori Iriminage — Shiho Giri variation...

The instant Uke grabs Nage's wrist Nage turns his hand palm down. He enters directly sideways leading with his elbow to take Uke's arm up and over as if preparing to do **Shiho Nage**. *Note this initial entry is similar to that for* **Morotedori Iriminage** *if it is done from the* **Soto** *or* **Ura** *side rather than the* **Omote** *or* **Uchi** *side.*

Nage must move in very close so he can lock Uke's elbow beside his head or else Uke can strike Nage's head with the elbow. Once Uke is locked against Nage, Nage brings his other hand forward to strike at Uke's face. The idea is to tip Uke's head over while at the same time cutting down with the hand that is still gripped by Uke. The pictures clearly show how quickly Uke is tipped over and his balance taken. *Note how far behind Uke Nage has entered...*

Uke is inHidari Hanmi

Uke is in Migi Hanmi

Sometimes this technique is not finished as a throw but is turned into a strangle hold. Nage reaches right around Uke's head and grasps Uke's hand which is still holding his wrist. By tightening his arms he will lock Uke's head and arm together effectively cutting off blood supply to the brain. This is a dangerous technique and should only be practiced by senior students, and even then only under supervision of a properly qualified instructor

Entering deep behind Uke's centre gives Nage complete control of Uke's balance. Continuing to enter behind Nage makes Uke so unbalanced he will fall down.

Since Nage's leg is in the way Uke must make a slightly circular breakfall around it or he will injure his lower back falling onto Nage's knee. One other alternative is to allow himself to slide down Nage's leg so he can fall in front of the knee.

Note in the examples shown from both sides above and below, Uke has maintained his initial grip on Nage's wrist. This tends to help keep him close to Nage and he can use the grip as support to lessen the impact he makes when he hits the mat.

To finish, Nage maintains **Zanshin** and moves back allowing Uke space to get up to ready himself for another attack.

Zanshin is often defined as a lingering spiritual awareness or contact, an invisible connection between Uke and Nage that should be maintained at all times during practice.

On a more peripheral level both partners should also be aware of the positions of anyone else training in the dojo so that neither one will throw the other accidentally into someone practicing nearby. If everyone maintains good Zanshin there is much less likelihood of injuries occurring in the dojo.

Gyaku Hanmi Katatetori Iriminage — Chudan entry...

The chudan method of entering is the one most commonly practiced. It is usually the fist method taught, and although it appears simple it is not as easy to enter from this position as it is from **Ai hanmi Katatetori** *(page 166).*

Once Uke has gripped and both partners are in **gyaku hanmi,** *(see pages 78 - 79 for some methods to break this grip)* Nage turns his body slightly so that the grip is in front of his centre. He rests his other hand on top of Uke's grip, and shifts his body past Uke until his centre is parallel to Uke's centre. By this time the grip has been broken and Nage can grasp the back of Uke's neck in preparation to enter behind. He will draw Uke's head in close as he prepares to take a **Tenkan** step.

Gyaku Hanmi Katatetori Iriminage — Jodan entry...

With the Jodan entry Nage raises his arm up to head height as if preparing to do **shomen uchi**. This opens Uke's grip on his wrist enough to loosen it and draws Uke forward so his weight is on the front foot. Nage rests his other hand underneath Uke's grip and steps at an oblique angle past Uke's centre to enter behind.

As in the **Chudan** example above, the hand that has broken away from Uke's grip is now used to grasp the back of Uke's neck. He draws Uke's head in close to that when he takes a **Tenkan** step Uke will have to follow.

Nage steps to the rear with the continuation of his entry which in both the **Chudan** and the **Jodan** example is **Tsugi Ashi Tenkan** or **Issoku Irimi Tenkan**.

He cuts Uke's arm down while extending Uke's head down in a spiral until Uke drops to the mat.

As he continues to move behind Uke, Nage now allows Uke enough freedom to try and stand up. Using Uke's upward movement Nage then tips Uke's head over which combined with Uke's legs moving forward completely unbalances Uke so he must fall to his rear. In this case there is often no time for Uke to position himself for a backwards roll. His only option is to take **ukemi** in the form of a breakfall as his legs fly out in front.

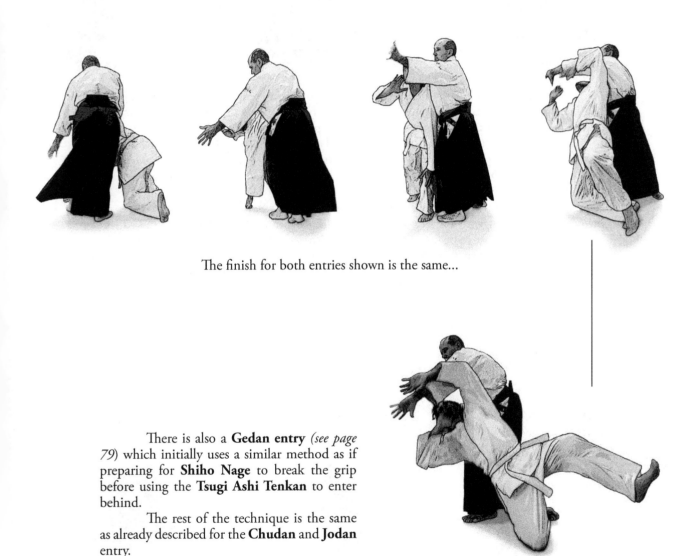

The finish for both entries shown is the same...

There is also a **Gedan entry** (*see page 79*) which initially uses a similar method as if preparing for **Shiho Nage** to break the grip before using the **Tsugi Ashi Tenkan** to enter behind.

The rest of the technique is the same as already described for the **Chudan** and **Jodan** entry.

Yokomen Uchi Iriminage Omote

Uke attacks with **Yokomen Uchi.** Nage steps across so his left foot is lined up with Uke's centre. This is actually **Irimi Tenkan** becaause the side step is the **irimi** and the back foot drifts back for the **tenkan.** Nage sweeps Uke's hand past his centre to twist Uke off balance.

Normally for this **omote** form Nage would continue to sweep Uke's hand around into his face while stepping in towards his centre (*with the left foor because in this example that was the foot that moved for the initial irimi... Uke could have attacked with the other hand which would make everything above be reversed.*)

However in this case above nage steps with his right foot behind Uke's front leg and then follows through with his left foot to enter deep behind Uke as if having walked right through his centre. Notice below how Nage's hip displaces Uke's hip forcing Uke's pelvis forward while Nage cuts through Uke's head with his arm. Dropping his arm while turning his hips as if he himself is cutting down with a **yokomen** strike wraps Uke around his hip which means Uke can only make a side breakfall to save himself *by rolling around Nage's hip.*

Although this is basically an **omote** entry and finsh, it contaians elements of the **ura** entry and finish which makes it somewhat amorphous. *In more advanced practice there is no strict omote or ura, but only combinations of both which continually vary depending on the movements of both Uke and Nage.*

Ushiro Ryokatatori Iriminage

All techniques applied to an attack from behind are difficult...

As Uke comes forward and grabs one shoulder, Nage steps with a small movement to the side which encourages Uke to come in closer to reach for the other shoulder.

When Uke makes contact with the second grip Nage steps forward on that side which also continues to draw Uke forward in a circular manner. This opens a space through which Nage can suddenly step back (*using the same leg he previously stepped forward with*) to destabilise Uke.

To get under the arm that made the first grab Nage must drop his centre slightly.

The actual stepping back will break the second grip, and to break the first grip Nage will use his head to extend forward against Uke's forearm. The moment this grip breaks Nage commences to step behind Uke for a sweeping **Irimi Tenkan** movement while at the same time he takes hold of Uke's neck and cuts down Uke's lead arm with his **Tegatana**. (*Hand blade*)

As he continues the Tenkan movement he spirals Uke down towards the rear.

With Uke's balance completely gone he leads Uke in a continuing rearward circle allowing him to rise.

As Uke rises Nage strikes with an open hand into Nage's face.

It could be the inside of a fist rather than a striking hand, but shown here the hand is open, minimising the chance of accidental injury.

This strike twists Nage's head around and over backwards.

Uke's upper body has now started to move back while his lower half is still moving forward.

In the finish shown below the technique has been done slow enough to allow Uke time to get one leg behind so he can receive it with a backwards roll. (***Ushiro Kaiten ukemi***)

In practical terms it would be done so fast that Uke's legs would fly out from underneath and he would fall flat on his back.

It is often emphasised that we should never be caught, or allow ourselves to be caught from behind. But with the possibility that this could happen sometimes we practice against attacks from behind.

We practice these in two ways:

1. Static, where Uke is allowed to step up behind Nage and grab his shoulders, or elbows, or wrists, or the back of the collar, which are the most common attacks used.

2. Moving, where Uke is encouraged by Nage to come around behind, and is in fact led by Nage into moving in a circle behind to complete the two handed grabbing attack.

Most applications depicted in this section of the volume are from a moving start...

Ushiro Ryotetori Iriminage

This technique is basically the same as the previous **Ushiro Ryokatatori Iriminage**, the only difference being the **maai**. Because Uke is grabbing Nage's wrists instead of his shoulders, there is more space between them which makes it easier for Nage to slip under Uke's arm after he has led him around to the rear and extended him forward on the opposite side to where he initially entered.

Uke is encouraged to come around to the rear to grab the other hand which Nage holds out in a position slightly in front of his centre line as seen laterally through his body.

As Uke grabs the second hand Nage steps forward to continue leading him, while at the same time raising his arms which has the effect of also raising Uke's centre. This makes Uke feel top heavy and not too stable.

As Uke finishes his step to take him slightly past Nage, Nage immediately steps back. As he steps back he keeps up high the wrist first grabbed by Uke and drops the other one. This gives him the space to step back under the arm while at the same time causing Uke to loose the second grip.

At this point Uke will feel as if he is going to fall forward so he naturally takes a step to compensate. As hUke takes this step Nage cuts down the arm he stepped back under and enters behind Uke with **Irimi Tenkan.** He reaches for the back of Uke's neck and draws him down until Uke's head is resting against his shoulder.

Nage continues his **Tenkan** step to the rear making Uke take more steps, so in effect he begins to spiral around the periphery of a large circle at the centre of which is the point where he is connected to Nage.

Because Nage is in the centre of the circle and Uke is travelling around the periphery, Uke will find his legs and feet getting further away from his upper body as he completes 360 degrees (*sometimes more, sometimes less*) and is back at the point where he first attacked Nage only this time he is completely unbalanced and controlled by Nage.

If Nage continues to draw Uke through into the start of another circle he will fall with little effort needed from Nage to make this happen.

Nage will step through behind Uke as he starts to fall, dropping his lead arm to take Uke's centre down to the mat, or extending his lead arm to tip over Uke's head before cutting it down.

Shown here is a classical finish
with Uke taking a back roll.
(Ushiro Kaiten ukemi)

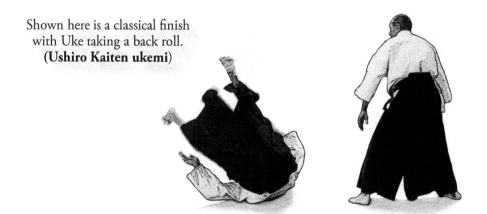

Eridori Iriminage

Eridori is always an attack from the rear. **Eridori** means collar grab. The collar is at the back of the neck. The front part is the lapel and if this is grabbed it is called **Munedori**

The instant Uke grips the collar Nage steps forward at a slightly oblique angle. Rather than stepping directly ahead he steps off to one side at an angle of about 15 degrees.

The moment his front foot touches he turns (**Kaiten**) 180 degrees back to face Uke.

The act of stepping forward clearly stretches Uke out, and going off the line at an oblique angle disturbs Uke's balance tipping him slightly backwards. As Nage finishes the **kaiten** he extends his open hand into Uke's face while at the same time moving laterally past Uke's centreline. This tips Uke over even further backwards.

Continuing to extend with his open palm strike, Nage steps forward past the line Uke is standing on. This tips Uke over backwards to such a degree any semblance of balance will disappear completely and Uke will finally let go and take a fall.

It doesn't matter which hand Uke uses to grab Nage's collar, or which way Nage turns. Once he is facing Uke the palm strike and body movement off line will work and have the same effect. In the case shown here Nage is on the inside of Uke's arm and the technique is **Omote** (*or an **Uchi** form*).

If Nage had turned the other way he would finish up on the outside of Uke's arm and the palm strike would be under the arm up into Uke's face with exactly the same effect. This would be an **Ura** (or **Soto**) form. The core of the technique is the same. Nage stretches Uke forward while unbalancing (*because of the oblique angle*) Uke's centre to his rear. The final entry is simply a body movement laterally past Uke to take his centre further off balance so he has no option other than falling. **The palm strike to the face is an added incentive for Uke to fall backwards.**

These three images are the same as those above only seen from the opposite side.

KOKYUNAGE — Breath Throw.
...unravelling confusion — perhaps...

What is Kokyu?

The word **Kokyu** generally is translated to mean 'Breath'.

In the context of Aikido it doesn't mean an emphasis on breathing in or out in relation to aspects of a technique, for example breathing out explosively (*sometimes with kiai*) when throwing Uke. This is forced breathing.

Unlike the breathing exercises utilised for **Misogi** where the inhalation and exhalation of air is used to cleanse the blood, filling it with oxygen and energy, while strengthening the lungs, purifying the body and teaching us how to focus and be grounded, **at all other times our breathing should be natural, unforced, and something we are not really aware of,** *just as breathing in everyday life is something we rarely consider.*

Kokyu, apart from meaning breath, is also associated with the concept of Life, for without breath or breathing we cannot live.

Kokyu can therefore be seen as a means of making Uke come alive; a way of making Uke move so that the movement can be channelled into a throw.

In Aikido it is believed that Kokyu is the channel through which Ki (*energy or spirit***) can be expressed.** This expression can be calm and gentle or explosive and dynamic. It all comes back to the interaction between Uke and Nage.

What is Ki?

This is the central character in the word AIKIDO, and is an almost impossible concept to explain.

Loosely, it means Energy, life force, spirit, mind, feeling, and it is used in a number of other ways that seem to be barely related. It is used in the words for light, electricity, and lightning amongst others where the major component is energy.

In Aikido it is the energy, life force, and spirit, aspects of the concept that we relate to, but these are all intangible.

The student will develop an awareness of **Ki** through practice of movement and technique both as Nage and Uke.

An individual and personal understanding of **Ki** will evolve over time, and is not something that can be forced or explained intellectually.

There are however some exercises that can be taught which can enhance the awareness of **Ki**, thus allowing us to begin developing it.

Kokyunage is translated as Breath Throw. *We are often told that it is the energy generated by proper breathing as we move that gives power to the throw.*

On a more prosaic level the keen observer will see that once Uke has been led into a position of unbalance, any slight movement on Nage's part will release the energy within Uke's attack causing him to fall. Of course gravity will ensure Uke falls, with only a little extra help from Nage to add emphasis to the fall.

Looking at a number of different **Kokyunage** we could conclude that this is a throw that primarily uses a whole body movement by Nage in combination with a redirection or leading of Uke's attacking energy to a point of complete unbalance that creates what appears to be a throw. Nage must enter in some manner to do this, and here lies the confusion as to what the difference is between **Kokyunage** and **Iriminage**.

Iriminage is an entering throw. Primarily Nage enters into Uke's space and unbalances him by directly attacking Uke's centre, often tilting, and twisting or turning Uke's head to unbalance him in preparation for the throw, but not always. Historically **Iriminage** was a series of neck breaking techniques in response to attacks with a sword or spear. These techniques through evolution have become head twisting or tipping back so that Uke is not seriously hurt but simply unbalanced ready for the continuation of the entering movement to create the throw. **The important difference between Iriminage and Kokyunage is the direct attack to Uke's centre.**

With Kokyunage, Nage can attack any part of Uke's body to create a movement, as if breathing extra life into Uke, which will unbalance him to the point of falling over. Further movement or extension from Nage will guarantee Uke to be propelled into a fall, or what appears to be a throw.

There are many different **Kokyunage** and most of them don't have a specific name which can be confusing when an instructor or teacher asks for the student to do **Kokyunage**. He may have no idea which one the instructor wants to see unless the instructor has previously demonstrated it.

Any technique that doesn't have a specific name is probably going to be called Kokyunage.

Some related martial art schools teaching **Aiki-jutsu** do have names for every single technique and variation which can also be very confusing because these names are often quite long being virtually a description of the technique.

It is therefore not such a bad idea that in Aikido there are hardly any names for Kokyunage other than that generic name itself.

There are three main concepts in the execution of Kokyunage which are: those that **keep Uke going in the same direction he was travelling** when attacking, those that **turn Uke to either the left or right side**, and those that **turn Uke completely around to send him back** in the direction he came from. Of course anywhere in between those three directions is okay as well since nothing is ever fixed as rigidly as that.

This way students only have to learn one or two **Kokyunage** from each of the three groups rather than hundreds of slightly different and varying techniques. So when we deal with attacks such as **Shomen uchi**, **Chudantsuk**i, **Y**okomen uchi or various one and two hand grabs, a technique from one of the three variations can be selected.

Thus the same technique can be done in response to any attack, and each time it will look and feel different because the attack is obviously different, and therefore the timing and **maai** will also be different.

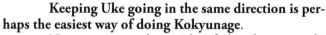

Shomen Uchi Kokyunage Omote

Keeping Uke going in the same direction is perhaps the easiest way of doing Kokyunage.

Nage enters to the inside of the **shomen uchi** strike. He continues the downward movement of Uke's strike by cutting Uke's striking elbow down while simultaneously raising Uke's other arm up from under the elbow.

*It is advisable to attack the elbow and thus control Uke through the upper arm and the shoulder joint. Attacking the wrist usually leaves too much room for Uke to flex his arm and avoid being taken off balance, giving him a strong possibility of **kaeshi waza** or counter attacking.*

Nage's body movement is **Irimi Kaiten** followed by a small step forward to add momentum to the throw.

Alternatively Nage could strike with an **atemi** using **tegatana** to Uke's neck cutting the head down at the same time as he cuts Uke's arm down rather than raising the elbow up and over. Nage's movement is exactly the same, entering **omote** (**uchi** side) of the striking arm with **Irimi Kaiten**, then utilising the **Kaiten** turn to cut the striking arm down while either raising the other arm or cutting the side of the head or neck down. The technique is finished with Nage stepping forward as he cuts Uke down towards the mat.

Note Uke enters with irimi kaiten, that is he enters and turns back to keep Nage travelling forward along the same line of attack...

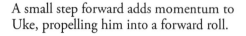

A small step forward adds momentum to Uke, propelling him into a forward roll.

Another simple **Kokyunage** is where Nage enters as Uke is raising his arm in preparation to strike **shomen uchi.** This only works if Nage's timing is such that he enters before Uke commences the downward strike. Reaching for Uke's elbow with a strong extension Nage continues his forward (**iri-mi**) movement straight through. This turns Uke completely around to face back towards the direction he had come from. With Uke's body twisted around and off balance Nage cuts down which takes Uke so far off balance he must take a forward rolling **ukemi.**

We can see that Nage has entered the moment Uke commences to raise his arm. Nage forces Uke to continue raising his arm beyond a comfortable position for striking which has the effect of raising Uke's centre up, making him unstable and light enough to turn.

Note:Nage enters in a straight line to turn Uke around to send him back towards where he came from.

This is a variation of the previous kokyunage where Uke is turned around and sent back...

If Nage misses the timing to enter before the **shomen uch**i commences and the strike is on the way down, a different form of control must be attempted because it is not possible to stop the striking arm without considerable difficulty.

Trying to block rather than blending and redirecting won't work especially if Uke is bigger and stronger. **In Aikido we try to be relaxed and avoid attempting to do techniques by using physical strength. If we focus on harmonising with and redirecting Uke's movement without attempting to stop it we will begin to develop an awareness of Ki and Kokyu, and how to use this effectively.**

When the opportunity is missed to enter early enough to catch the rising arm **Nage enters to the Ura side with one hand underneath Uke's elbow and the other on top.** The downward movement of the strike can be followed and redirected. Nage must grip firmly but without trying to stop Uke's movement. As Uke's strike finishes its arc down Nage extends it further forward to tip Uke onto his front foot.

Nage can then raise Uke's arm up which will have Uke floating on his front foot. By half turning suddenly (**kaiten**) to face the rear he can flip the arm over to turn Uke completely around to his rear, with both Uke and Nage finishing in the same position already described for the previous Kokyunage. Nage continues to cut down as before and Uke will have to take a forward roll.

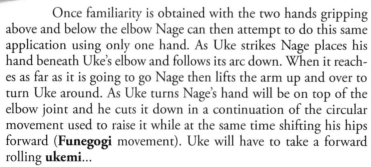

Once familiarity is obtained with the two hands gripping above and below the elbow Nage can then attempt to do this same application using only one hand. As Uke strikes Nage places his hand beneath Uke's elbow and follows its arc down. When it reaches as far as it is going to go Nage then lifts the arm up and over to turn Uke around. As Uke turns Nage's hand will be on top of the elbow joint and he cuts it down in a continuation of the circular movement used to raise it while at the same time shifting his hips forward (**Funegogi** movement). Uke will have to take a forward rolling **ukemi**...

Uchi — Omote

Soto — Ura

In both thses kokyunage the movement of Nage is almost exactly the same except one starts outside and finishes inside while the other starts inside and finishes outside

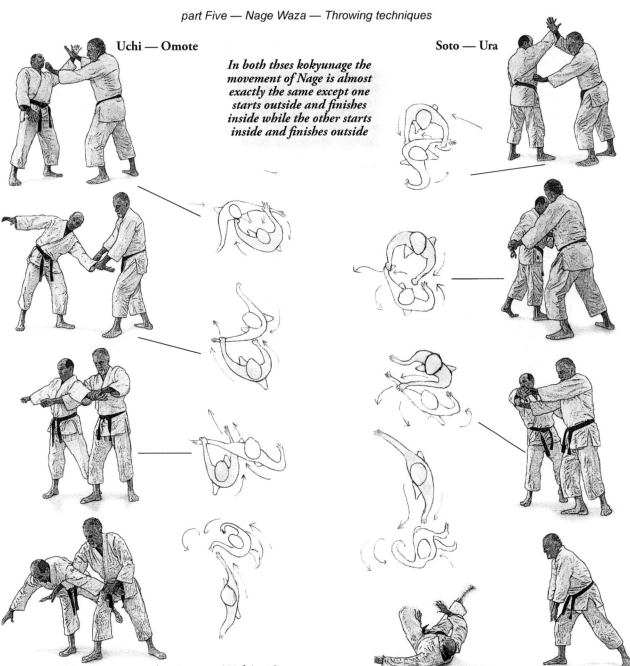

Nage enters to the **Omote** (*Uchi*) side. There is the **atemi** (*this time to the face*), sweeping down and catching the wrist, but as the arm is extended Nage brings his free arm up under Uke's upper arm to raise Uke's centre making him weak and easy to throw. The use of Uke's arm creates the throw. This again turns Uke 90 degrees for the throw.

Some times it is called **Udekiminage** *or even* **Hijikime Jujinage,** *although* **Jujinage** *is generally when Uke's arms are crossed with one locking the elbow. Here the elbow is locked with Nage's arm crossing under Uke's arm.* Pressure against the elbow will encourage Uke to take **ukemi**.

This kokyunage turns Uke around to project him at a 90 degree angle to his line of entry, although anywhere between there and a full half circle is fine.

Nage enters offline to the **Ura** (*Soto*) side with **atemi** to the lower ribs while the other hand cuts the shomen strike down. The hand that strikes the ribs catches Uke's wrist, extending the arm to turn Uke. Another **atemi** to Uke's face is deflected, and falls on Uke's elbow. Nage steps forward extending the elbow towards the mat to throw Uke. (*Aiki Otoshi... it is also done from gyaku hanmi katatetori*).

Dealing with attacks from behind helps develop awareness (like a sixth sense) of what is happening to you even though you can't see it. Almost like training with eyes shut and using only the feel of the person and his energy as they attack to create the technique. Consequently Ushiro Waza (rear attacks and techniques) are more advanced and require the student to have at least mastered basic body movements coupled with some ability to blend and harmonise with a partner.

Ushiro Ryokatatori Kokyunage Omote

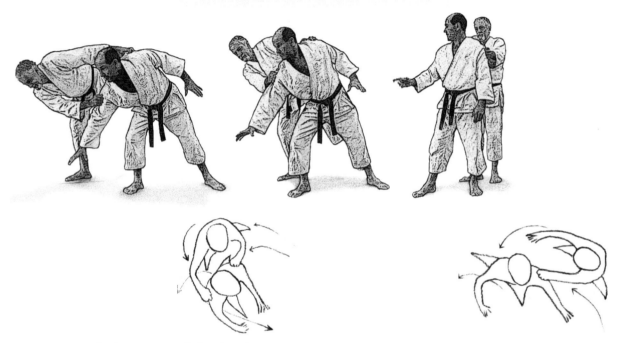

Uke has come up behind and grabbed Nage on both shoulders. Immediately on feeling the hands locking on Nage steps forward which leads Uke around to the extended side. Further extension coupled with a slight twisting of the body will send Uke forward enough to make him take a fall; in this case **Mae Kaiten Ukemi.**

The above is shown from a static start with Uke standing behind Nage and grabbing while Nage has yet to move. (*Image on right.*)

Once the form is understood it is practiced with movement.

As Uke comes in to grab Nage from an angle he will grab one shoulder first, reaching around to grab the other. Nage will move a little in the same direction as Uke in order to lead Uke in. This will centralise Nage's body and encourage Uke to enter behind to grab the other shoulder.

As soon as Nage feels Uke coming behind and grabbing the shoulder he starts to move forward. Uke's forward movement is given added emphasis and he suddenly finds himself flying past Nage and is no longer hanging on to make some attack but finds himself hanging on so he won't fall. *This is a subtle subconscious reaction of which we have little control over, at least for a fraction of a second.*

Before Uke can recover Nage continues to move or extend forward using his shoulders to extend through Uke's arms. Uke will have to let go (as he heads face forward into the mat) in order to take a forward roll. (*Image on left*).

Note: as the drawings indicate, Nage's movement is partially circular, with the hips turning to add energy and momentum to the projection.

Ushiro Ryokatatori Kokyunage Ura

Uke is thrown to his rear...

As Uke comes around to grab the second shoulder Nage steps just forward enough to cause Uke to lean over. This movement also clears a space which will allow Nage to step through to enter behind Uke's front leg. As Nage straightens his body it causes Uke to bend over backwards, and now (*once again*) he is hanging on so he won't fall. He can't step back to regain his balance so he hangs on. This is the same subconscious effect as in the previous example.

Because Uke is hanging on, when Nage turns towards him and drops his body slightly, he will make Uke fall straight down to the mat. There is nothing Uke can do to stop this as he is totally unbalanced. For his own safety he will allow the trapped leg to fly around past his other leg to take a turning to the rear side breakfall. (*See pages 43 to 48 for examples of side and rear break falls.*)

Please be aware that this is **Kokyunage**. Nage has not attacked Uke's centre as he would for **Iriminage**, but has moved aside and behind in such a way that Uke is totally unbalanced and can be made to fall very easily. If anything, Nage has responded to the double shoulder grab by in effect attacking the grabbing hands and arms with his body movement.

In the examples shown previously Nage has attacked the arm or the elbow and used movement or extension of that to throw Uke.

Mundakeshime Kokyunage Omote

A form of bear hug, and just like the **Ryokatatori** attack, at the moment Nage feels Uke's arms coming around to lock and squeeze he extends both his arms out with fingers open to extend **Ki**. This prevents Uke getting a firm grip. Before Uke can tighten Nage is already moving forward in exactly the same manner as **Ushiro Ryokatatori Kokyunage Omote**. Again he is extending through his shoulders to destabilise Uke. Uke will find himself flying around past Nage and heading down face forward to the mat.

Eridori Kokyunage Ura

Eridori is a collar grab from behind with one or both hands. Here Uke is grabbing with one hand.

The moment Nage feels his collar grabbed and he is pulled backwards he steps back and to the side (*at an oblique angle*) until he is parallel to Uke. Moving his body back against Uke's arm will cause Uke to lean back. Nage can take advantage of this by striking with his fist, forearm or elbow to Uke's face, extending through to tip Uke further backwards.

Stepping in behind Uke as he strikes will guarantee Uke is unbalanced backwards. He can't step back to escape and he can't make a backwards roll either.

As soon as Nage drops his centre, the weight of his arm on Uke's face or upper chest area will add momentum to Uke's back fall. Uke will have to go around Nage's leg to escape with a breakfall to the side.

Note: Nage does not turn or twist the hips, he simply moves in a straight line behind Uke once the initial back step has been made. Nage moves without changing his body angle, moving the whole body as single unit from beside to half behind Uke.

Ushiro Ryotedori Kokyunage Omote

Uke comes around behind Nage to grab both wrists. Nage leads him forward the moment he has grabbed the second hand by raising his arms up to bring Uke around past him on the other side from his initial entry.

Extending forward and dropping the arms accentuates Uke's forward momentum into a fall. Uke will take a rolling **ukemi**.

Munedori Kokyunage

Above: Uke grabs Nage's lapel with one hand.

To do this **kokyunage**, Nage simply turns his body so he is facing to same direction as Uke and drops to one knee (*or steps forward*).

In the example above Nage extends his arm through a point just above Uke's elbow after entering (**Irimi Ashi**) to the inside (**Uchi**) which enables the technique to be done without any pressure against Uke's elbow. As he finishes the entry with a **Kaiten** turn he extends forward with his shoulder and drops to one knee.

Falling face forward Uke will let go and take a forward rolling **ukemi**.

Nage could also turn the other way, to the outside (Soto) of Uke's arm, and without having to extend through, the pressure of his upper arm and shoulder against Uke's elbow will force Uke to come forward to prevent damage to the elbow since this move from the outside goes against the way the joint moves rather than with it as in the example above. Once again Uke will let go and take a forward roll to escape.

In the example below, which is also **Munedori Kokyunage** (*with a two hand grab*), it can clearly be seen whichever way Nage turns his upper arm or shoulder will be extending Uke's arm in a manner which goes against the elbow joint. Again as Nage turns and drops Uke will have to take a sudden dive into a forward rolling **ukemi** which is almost a breakfall.

With this two handed grab attack Uke will have to respond quickly because any very sudden turn by Nage could cause severe damge to his elbow.

Chudantsuki Kokyunage

Uke steps forward with a punch to mid level (Chudantsuki). Nage waits until the punch almost reacahes his mid section then steps to the side to enter and redirect the punch.

Timing is important because if Nage moves too soon Uke can change direction to follow the movement, so Nage must wait until the strike is fully committed so Uke will have the impression he will hit his target. Then when Nage moves it is too late for Uke to change direction, and Nage has a brief opportunity to create a response to the strike.

Nage moves in close enough to touch Uke's elbow. He redirects the punch downwards, but only far enough to grasp Uke's sleeve. He raises Uke's arm up and outwards just enough to enable him to slip past to enter directly into Uke's centre. He strikes an **atemi** (*using **tegatana***) to Uke's face as he enters. T*he **atemi** could be a fist in the face with an elbow strike to the chest.*

For purposes of training the strike does not make contact, but Uke must get them impression that if he doesn't pull his head back he will be hit.

This pulling back combined with Nage raising Uke's arm up lifts Uke's centre making his balance weak and his body easy to manoeuvre.

Nage continues to enter with a small **Irimi Kaiten**. He shifts his **tegatana** to the side of Uke's neck and dropsto one knee cutting down with the **tegatana** as well as the hand holding Uke's arm. Uke suddenly finds he is falling forwards into some kind of breakfall.

Seen from the opposite side: Nage has entered under the raised strike with a **tegatana** towards Uke's face.

Shifting the **tegatana** to Uke's neck Nage begins to cut down lowering his centre.

He drops to his knees to finish the movement. He hangs onto Uke's arm where he initially grabbed it to encourage Uke to drop suddenly rather than trying to step forward into a roll.

Uke's forward roll will be shortened into a brakfall.

Morotedori Kokyunage Ura or Morotedori Kokyu Ho

Along with Gyaku Hanmi Katatetori Kokyunage, this basic Kokyu Nage is possibly the first that most students learn. It is a logical extension of the exercises **Katatetori Tai no Henka** and **Morotedori Tai no Henka,** which are **Tai Sabaki** exercises often practiced at the commencement of a general class. (*See pages 65 and 66.*)

Morotedori Kokyunage begins in exactly the same manner as **Morotedori Tai no Henka**, but instead of finishing with arms at waist level and extended forward, Nage continues to raise both arms to lift Uke's centre up making him lighter on his feet. As the arms reach forehead height Nage steps behind Uke (*preventing Uke from stepping backwards*) and turns his upper body slightly to the rear while extending the arm that is grasped.

Uke will be unbalanced to the rear and because he can't take a step back he will have to make a semi circular break fall to the rear. He does this by swinging the back leg around across his front leg and falls on the side away from Nage.

There are other ways of falling and each person will discover through practice 'ways that suit their particular physiology. Apart from that, each time the technique is done, there will be variations which may necessitate falling slightly differently. **There is no fixed way, only that which can be adapted for the moment.**

Gyaku Hanmi Katatetori Kokyunage can be done a number of different ways with each way focussing on a specific aspect and a different entry such as a direct line in at an oblique angle or a more circular **Tenkan** movement with expanded awareness of what goes on around the partners, and so on.

At its most basic and static form Nage begins as if doing Gyaku hanmi Katatetori Tai no Henka, then from that position he slides obliquely behind Uke while extending the arm that is grasped across Uke's face.

As Uke loses balance to the rear, the rest is as already described for **Morotedori Kokyunage**. Uke will also finish in the same way.

This breakfall (**Yoko Ukemi**) is the same for both techniques just described.

It is semi circular with Uke finishing on his side facing away from Nage and partially behind Nage's finishing position. (*See pages 43 to 48 back and side Break falls.*)

> **Moroteddori Kokyunage Omote**

Again the beginning is the same as **Morotedori Tai no Henka**, except that once Nage has raised Uke's centre enough to disturb his balance Nage steps forward and extends his arm down at an angle of approximately 45 degrees. Uke will find himself falling forward, so he steps forward to compliment Nage's forward movement and positions himself for a rolling **Mae Kaiten ukemi.**

At a more advanced level Nage doesn't step or slide forward as shown here, he simply drops his arm while doing funegogi forward with his hips.
This forward movement of the hips will stranslate through the dropping arm and will be enough to project Uke into a fall.

Gyaku Hanmi Katatetori Kokyunage

As you continue to practice basic concepts such as gyaku hanmi kata-tetori kokyunage, the training must go beyond static and mechanical and become fluid and flowing. The idea of a specific technique no longer applies. What Nage is looking for is a way of moving through Uke while unbalancing or throwing him regardless of how Uke attacks or what he does, while not leaving gaps or holes that will allow Uke to make kaeshsi waza.

As Uke rushes forward Nage extends what could possibly be a fist towards him. Involuntarily Uke will attempt to grab the wrist to prevent being struck.

The moment Uke's hand touches Nage's wrist, Nage enters before Uke's grip can tighten. He enters directly towards Uke's centre at a slightly oblique angle so he can tip over Uke's head (***with atemi to the side of the jaw which slides on past as Uke pulls his head back***). He enters deep enough to displace Uk'es centre. Note Nage's lead leg is behind Uke's front leg so he can't step back to escape. By this time Nage has allowed Uke to grab his wrist.

While the lower half of his body is still moving forward Uke struggles to hang on . He is now trying to prevent himself from falling. Nage lets his arm become empty so there is nothing for Uke to hold on to. It drops, (*or cuts down as if making kesa giri with a bokken*). The fact that Uke's upper body has been stopped and tipped over backwards while the lower half continues forward guarantees he will fall the instant Nage's arm starts to drop.

Chudantsuki Kokyunage

This is similar to the kokyunage shown of page 198. It is however more advanced and a little harder to do as timing needs to be more precise when dealing with a punch than it does with Shomen Uchi.

Once again we have gone from static mechanical training to more fluid movement. Uke attacks with **chudan tsuki**. As the punch comes close Nage begins stepping off line to the outside (**soto or ura**). Note he is preparing to do what appears to be a **gyaku yokomen** strike down towards the attacking punch. **This is not a blocking movement.**

It is essential that Nage shifts Uke's punch off its line of attack.

His forearm makes contact beneath Uke's elbow. *This is not Gedan Barai or a lower block, it is a redirection of Uke's attacking arm,* which enables Nage to accurately position his arm beneath Uke's elbow.

Uke's body is controlled through his elbow and upper arm so rotating Uke's elbow up an over in a vertical circle will spin Uke completely around to face back the way he came

Once Uke is turned completely around Nage continues the downward arc of the vertical circle. While Uke's elbow has been rotated up and over, contact has been maintained by Nage with Uke's elbow. The first point of contact was directly underneath against the point where the Ulna fits into the elbow socket. As the arm is rotated up and over, Nage's contact shifts to the inside of the elbow joint and throughout this movement contact is not lost.

Nage's downward arc which is a vertical line paralleling his own centreline will take Uke straight down towards the mat. Uke will either make a very tight forward roll, or if Nage takes a positive grip and pulls back at the bottom he would flip Uke completely over onto his back into a break fall.

Note: this is different from the chudantsuki kokyunage on page 204. Uke is not turned around there because Nage enters inside under the arm, turns and throws Uke so he continues in the same direction. In this one Nage stays outside of the attacking arm and turns Uke so he goes back in the direction he came from.

In these views from the opposite side Nage's arm beneath Uke's elbow is clearly seen as he begins to rotate Uke's arm up and over. Uke will spin on his front foot, allowing his back foot to fly around as his upper body turns to position itself for a forward rolling escape.

It is because Uke can receive, or take ukemi, that practice at high speed with full committment can be achieved without anyone being seriously hurt. It is therefore advisable that ukemi practice should be a regular part of everyone's training no matter what level they have achieved..

Hijitori... Kokyunage ... Shihonage...

Using the principle of **Kuzushi** and not being concerned with any specific application allows Nage considerable freedom to see what can be created by the way both partners move...

Once a certain level of understanding regarding basic techniques is attained it is time to go beyond the rigidity of having to do something specific.

Here with **Hijitori** we are looking at the principle of **Kuzushi** (*Unbalancing Uke*). In the process of stepping off line and extending Uke's elbow to take away his stability Nage finds

he can do a number of different things. In the example on this page Uke's position allows Nage to do a simple **Kokyunage**.

By stepping back and dropping the arm used to extend Uke's elbow, or cutting down with it, takes away the last vestige of Uke's stability and he has no option but to fall.

Seen from the opposite side, the start is exactly the same: Uke grabs Nage's elbow but before he can do anything else Nage steps offline, reaches over Uke's arm and takes his elbow. Making a slight **Irimi kaiten** move Nage extends Uke's elbow forwards to take away his balance. Nage then takes Uke's wrist from underneath with his free hand (*breaking Uke's* **hijitori**) and using the hand first used to extend Uke forwards, he takes Uke's freed hand on top to apply **shihonage**. (*This is not unlike doing it from* **gyaku hanmi katatetori**.) Nage cuts Uke's hand straight down behind his shoulder. Since Uke is already leaning back almost ready to fall there is no way he can stop the **shihonage** from being applied. To finish, having dropped Uke onto his back, Nage moves away while keeping attention focussed on Uke.

Another finish could be where Nage stretches Uke's arm out behind while he is on his back in a variation of **kotegaeshi** with his elbow pointing up and his palm firmly flat on the mat. Any downward pressure on the elbow will convince Uke not to resist.

Part Six

> ## Adding Complexity and a degree of difficulty

Suwari Waza Ikkyo...

Hanmi Handachi shomen uchi attack...

Hanmi handachi Ushiro Ryokatatori attack...

As students progress into higher Kyu levels a number of interesting, and sometimes very different techniques are introduced.

These techniques are generally variations built around the core techniques studied from the beginning, Shiho Nage, Irimi Nage, Kokyu Nage, and Katame Waza.

The serious student will have realised that the variations are only in the way Nage is attacked by Uke and not in the technique itself. The actual technique is the same, and if there is any confusion in the mind of the student, returning to the basic, fundamental, or core technique should assist in resolving that.

A thorough understanding of basic technique is required for more advanced study and returning to these techniques is always beneficial. As students we should always go back to the core techniques to study them in detail in preference to looking for new and more complicated things.

Ikkyo is taken as a basis to explore the other Katame Waza that logically follow, these being **Nikyo**, **Sankyo**, **Yonkyo**, **Gokyo**, and **Rokyo**. (*See pages 81 to 109.*)

Attacks from behind, **Ushiro Waza,** are introduced. Some of these have are shown in other parts of this volume where they relate to a more advanced form of a technique being explained. (*For example see page 98 for **Katatetori Kubishime Sankyo Omote**. Also pages 158 to 159 for **Ushiro Riokatatori Shihonage** and pages 200 to 201 for **Kokyunage** coming out of attacks from behind.*)

Techniques in a seated position, **Suwari Waza,** are introduced, as well as **Hanmi Handachi Waza,** standing attacks against a seated Nage. For the person seated these are much more difficult to do than the standing (*Tachi Waza*) version of the same technique, and study of **Shikko** is essential to be able to move smoothly. (*See pages 36 to 40.*) **Ushiro** attacks are also applied in **Hanmi Handachi** adding a further amount of difficulty.

Combined attacks, often a grab followed immediately by a strike to the face (***Gyaku Hanmi katatetori men Tsuki***), or double punches, or depending on the level of the student's ability to receive, even kicks such as **Mae Geri** or **Mawashi Geri** could be introduced.

Attacks with and against weapons such as **Bokken, Tanto,** and **Jo** are also introduced at higher levels. These are not studied as weapons systems, *but because the use of weapons requires more focus and precision,* we use them as a means of understanding extension, timing and distance, and how this relates to general Aikido principles. We use them to improve our Aikido.

Ushiro Waza

Dealing with an attack from the rear is more difficult than dealing with a frontal attack simply because Nage can see what is in front and has time to deal with it, whereas an attack from the rear can be totally unexpected often giving Nage no time to react before the attack is finished.

To develop awareness of how an attack from the rear feels these attacks are practiced in a controlled manner initially from static positions before movement is introduced.

If the practice is initially static, Nage will allow Uke to take the appropriate position behind with whatever attack is to be practiced before dealing with it and completing the technique. To complete the technique he will have to generate movement in Uke which can allow Nage to position him for a throw or take down to a pin.

When movement is introduced it is usually in the form of Nage leading Uke in and encouraging him to come around to the rear for the final attack which often is a combination of hand, wrist, arm, shoulder or collar grab with one or two hands, or some kind of choke hold combined with a grab, or a variation of a bear hug.

Uke will attack from one side before moving to the rear to complete the attack. This gives Nage time to harmonise and lead Uke into a position where he can be easily thrown or taken down for a pin.

Both forms of practice are useful because there will be times when Nage is caught unawares from behind by Uke, usually in a multiple attack situation such as **jiyuwaza** or **randori** practice, and suddenly has to deal with a bear hug or a stranglehold. Static practice teaches how to deal with that situation.

Of course no amount of practice will teach us to deal with an unprovoked attack with a strike such as a punch or kick to the lower back from behind or a strike to the back of the head with a club or a bottle from the rear if we cannot be aware of it coming.

We can only hope that with a lot of practice we can in time develop a kind of sixth sense that will warn us of this type of attack which could give us a small window of time to react soon enough to prevent serious damage.

If however, the unprovoked attack includes a grab, then most likely we will be able to instantly deal with it. This is what we train for in the dojo when doing **Ushiro Waza.** Sometimes to heighten awareness within Nage we will practice with eyes shut so he cannot see who his Uke is, how big Uke is, or exactly how he got to the position where he applies the attack. Nage has to deal with it by feel alone. He must move Uke, unbalance and throw him while keeping his eyes tightly shut and using only his body awareness to understand how he is moving and throwing Uke.

Uke of course has his eyes open so he can see where and how to attack and where to position himself when he takes **Ukemi.** Training where Nage has his eyes shut is only practical where grabs are involved, as contact is needed in order to blend with Uke's **Ki** to be able to redirect it.

Ushiro Waza static practice. Nage waits for Uke to come around behind to grab his wrists before starting to respond with a technique

In advanced practice Nage induces Uke to attack by attacking first so Uke's response is to counter and seek an advantage. Nage leads Uke into an ushiro attack which he then controls to finish with an application...

> **Ushiro Ryotedori**
> **Juji Garami Nage**

The moment Uke grasps Nage's hand, Nage draws Uke in leading his momentum so Uke comes around behind to grab the other hand. As Uke grabs the other wrist Nage continues to lead him forward, raises his arms, (*to raise Uke's centre*) and brings him past so Uke is now on the other side from where he started.

At this point Nage grasps Uke's wrists and draws the outer lower arm in towards his centre while crossing the upper arm over the elbow to lock the arms in a cross position.

Turning the upper arm over so the elbow is locked tight and the arm is straight Nage can now extend over the lower arm. This extension of the lower arm over and down around the locked elbow joint will quite painfully tip Uke's upper body over towards the mat.

Maintaining the extension Nage can now steep through with a sliding step, throwing Uke down onto the mat. Usually Nage lets go so Uke can take a forward roll.

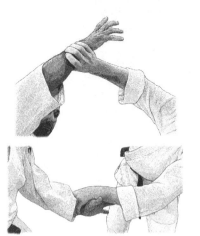

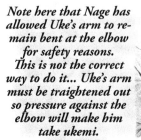

Note here that Nage has allowed Uke's arm to remain bent at the elbow for safety reasons. This is not the correct way to do it... Uke's arm must be traightened out so pressure against the elbow will make him take ukemi.

Hand positions for Ushiro Ryotedori Juji Garami Nage.

Once Nage has led Uke around to the front his top hand drops directly down onto Uke's wrist to take a firm grip. Uke's arm is turned forward and straightened so it can be locked against the lower arm.

Nage's bottom hand is positioned with the fingers and thumb extended so it simply rises up to grasp Uke's other wrist. Nage draws the arm through until the elbows are crossed. With the top arm straightened, the forearm of the bottom arm can be used to rotate around the elbow to tip Uke over into a fall. If Nage lets go of both arms Uke will take a forward roll but if Nage maintains his grip on the arm used to lever Uke over, Uke will have to take a breakfall as if coming out of Koshinage. (*See page 48.*)

Ushiro Ryotedori Juji Garami Nage

With full committment we can see there is a lot of movement. Nage is moving while Uke is attacking; moving to draw Uke in and encourage him to come around behind. This is much more dynamic than the previuous example which at beginner level is vitrually a static exercise to understand the relative positions of both participants. There should be no stopping and starting again once Uke's attack has commenced.

As Uke comes around and reaches for Nage's other hand, Nage is already slipping back under Uke's first arm, while raising it up and taking the top grip (as *described on the previous page*). As he finishes slipping under the arm his other hand has already taken the bottom grip and drawn Uke's arms across each other. He cranks him over and steps forward to project Uke into the forward roll below...

Ushiro Ryotedori Juji Garami Katame Waza

From this position: —————————

Instead of stepping forward to project Uke, Nage either stays exactly where he is or allows his back leg to slip back a little which opens a small space directly in front of his centre. At the same time as this while maintaining a firm grip on Uke's arm (*used to lever him over*) he cuts down into this empty space as if making **kesa giri** with a **bokken**. Uke is flipped over into a breakfall (*see breakfall exercise on page 48*). Nage maintains the grip so he can apply pressure against Uke's elbow with his knee to demonstrate that if neccessary he could snap the elbow and cause serious damage.

Nage uses pressure against Uke's elbow but instead of levering Uke over, he uses the stretched out arm to swing Uke around so he is facing him. He steps back slightly with his front foot as he does this to create a small space to bring Uke into.

He then extends both crossed arms down at a steep angle into Uke's centre which causes Uke to collapse or drop to his knees.

Continuing the downward extension makes Uke sit back so he can fall onto his back. As he starts to fall Nage enters behind keeping Uke's arms ccrossed.

Continuing to extend Uke's crossed arms down into his centre further collapses Uke.

Nage moves around behind as he pins Uke to the floor, finally stepping away while still holding Uke down with one hand.

An alternativbe finish here would be to kneel on Uke's crossed arms which in effect would create a strangle hold.

Once Uke is suitably subdued, Nage moves away.

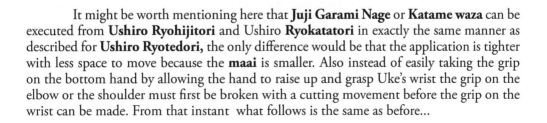

It might be worth mentioning here that **Juji Garami Nage** or **Katame waza** can be executed from **Ushiro Ryohijitori** and Ushiro **Ryokatatori** in exactly the same manner as described for **Ushiro Ryotedori,** the only difference would be that the application is tighter with less space to move because the **maai** is smaller. Also instead of easily taking the grip on the bottom hand by allowing the hand to raise up and grasp Uke's wrist the grip on the elbow or the shoulder must first be broken with a cutting movement before the grip on the wrist can be made. From that instant what follows is the same as before...

Tekubi Mochi Eridori Juji Garami Nage

Tekubi Mochi Eridori...

...is an attack from the rear where Uke has come from behind and grabbed Nage's collar and wrist at the same time. His intention may be to pull the neck and arm back while kicking one of Nage's legs from behind the knee to extend it forward as he pulls Nage down onto his back.

Nage must not give Uke any opportunity to do this or anything else. The moment he is grabbed he immediately extends his arm and turns his body so it is at an oblique angle to Uke. Uke is now within the range of Nage's peripheral vision and the extension helps prevent Uke from pulling back the wrist. In fact the extension of the arm has a tendency to lead Uke slightly forward, and this creates a space into which Nage can step back.

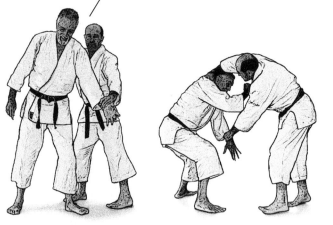

As Nage steps back underneath the arm he drops his centre so he can get his head past the grab on his collar. He strikes an **atemi** at Uke's face and extends the arm that Uke is grasping across his centreline and downwards. This turns Uke's upper body over into an awkward unbalanced position.

The hand that made the **atemi** to Uke's face slides under Uke's upper arm and turns the elbow over to further turn and twist Uke into a more unbalanced position in which he is leaning forward while being twisted.

Nage's other hand rises up and grasps Uke's wrist. This breaks Uke's grip on Nage's wrist and allows Nage to draw Uke's arm right through so it can be locked against Uke's other elbow.

Rotating the lower arm over the elbow Nage now finishes by stepping forward and extending through Uke's shoulder rather than putting pressure against the elbow.

(Note: *This is for safety reasons so Uke will not be injured. In the street if this was done the arm would be locked over the elbow joint and pressure applied to force the assailant over or have his elbow badly damaged.*)

Left: Uke has stepped forward in preparation to take a forward roll. Nage will let go as he extends, allowing Uke to take the roll.

In this example Uke's crossed arms can be seen and hasn't stepped forward.

Rotating the arm pointing up over against the locked elbow tips Uke over face down into a precarious position. Nage drops his centre slightly taking both of Uke's arms directly down his centreline towards the mat. This tips Uke right over without allowing him to step forward.

Nage finishes the throw by drawing in towards his centre the arm he used to crank Uke's upper body over. At the same time he releases the other arm which gives Uke enough impetus to flip over into a breakfall. Nage maintains his grip so he can finish with an arm bar or a pin.

Another finish, more difficult to receive, is for Nage to come behind Uke without letting go of either arm and to drop Uke straight down onto his back. Nage then uses one arm to press the other arm against Uke's neck in a strangle hold. Nage then rests one knee over the point where the two arms cross pressing down to increase the pressure on Uke's neck to make sure he is immobilised. Nage then has both hands free to deal with another attacker if necessary while keeping Uke pinned to the floor. (*Page 217*)

Shomen Uchi Juji Garami Nage

Nage moves off line as Uke strikes **shomen**, reaches towards the striking arm and follows it down. One hand is underneath to catch Uke's wrist when it reaches the bottom of the strike while the other on top guarantees the striking arm goes all the way down until it is caught from underneath.

 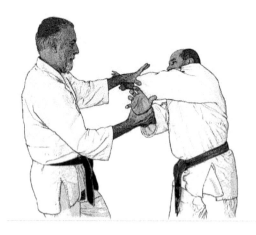

The instant the striking hand is caught Nage strikes with a back fist (**Uraken**) to Uke's face. Uke will naturally block this to avoid being hit in the face.

At the moment of contact Nage allows his **Uraken** to rollover into a grab.

He stretches Uke's arm across the lower arm and steps in towards Uke's centre. The **Irimi** is finished with a **Kaiten** body turn

Nage uses the lower arm to lock against the elbow, extending forward to turn Uke's upper body over into a position ready to receive the throw or takedown as already described.

Morotedori Juji Garami Nage

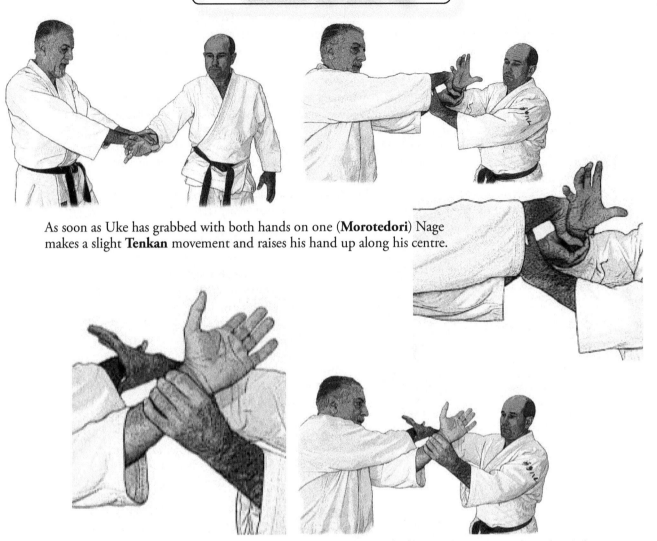

As soon as Uke has grabbed with both hands on one (**Morotedori**) Nage makes a slight **Tenkan** movement and raises his hand up along his centre.

This opens both Uke's wrists and makes the grip weak allowing Nage to reach under and grasp the (left) wrist that is highest along his arm. As he pulls it through to lock it against Uke's right elbow Nage allows his other hand to fall over on top of Uke's right wrist. Pulling the right arm straight and turning it so the elbow is facing him, Nage uses Uke's left arm as a lever to turn Uke's upper body over in preparation for the throw or the takedown.

Basic Koshinage

Many people are frightened when it comes to receiving **Koshinage** and perhaps this is only because not enough preparation has gone into how to receive it as Uke, or how to position Uke from the point of view of Nage. Often Uke will try and roll out of it only to injure neck or shoulder by coming down too vertical. *In fact, in some places they try to teach you how to roll out of it but in my view this is not koshinage but more kokyunage with Uke diving headfirst over Nage's hips to make a forward roll.* **If Koshinage is applied properly Uke cannot roll out of it. Uke will be slammed down onto the mat so it is essntial to learn how to breakfall out of the throw to receive it safely.**

When first attempting **Basic Koshinage** both Uke and Nage need to cooperate so each is in control of what they are doing. If both partners are in control then no one will be hurt and they can practice it many times in safety.

Partner **assisted practice for the ukemi is essential** *and the exercise shown on page 48 will help prepare Uke for receiving Koshinage. The exercise should be practiced before introducing a basic form of Koshinage,*

Points to consider as Uke when practicing

Koshinage are:

1. Making yourself lighter as Nage prepares to load you onto his hips.

After deflecting the **atemi** to the face, which Nage uses as a distraction to make enough time to turn and position himself to load Uke onto his hips, Uke makes himself lighter by rising up onto his toes. Nage moves in very close so his hips are touching Uke's centre.

2. Sitting comfortably on Nage's lower back.

Uke reaches around and grasps Nage's arm as he is loaded onto Nage's lower back. He lets go with his other hand — the one he originally used to grab Nage's wrist — in preparation to use it to break the fall when he hits the mat. This position across Nage's lower back is easy to maintain as it is simply a matter of balancing on Nage's hips. Nage should have his back arched upwards as if he is looking up to the ceiling. This upward curve keeps Uke sitting on the hips without strain on the lower back.

3. Controlling the fall or the roll off Nage's back.

Only Uke can do this as he is the one balancing like a see-saw Across Nage's hips. As Nage lowers his extended arm which Uke is hang-

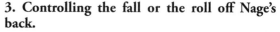

ing onto, Uke will naturally tip over towards the mat. To avoid landing on his face Uke needs to fling his legs over in an arc so his body actually pivots around his shoulder and the grip he has on Nage's arm. He could alternatively simply roll sideways over Nage's lower back to fall directly behind. How Uke lands is often different each time depending on the speed of the technique. The moment he touches the mat Nage will straighten which pulls up on Uke's grip thus helping to raise Uke at the moment of impact, making the fall easier.

Koshinage requires practice, but if done carefully, should not present problems.

Gyaku Hanmi Katatetori Koshinage

Starting from **Gyaku Hanmi Katatetori**, Nage strikes **atemi** towards Uke's face as he steps in to a position between Uke's legs.

As soon as he has stepped in, he turns his body so the position is at right angles to Uke. He allows the arm Uke has grasped to come over the top of his body as he turns into the right angle and extends that arm upwards. At the same time he looks up in the direction his arm is pointing and makes sure that his hip is actually touching Uke's centre. With his knees bent and his upper body angled upwards Nage can now make a large downwards arc with his arm which will roll Uke over onto his hip.

In effect when Nage enters into the position he should be visualising that he is going right through Uke's centre which is what makes Uke roll over onto Nage's lower back.

Uke maintains his grasp on Nage's wrist and allows that upper extension to raise him. This is where cooperation comes in. Rather than have Nage pull him over across his back as a dead weight, Uke comes up onto his toes to make himself lighter, making it easier to lean across Nage's lower back to position himself for the throw as Nage makes that downward arc with his arm. If Nage dumps Uke as a dead weight it is a very hard fall for Uke to receive. If Uke participates by making himself lighter the resulting fall will be softer and easier to manage.

Once Uke is rolled across onto Nage's lower back he reaches around and grasps Nage's extended upper arm and lets go of the hand he originally grabbed in the **gyaku hanmi katatetori** attack.

For the first few times the exercise will stop here as both Uke and Nage position themselves ready for the final throw while practicing how to enter safely in preparation for the throw.

Practicing to this point helps build confidence in both partners, although when first attempting **Koshinage** it is best if Nage has had more experience than Uke and so is able to guide him into the correct position for receiving the fall.

When both partners feel comfortable with what they have achieved the final part of the technique can be practiced.

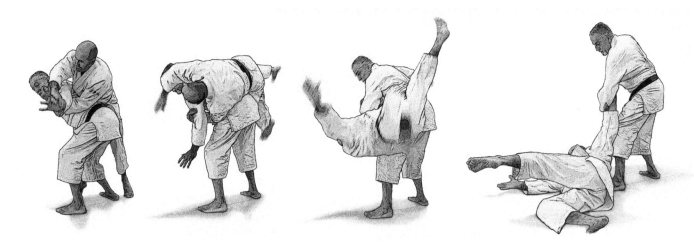

There are two ways the fall can take place. Firstly Nage could simply stand up straight and Uke will roll sideways off Nage's lower back into a breakfall exactly the same as practiced earlier with a partner (*page 48*) except it happens from a slightly higher position. If Uke maintains his grasp on Nage's extended arm his impact on the mat will be less because he is holding himself up as he falls. His free hand helps break the fall as he comes down.

The second way is if Uke initiates the fall by rotating his body over the point where he is grasping Nage's extended arm. This means he actually flings his legs over so his whole body goes over Nage's hips. He will probably come down on one foot first which combined with hanging on to Nage's arm for support as well as taking some weight on his leg he can actually lower himself reasonably softly to the mat.

Nage will also assist by standing up slightly and hooking his arm around Uke's grasp in order to support some of the weight which also helps to lessen the impact on the mat.
In other words both partners are controlling what they do in order to make the practice easier and more enjoyable.

Practicing at a more senior level Nage simply moves into and through Uke's centre so fast and deep that Uke will be flung over the hip very quickly and perhaps will not have time to grasp Nage's arm but more likely will roll across in the air as he comes down over the hip and drop into a side breakfall. (*See page 51 for an example of this exercise. In koshinage however Nage is unlikely to be on his knees, so the roll over into the air will be higher, and the consequent drop will be from a greater height than that shown. However the way of executing the fall is basically the same.*)

Koshinage, like every other technique, **can be done from any attack and there are many different ways of doing it.** Before attempting any more advanced way a thorough understanding of the basic form from **Gyaku Hanmi Katatetori** is a requirement as a base from which to expand into other possibilities.

Katatetori Ushiro Kubishime Koshinage

The technique most often practiced from **Katatetori Kubishime** is **Sankyo** (*see page 98*), but there are many techniques that can be done from this attack. A more advanced method to deal with this attack is **Koshinage**.

Uke has grasped one hand (**Katatetori**) and come around behind to apply a strangle hold (**Ushiro Kubishime**) in preparation to pulling Nage backwards while strangling him.

The instant Uke's hand has come around the neck and grasped the shoulder to give pressure for the strangle hold, Nage drops his centre to prevent himself from being pulled back, and at the same time drops his chin to prevent being strangled.

Nage raises his grasped hand vertically which has the effect of raising Uke up so his centre of balance is weak. When Nage's hand reaches head height he leans his upper body to that side and shifts his arm and Uke's grip over his head, extending up towards the sky. Because Uke is still hanging on thinking he is attacking this extension makes him lean across enough for Nage to roll him onto his hip.

Nage loads Uke onto his hips (**Koshi**). To throw Uke, Nage simply straightens his back and Uke will roll over and fall.

To prevent getting hurt, Uke maintains his grip on Nage's shoulder for as long as possible while releasing his grip on Nage's wrist so when he rolls over and falls he can use that free arm to break his fall while holding himself up with the other.

If he wanted Nage could flip Uke off with a sharp movement of the hip which would mean Uke has to take a hard breakfall. But in the example above beginning from a static position both participants are studying the movement and helping each other, so the **ukemi** is softer and easier.

Koshinage does not allow Uke to make a forward roll; it has to be a break-fall. Trying to roll opens the chance of injury. Practice should always be with both participants cooperating.

There are many different ways of doing **Koshinage** and any throw where Nage lifts Uke onto his hips in order to roll him over them or to fling him off could be called **Koshi** (*hips*) **Nage** (*throw*).

In Judo or Aikijutsu each individual throw will have a different name, but in Aikido they are all called the same and grouped together simply as Koshinage.

What distinguishes each one is the attack from which it is done as this can determine the way in which Uke is loaded onto the hips for the subsequent throw.

Shown here are only a few ways of doing Koshinage, including the basic form first introduced (*at 3rd Kyu level*), **Gyaku Hanmi Katatetori Koshinage.**

Chudan Tsuki Koshinage

When Uke punches or stabs **chudan** level Nage enters with **Irimi Tenkan** to the **Ura** side and grasps Uke's sleeve just above the wrist.

Nage raises Uke's arm up as he steps back and turns his hips with a **Kaiten** move. This spins Uke completely around to face back the opposite way.

Nage then steps in towards Uke's centre and wraps his free arm around Uke's back. He drops his hips beneath Uke's centre and turns them enough so when he lifts Uke up he can lay him across his hips.

Continuing the rotation over his hip Nage draws Uke's arm down in an arc towards the mat while giving a small twist with his hips. The result is Uke will fly over.

The downward arc is straight down along Nage's centre line and as Uke rolls over Nage's hips because his arm is being drawn down and back in towards Nage, Uke will have no choice but to take a side or back break-fall.

Throughout the whole movement Nage maintains a strong grip on Uke's sleeve, and when Uke hits the mat Nage can use this grip to pull Uke back up slightly at the moment Uke hits the mat which helps to cut some of the impact. Nage can also maintain his grip with the arm across Uke's back, in effect lowering Uke down for a more gentle finish.

This is particularly helpful with Uke's who are uncertain of how to receive this fall. Nage is in complete control over how hard or soft Uke hits the mat because he is holding Uke's sleeve as well as around Uke's back.

In effect, for this form of **Koshinage** Nage does all the work. He lifts Uke up, rolls him over his hip, and lowers him down to the mat.

He could just as easily drop him from hip height or fling him off to make him roll in the air before dropping into a breakfall. In fact with senior students practicing at a more intense level this is what usually happens. Once Uke has started to roll across Nage's hips, Nage lets go and Uke is left to make the fall as best as he can.

For those unfamiliar with the technique practicing slowly, hanging on and maintaining control is the best way to study this technique.

The final picture in this sequence shows Nage still holding Uke's arm for support which guarantees that Uke will fall onto one side and not flat onto his back.

Falling flat onto your back will almost always knock the wind out of you, perhaps even damaging the lungs. Certainly it is harder to get back up if you can't breathe.

Falling onto one side is always much safer.

These kinds of side break falls should be practiced frequently so they become easy and comfortable to do, after which receiving **Koshinage** should not be a problem.

Flinging Uke across his back, Nage walks straight through Uke with Koshinage, Note how Uke is hanging onto one of Nage's arms to slow down the fall...

Shomen Uchi Udekiminage

Like Koshinage, Udekiminage is a throw or takedown many students fear because their arm is locked at the elbow with a figure four type hold. Uke is then thrown while this lock is maintained. If it is not done correctly severe damage could result to Uke's elbow and shoulder.

From **Shomen Uchi** it begins exactly the same as for **Ikkyo Omote,** but Nage does not take Uke down too far. The moment he grasps Uke's wrist he releases his hold on Uke's elbow and reaches around the striking arm, and underneath to take hold of his own wrist where he is grasping Uke's wrist. This locks Uke's arm in place. (*See close up images next page.*)

This technique is not practiced often but it is included here as a matter of interest for students to see how one technique can lead into another entirely different finish.

Nage now pivots in towards Uke's centre.

Because Nage's forearm is resting over Uke's elbow it is easy to bend Uke's arm in an upward spiral into his face. As Nage continues his turning entry he cuts Uke's locked arm over to the rear. Uke will turn with his arm to position himself for the takedown.

Shown here Uke takes a fall backwards. This is the easy option.

Much harder is for Uke to turn completely forward and dropping his shoulder he rolls over the top into a **Mae Kaiten Ukemi** which becomes a breakfall because Nage doesn't let go of the figure four lock.

To maintain the lock without dislocating the elbow or the shoulder or both, Nage must drop to his knees as Uke goes down.

Koshinage can also be executed instead of usual finish while still maintaining the figure four arm lock. It begins the same way, as if doing **Ikkyo** from the **Shomen Uchi**.

Once the arm has been locked and spiralled back into Uke's face, Nage turns completely around in front of Uke positioning his hips right against Uke's centre.

Extending the arm lock downwards a little will lay Uke across Nage's hips ready to be thrown.

This throw is also dangerous for the same reasons that Udekiminage is dangerous.

It is easy to dislocate the joints if Nage remains standing with Uke's arm locked while the rest of Uke's body is falling. Uke's own body weight and downward momentum will cause the damage.

Nage must lower himself down as Uke falls over so the arm lock stays in the same position relative to the rest of Uke's body

Detail of Nage applying the lock, and pivoting in towards Uke ready to throw.

From this position Uke can flip over the top if Nage cuts down, or turn back under to receive on his back, or alternatively Nage can drop his hips and slip under Uke's waist to position him for **Koshinage**. Whatever happens Uke should be aware enough to adjust his **ukemi** accordingly.

Ryokatatori Kubinage

Nage's defence to this two handed grab is the same whether Uke grabs **Munadori** (*each hand grabbing a lapel*) or as in the example above **Ryokatatori**. (*Grabbing both shoulders from the front.*)

The moment Uke grabs Nage's shoulders, Nage immediately extends forward with an **atemi** to Uke's face. This **atemi** may also be accompanied by a small sliding step forward which tends to put the two partners in **Ai Hanmi**. The object of this is to pre-empt whatever intention Uke has, and to make him pull back his head, which also tends to disturb his upper body stability.

Nage further destabilises Uke by immediately dropping his striking arm down onto Uke's elbow. He draws Uke's elbow in towards his centre shifting his own weight back as he does this. This creates a shallow arc or partial spiral downwards towards the space opened up by Nage's shifting of his weight back

The hand Nage used to cut down Uke's elbow now rises up and palm up reaches towards the back of Uke's neck.

As this hand wraps around the back of Uke's neck Nage also moves in with a sliding step to a position parallel to Uke, reaching over with his other hand he rests it palm down on the other side of Uke's head. The fingers of both hands are touching behind Uke's head and the head is held tightly with both of Nage's fore arms on either side of the head. Nage's head is now locked and he is bent forward in an unstable position.

At this point extreme care on the part of Nage is needed. If he simply jerks the head forward he could do serious damage to Uke's neck. If he hangs on when he throws, he could also damage Nage's neck because the weight of Uke's body as it goes over will either snap the neck or tear muscles and tendons. In either case serious problems both medical and legal could eventuate. A technique like this is only practiced at senior level with both participants fully aware of how to respond to what is happening.

Needless to say a qualified instructor must also be monitoring this practice.

Nage drops to his knees or at least to one knee, and leads Uke's head down into the space created by his **irimi** movement in beside Uke.

It is important to realise that Nage is not throwing Uke by jerking the head forward or twisting it and extending or any other way that one could attempt this. *It is too dangerous and serious damage will occur.*

What Nage is doing is cradling Uke's head and gently leading it down towards the mat... into the space created when he dropped to one knee.

Uke will in effect take a forward roll. His body is already in the forward roll position even though it seems otherwise because of the grip around his head and neck.

Nage lets go the instant he sees Uke commencing the forward roll.

In the case above Uke has maintained a one hand grip on Nage's shoulder and so takes a breakfall over the top rather than a forward roll. It is probably best, inially, to do this by taking a forward roll.

As Nage gets up and moves away Uke will finally let go.

Shomen Uchi Kubinage

When Uke attacks with shomen uchi Nage steps back and moves slightly inside the line of the strike. He reaches up to meet the downcoming strike and follows it down with his hand resting on top of Uke's wrist. When the strike reaches down as far as it is intended to go Nage's hand is already resting on top of Uke's hand.

Instead of taking a firm grip and proceeding to enter with Ikkyo — *note that this would be the same position for Ai Hanmi Katatetori Ikkyo* — **Nage trikes back up towards Uke's head with his tegatana as if doing gyaku yokomen.**

Nage's other hand, palm up, reaches

towards Uke's face. When the gyaku yokomen touches Uke's head Nage turns his hand so his palm cradles that side of Uke's head. Meanwile the other hand has recahed up and cradles Uke's head on the opposite side.

Nage is stepping forward as the cradling of Uke's head occurs. When the step is completed Uke should be stretched forward and beginning to bend over. Note he is reaching towards the mat in preparation to take a forward roll.

Nage begins to cut down in an arc towards the mat. Because he is holding Uke's head this downward arc makes Uke bend over fowards until he is touching the mat with his extended arm.

Note that Nage is cutting down inside the leg he used to step forward... into the empty space immediately in front of both of them. This is the point where a line drawn from Uke's centre forward towards the mat would intersect with a similar line drawn forward from Nage's centre. The point where these imaginary lines meet is the empty space into which Uke is being projected.

As Uke's forearm touches the mat in preparation for the forward roll Nage gently places Uke's head as close to the mat as possible.

This allows Uke to create his forward roll. Nage lets go as Uke rolls over.

If Nages cuts down steeply Uke will probably have to make his roll a breakfall, but if Nage extrends forward and downward at an angle between 30 to 45 degrees, Uke will be able to make a forward roll quite comfortably.

Once again any application involving Uke's head such as Kubinage must be done with extreme caution and full awareness with both partners cooperating to study this.
There should be no fooling about or game-playing here. It is far too dangerous.
It should not be practiced at all without a qualified instructor supervising.

Hanmi Handachi Eridori Kokyunage

The movement at the start is similar to the movement for **Tachi Waza Eridori Irimi-nage** (*refer to page193*) in that Nage moves forward slightly in an attempt to stretch Uke forward and to open a space he can use to move back under the arm and hand grabbing his collar.

The main difference here is that Nage is restricted in his ability to move because he is seated, whereas Uke has an advantage being in a standing position and able to move more freely.

Nage rises onto his toes, swivels one side forward as he would for **Shikko**, extending forward to stretch Uke out and make some space. He also moves slightly to the side away from Uke to give himself enough room to swivel back under Uke's arm.

Ducking under Uke's arm with **Hantai Tenkan** (*half Tenkan movement*) Nage turns his upper body and rests his head against Uke's wrist. This effectively traps Uke's hand in a twist of the collar and as Nage straightens (*sitting back up*) it bends Uke's arm even more and causes him to lean forward.

Continuing to lean forward makes Uke bend over even more. Using the arm that is now immediately behind Uke Nage pushes Uke's lower back forward. Eventually Uke will let go (*as his trapped arm straightens*) and fall forward flat onto his face.

Alternative finishes.

Among the many ways that Nage could deal with this attack from the rear are the following.

Nage could take Uke's elbow (*instead of pushing Uke's back forward*) and extend it forward, taking Uke's wrist with his other hand as Uke's grip is released, to finish with **Ikkyo Ude Osae**, (*similar to the Ikkyo finish on page 85 from **Ushiro Ryokatatori** or **Suwariwaza Katatori Ikkyo**.*)

Another would be for Nage to swivel forward bringing the leg he moved back on forward again and turning his upper body in the direction away from Uke. Because Uke's hand is still trapped in the collar he would have to come around in a partial circle to release his hand at which point he would be in a position to take a forward roll. This would also be **Kokyunage.**

Men Tsuki Ikkyo Omote

Men Tsuki is a punch to the head. It could also be called Jodan Tsuki, upper level punch.

Whatever it is called, as the punch almost reaches Nage's face he raises one arm (*as if preparing to do Shomen Uchi*). The object is to feel where Uke's attacking arm is rather than trying to deflect it. Once contact is made Nage can alter its trajectory slightly, so his position is then just outside of it rather than directl;y in front of the fist.

At the same time he drops down onto the inside knee (*the one nearest Uke*) and with his other hand **he delivers an atemi to Uke's groin.**

This will of course make Uke bend forwards even if hard contact to the groin is not made. *The thought in Uke's consciousness of the punch getting there is sufficient to have the desired reaction.*

By this time Nage is on both knees. The hand used for the **atemi** has gone up to take Uke's elbow which is rotated over to continue Uke's leaning over forward movement.
Taking a slight sideways step on the knee away from Uke allows Nage to lead Uke across and down into an empty space. Uke's elbow is rotated over and locked and as Nage leads him down he has no option but to follow this movement.

Uke will fall flat as if doing a push up, lowering himself to the mat with some control rather than falling straight onto his face as he would do if unable to receive well.

The finish is Ikkyo Ude Osae. *Note: this is not the usual Ikkyo Omote from Tsuki. Chudan Tsuki is the usual attack for Ikkyo exercise, but sometimes Jodan Tsuki is used and Nage must be prepared to try something different...*

Hanmi Handachi Ushiro Ryokatatori Sankyo

This application introduces two areas of difficulty or complexity. Firstly Nage is on his knees in **seiza**, and must move as Uke attacks, and secondly the attack is both shoulders being grabbed from behind. (**Ushiro**)

All responses to attacks from the rear are more difficult to deal with than a similar attack from in front. The movement used in **Hanmi Handachi Ushiro waza** is essentially the same as used for **Tachi waza Ushiro** attacks, but because Nage is on his knees the amount of movement he can make is more constrained. This makes the technique more difficult than the same technique if both partners are standing.

The moment Uke grabs one shoulder and reaches around behind Nage for the other, Nage moves that side forward forcing Uke to enter behind a little deeper and to overextend as he reaches for the second shoulder. Nage's movement is basically a pivot on one knee as he extends his upper body in a semi circular movement to the front.

This circular movement will bring Uke right around the rear to finish coming past Nage. As Uke passes Nage and is virtually in front and leaning forward, Nage will cut Uke's elbow down to further unbalance him in a forward direction. It is the arm that grabbed second that is cut down.

A space is now opened up for Nage to reach through and take the hand that grabbed first. Nage makes a simultaneous **atemi** to Uke's face with his other hand which should distract Uke enough to loosen that first grip so Nage can pull the hand away. At this point he should have a strong **sankyo** grip on Uke's hand.

Cutting the **sankyo** down will make Uke let go of his second grip to be able to use that hand to support himself so his face and upper body isn't smashed into the mat.

Nage can now move around to a position in front of Uke's arm, and moving backwards will grasp Uke's elbow to draw him forwards and down onto his face.

Hanmi Handachi Ushiro Ryokatatori Sankyo continued...

Nage is at an angle of about 45 degrees to the direction Uke's body is facing as he draws him forward. ***Standing and doing this as a tachi waza the angle would be closer to 90 degrees,*** but on his knees, nage is somewhat restricted so the angle in front is obviously going to be less since he can't move as far in one step as he could if he was standing.

Moving backwards is also restricting so Nage's approximately 45 degree angle allows him to draw Uke forward past him if necessary, before repositioning himself for the final hold down.

For the final pin Nage moves forward into the space between Uke's head and shoulder with one knee, and with the other knee hard into the ribs just below the shoulder. This locks Uke's shoulder and arm in one spot and stops him from moving forward or backward in an attempt to escape.

Nage should finish his forward step and be in a position to apply the pin at the same moment that Uke falls forward onto his chest.

Nage can now change hands grasping Uke's trapped hand in such a way that the palm can be placed flat against Nage's shoulder. ***It is important that the palm is flat against Nage's shoulder because this locks the elbow joint which makes the arm less flexible and unable to be rotated as it is for Nikyo.***

Nage's other arm draws Uke's elbow in towards his centre to lock the joint, making Uke's arm immobile. (*See pages 99 and 100*)

Any slight turn of Nage's body towards the back of Uke's head will put enormous pressure on Uke's elbow joint and shoulder. He will have no option but to submit.

Other techniques of similar difficulty and complexity are **Hanmi Handachi Shomen Uchi Iriminage** (*page 175*), **Hanmi Handachi Shihonage** (*page 151 and 162*), **Hanmi Handachi Tsuki Kotegaeshi** (*pages 140 – 141*), and **Katatetori Ushiro Kubishime Sankyo Omote** (*page 98*).

Suwari Waza — Seated Techniques.

Techniques done while both partners are seated are much more difficult to do than the same technique when both are standing. Because movement is restricted both partners need to move from their centre and both need to make their application of technique more constrained than they would if standing, in other words tighter and more focussed with smaller rather than bigger movements. **Shikko** (*pages 36 to 40*) **is essential practice for learning how to move in seiza and should be a part of regular practice wherever possible.**

Suwari Waza Katatori Ikkyo Omote

The moment Uke grabs Nage's shoulder Nage pivots with his free side slightly towards Uke so he can reach with an atemi to Uke's face. Uke will react by pushing this aside.

Nage allows his deflected hand to slide down along Uke's grabbing arm so he can draw Uke's elbow towards him while pivoting slightly backwards on that other side. This causes Uke to drop down losing some of his stability.

Nage then allows his hand to further draw in to grasp the hand Uke is using to hold the shoulder. By rotating his hips forward and extending Uke's elbow forward Nage is able to turn Uke over so he will end up facing the opposite direction and losing his grip on Nage's shoulder. All Nage has to do is maintain his grip on the hand that was grabbing his shoulder. He doesn't have to pull it off since it will come off as Uke is twisted forward and down towards the mat. Holding it there as he moves forward also helps tip Uke over before he loses his grip completely.

Nage now moves forward extending through Uke's elbow and hand to guide him into the empty space in front between the two of them. As Uke falls face down on the mat Nage maintains the forward extension down Uke's arm through his shoulder to pin him to the mat and hold him in place while he positions himself to apply **Ikkyo Ude Osae**.

Note that the grip Nage has on Uke's hand is the same as Nikyo. He does not let go of this grip while he takes Uke down onto the mat. He maintains this **Nikyo** grip to finish the **Ude Osae** (*see page 23 for the two ways of pinning Ude Osae — Ikkyo— that are commonly used in Aikido practice.*) There are other more drastic ways to pin using **Ikkyo** variationss but we don't need to go into those here.

Applying the pin: Nage eases Uke's arm down over his knee so he can feel the tension increasing. If Uke is not very flexible in the elbow and shoulder he may tap (*submit*) at this point, and Nage will release and move away, but usually Nage can slide Uke's wrist down over his knee until it reaches the mat. He then turns the fingers of Uke's trapped hand towards Uke's face which vastly increases the pressure on Uke's wrist. He will usually submit at this point because firstly he can't move, and secondly the pain of the wrist rotation becomes quite intense.

Again, as in all practice, Nage must be aware of Uke's increasing discomfoort and be ready to release his hold down. Uke must be aware of his own pain threshiold and be prepared to submit by tapping out so Nage can release the hold down.

There is no point in trying to prove how tough you are or how much pain you can accept; only injury results from this attitude. This also applies to Nage, there is no point in continuing to apply pressure once Uke has been restrained. It doesn't make Nage tougher; it only shows Nage is a bully. After all. Uke has lent his body for Nage to practice the application. Nage should respect that, and release as soon as Uke taps and submits.

Suwari Waza Shomen Uchi Iriminage Ura

This is essentially the same as the **Tachi Waza** form (*on page 167*), but is only made more difficult by the fact that both partners are on their knees.

Above Nage enters with **Irimi Tenkan** but the movement is smaller and tighter than the standing form. As Nage completes the turn he has hold of Uke's neck and has cut down Uke's striking arm so all of Uke's upper body weight has fallen forward and is supported by the hand resting on the mat.

As Nage finishes the turn and draws Uke forward, Uke uses the hand on the mat to support his weight so he can step forward in an attempt to either get up, or at least to follow Nage's leading movement.

But because Nage turns back towards Uke and uses his free hand to strike at Uke's head, Uke's upper body movement is stopped and his legs slide out from Underneath. If this was a standing form Nage would most likely step through behind Uke's lead leg to tip him over backwards. This step is not possible in a seated position so a simple twist of the body towards Uke is sufficient to achieve the same result.

Uke finishes falling flat onto his back as his legs continue forward. Sometimes a back roll is possible, other times not. In this example it was a back breakfall...

Suwari Waza Shomen Uchi Sankyo Omote

This begins the same way as **Shomen Uchi Ikkyo**. Uke's strike is redirected by Nage's forearm to shift Uke off the line of his attack. At the same time Nage takes Uke's elbow and rotates it over to continue turning Uke's upper body off the line of attack. Nage also moves forward slightly as he does this.

Nage now steps forward with the leg closest to Uke to continue the forward turning into a downward movement. Uke will brace himself with his other arm in order to stop being pushed face down into the mat. The instant Nage feels this resistance he extends Uke's elbow forward and allows the grip he began to take on Uke's wrist slide down to finish grasping the fleshy part of Uke's hand, trapping the little finger along with the ring finger. (*See page 96- 97 for detailed description of sankyo from Tachi waza Shomen Uchi attack.*) Uke's arm is further extended which adds an upward twist to Uke's upper body.

Continuing to move forward while extending both Uke's elbow and hand will take Uke down onto the mat. Nage now moves his outside leg forward, drops his hand from the elbow and takes hold of Uke's hand from underneath to maintain the inwards twist (*Kote Hineri*) of the wrist. This allows him to release the hand he first used to make an **atemi** to Uke's face while preparing to step forward (*again with the outside leg*) in a circle around to the other side of Uke's trapped arm.

Coming around the arm Nage faces Uke. He takes hold of Uke's elbow with the hand used for the **atemi** while not releasing the grip on Uke's hand. Nage moves backwards and draws Uke forward so he falls flat onto the mat. Note that once the **Sankyo** (*Kote Hineri*) grip has been taken, Nage does not release it until he places Uke's hand against his shoulder to apply the final pin *(Katame Waza)*.

To finish the **Sankyo** pin Nage releases Uke's elbow, takes hold of Uke's hand and holds it palm forward flat against his shoulder. With the hand he previously used to maintain the wrist twist throughout the movement to this point, he now uses to draw and lock Uke's elbow in to his centre. Uke is now unable to move or escape.

Nage only has to turn his upper body towards Uke to put intolerable pressure against Uke's elbow and shoulder. Uke will have no choice but to submit.

Suwari Waza Kokyu Ho

Suwari Waza Kokyu Ho is always practiced at the end of a Test for Kyu grades as well as Dan Grades. It is practiced almost always at the end of regular training classes, and sometimes even at the beginning of a class. Sometimes it is called **Suwari Waza Kokyu-ryoku Ho. Kokyu Ryoku** means breath power. Breath power involves the whole body. It is the imbuing of the body with power gained from correct breathing and the execution of technique using the whole body. *The esoteric belief is that breath is exuded from every pore in the body and is not only what is expelled from the lungs or breathed into them.*

Kokyu can also imply or mean timing, so distance and timing are all involved with the development and execution of **Kokyu**.

There are several exercises where this is practiced standing but probably the most important exercise is the seated form commonly called **Suwari Waza Kokyu Ho.** This specifically teaches us to extend and move from our centre since we are seated and can't use legs.

Uke and Nage face each other. They should be close enough to for neither to stretch forward for one to grasp the other's wrists. As Nage extends towards Uke's upper body, Uke will find his arms and in particular his elbows rising. This raises his centre and makes him weak and unable to resist further extension from Nage. As soon as Nage knows Uke has lost strength he will cut one hand down to one side while extending the other in towards Uke's Face. Uke will find himself toppling over to that side.

Nage will immediately slide in to hold Uke down flat on his back. Both of his hands will extend towards Uke's face and Uke will hang on so he can't be hit. Uke allows one of his legs to cross over the other as he is held down, making use of this movement to stretch and relax the lower back, one of the reasons it usually done at the end of a training session.

Nage sits back on his heels with his body position approximately 45 degrees to that of Uke. The feeling he should have is of extending energy way beyond the actual reach of his hands. He will hold this position for several moments, before moving back enough to allow Uke to regain his seated position. However at the moment Uke is about to regain his seated balance Nage repeats the exercise on the other side.

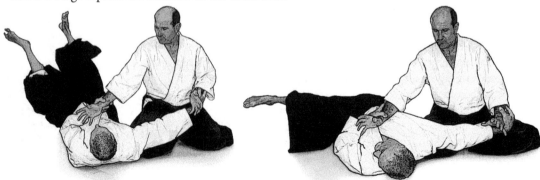

Looking for Openings...

As Uke and Nage become more adept at doing a particular technique — **Irimi-nage** for example — and no longer need to think about what they are doing, each can look for weaknesses in the other's technique and make an attempt to counter it.

If Uke attacks with **shomen uchi** and Nage's response is weak or isn't applied in such a way as to take Uke's balance or be immediately in complete control of Uke's movement, then the possibility for Uke to counter this attack is very strong.

A successful counter in which Nage ends up being thrown or projected by Uke is called **Kaeshiwaza**.

Kaeshiwaza isn't only reversing the technique, although that is what is commonly practiced — *Ikkyo to Ikkyo usually being the first kaeshiwaza taught* — it can also be applying a totally different technique as a counter to a poorly applied technique.

For example if there is a weakness in the application of **Nikyo**, Uke can reposition himself and counter with **Sankyo** to take Nage down and pin him, or he could apply **Kokyunage** or **Iriminage**; there are literally any number of responses which depend only on what kind of weakness or opening there is in Nage's original attempt to deal with Uke's attack.

Any technique can be countered with the same technique if the principle within that technique isn't applied correctly. Some examples are **Sankyo** to **Sankyo**, **Shihonage** to **Shihonage**, **Kaitenage** to **Kaitenage**, and so on. And of course any technique can be countered with an entirely different technique.

The more advanced student should always strive to apply principles correctly, and should not rush into a technique on the assumption that doing it fast will make it happen. This usually ends up with mistakes being made, especially if Uke allows the technique to happen knowing this is only practice and not real. Apart from creating a false sense of one's ability, mistakes practiced too often become ingrained and are hard to get rid of later.

Another form of more advanced practice is where Uke attempts to counter Nage's response to an original attack with a totally unexpected counter attack. If this works it would simply be a **kaeshiwaza**, but if Nage sees it happening he can react and use that attempted counter to apply the same response he began with in a slightly different way or with a totally different response then this is not **kaeshiwaza** but simply Nage finding another opening (**Suki**) which allows him to complete his response to project or take Uke down. Nage and Uke both should always look for openings or weaknesses in each other which will give either one an opportunity to complete a technique or response.

Another advanced form of practice is where Uke knowing what Nage is going to do offers some resistance to Nage's attempt to apply the technique. Rather than trying to use force to counter the force Uke is using to resist, Nage simply forgets about the original technique he was going to apply and looks for an opening elsewhere and does an entirely different technique that Uke is not expecting. For this reason *Uke should not anticipate and start to fall in a certain way, but should wait to see and feel what Nage is doing before taking appropriate ukemi.*

> **Iriminage to Iriminage**

In this example Uke is attacking with **Shomen Uchi**. The initial response from Nage is to enter for **Iriminage**, but if the **irimi** is not to the right position, it will be weak.

The moment Uke feels this weakness he responds by striking back with an elbow towards Nage's face. Nage senses this and changes the hand that would have taken Uke's neck to take the striking elbow while his other hand now takes Uke's neck instead.

Nage reverses direction and moves back around Uke's other side, or back in the direction he had entered from at the beginning. He draws Uke's elbow down and as Uke follows this movement around Nage finishes with **Iriminage** on the opposite side to that which he originally intended.

Iriminage to Kokyunage

As soon as Uke strikes shomen Uchi and Nage enters Uke brings all his weight down on the striking arm to prevent Nage from attempting Iriminage. Feeling this resistance Nage abandons the **iriminage**, reaches across Uke's back and slides his hand in under Uke's other arm.

Nage draws Uke's other shoulder towards him while at the same time he abandons the striking arm and lets his hand drift up to the shoulder above it and pushes this shoulder forward. This spins Uke around in a circle.

As Uke spins around, the hand Nage has under Uke's shoulder slides down to Uke's elbow. Stepping forward Nage cuts this elbow down right in front of Uke's lead leg, the object being to put it on the mat right in front of Uke's centre. Uke will flip over forward to receive with **mae kaiten ukemi**.

Kaeshiwaza from Nikyo

Examining some examples of **Kaeshiwaza applied from Nikyo**, we look firstly at an application of Nikyo. from two different attacks: **Chudan Tsuki** and **Gyaku Hanmi Katatetori.**

Uke attacks Nage with a punch to the mid level, **Chudan Tsuki**.

Nage shouldn't anticipate and move too soon or Uke will simply adjust his attack to compensate for Nage moving out of the way.

Nage should instead wait until the punch is fully committed and has almost reached its impact point before moving. It is then too late for Uke to change his attack.

Once Uke is committed to the attack — his lead foot is still in the air not having finished the forward step, and the punch is past half way to its target — Nage moves a fraction offline and simply rests his hand (Palm up) on Uke's wrist. As the punch finishes the moment Uke's front foot hits the mat, Nage immediately moves to the rear of Uke, sweeping the attacking arm down and back to stretch Uke and disturb his balance. Nage finishes this movement with a half **Tenkan** step so he is **sideways to Uke facing directly towards Uke's centreline.** *This is not a series of movements but one continuous movement coinciding with Uke's movement.*

Continuing to move in a circle to the rear, as Nage maintains the sweeping motion, his hand rotates underneath Uke's wrist into a position to take it in a firm grip from underneath.

Making sure that Uke remains unbalanced to the rear Nage brings Uke's wrist up towards his shoulder and shifts his body forward

This position is exactly the same as that shown above except Uke has grabbed Nage's wrist.
See page 250

until it makes contact with Uke's wrist. This means Nage does not pull Uke towards him — which might encourage Uke to take a step to regain his balance — but Nage moves in close enough for his shoulder to make contact with the wrist he is holding.

As soon as he has entered enough to make this contact Nage immediately uses his free hand to lock Uke's wrist against his shoulder with **Nikyo** (*Kote Mawashi*).

This is an Ura form of Nikyo so once Uke's wrist is locked into Nage's shoulder Nage will apply **Nikyo** to drop Uke to his knees.

This application of Nikyo is a continuation of the movement Nage used to move in.

The energy of the forward movement is transferred into a downward angle which puts intense pressure on Uke's trapped wrist, so Uke has little choice but to drop under it to avoid damage and pain.

Once Uke has dropped Nage takes the wrist away from his shoulder but maintains the **Nikyo** lock with a firm grip. Releasing the initial grip he took underneath Uke's wrist he moves that hand to Uke's elbow and rotates the elbow over in a downward angle to the mat.

This will turn Uke over and project him forward onto his face.

Uke supports himself with his free hand so he is able to control or lessen the impact on the mat.

The takedown move in preparation for final pin shown here is not quite Ura but more like Omote. To do **Ura** a deeper entry behind Uke is needed and Nage must make a full **Tenkan** in order to spiral Uke completely around.

The actual finish is often determined by the relative positions of both Uke and Nage at any given moment so sometimes a strictly **Omote** or **Ura** finish is not possible but a combination of both can work well. It all depends on how Nage perceives the final result while doing the actual technique.

There is always a constant adjustment between Nage and Uke no matter what the technique because each time they do something it is never exactly the same as the way they did it a moment before.

Similarly with **Gyaku Hanmi Katatetori,** once Nage has moved to the rear and brought Uke's wrist to an appropriate height Nage moves in to apply Nikyo.

Note the grab Nage uses to take Uke's wrist is exactly the same as that shown in the Chudan Tsuki response on page 248.

It is at this point, if there is a weakness in Nage's application, that Uke can create a counter response which, whatever the technique, can be referred to as Kaeshiwaza.

An important aspect for Uke to consider is how he will position himself when he drops down as the Nikyo is applied.

If he drops down onto the knee away from Nage (*outside knee*) keeping the inside knee up as shown here in this sequence, then if Nage decides to move to the side or back, Uke can follow and maintain his position. If he thinks there might be a weakness he is in a position to move in against Nage to counter. (*Shown below*)

The Kaeshiwaza here is to enter and take Nage's leading leg, to hold it tight while extending through Nage's shoulder or upper chest to topple him over backwards, after which an atemi to the face is applied.

If he drops with the inside knee down and the outside knee up he is not is a position to counter and is in fact assuming that Nage is going to enter to the rear with **Irimi Tenkan** to spiral him around for the **Ura** finish. *This may not be Nage's intention and so Uke is then left in an awkward position with little ability to apply a counter or kaeshiwaza.*

Kaeshiwaza ... Kokyunage from Nikyo

The weakness here is that Nage has his elbow raised (*instead of holding it tight against his side*) and is unable to correctly apply the hold against his shoulder. He is unable to make Uke drop.

Uke lowers his centre slightly as well as the almost trapped arm making an **atemi** with his elbow towards Nage's centre. At the same time Uke starts to move around Nage with **Irimi Tenkan.** As he finishes the **Tenkan** Uke rotates Nage's elbow over ready for projection into **Kokyunage** (*Ikkyonage*)or a take down which would be **Ikkyo Ura** or any other **katame waza.**

The finish here is **Kokyunage.**

Uke immediately steps forward as he rotates Nage's elbow over. he extends both arms as he steps forward and this projects Nage downwards at a rough 45 degree angle from which Nage can only take a forward roll.

Note: ***the terms Uke and Nage really are not applicable in a kaeshiwaza situation because Nage becomes Uke and Uke becomes Nage and if the kaeshsiwaza isn't applied properly it can be reversed so the roles again reverse...***

Kaeshiwaza ... Nikyo to Sankyo

The weakness is again with the elbow being left up and not locked in tight against his body. Uke deliberately drops right to the mat and dropping his elbow rotates his hand in towards his face. This turns Nage's other elbow up into the air and shifts his upper body balance causing him to lean over away from Uke.

Uke can now take Nage's hand — where it is still holding in an attempt to maintain a **Nikyo** grip, but is powerless — and applies **Sankyo**.

Uke steps up in a spiral move in towards Nage's unbalanced centre and the **Sankyo** grip he has taken comes into effect. Uke can now finish with either **Sankyo Omote** or **Ura**. Shown here is **Sankyo Omote** and rather than a seated pin Uke has applied a standing pin.

A standing pin is usually used if a weapon such as a tanto is to be taken.

Mae Geri — Front kick

Techniques are not generally practiced from Mae Geri (Front Kick) attack unless students are very good at receiving with a breakfall from a height.

There is also the philosophical reason that to attack someone with a kick leaves the person attacking vulnerable because he has one leg off the ground and is therefore easy to unbalance and throw.

However those who train in an art that uses kicking are usually very fast and have powerful kicks and can often deliver these kicks before the person being attacked can react to them. Students should take some time to learn how to kick, before attempting to practice against kicks.

With that in mind, we should practice against kicks and related attacks, because they are commonly used in brawls and situations of a similar nature which one day we may find ourselves in, although one would hope not. So we can practice dealing with kicks in a controlled dojo situation. **Using similar techniques that are used to prevail against Tsuki attacks** we can study how similar the front kick (**Mae Geri**) is to a straight punch (**Chudan Tsuki**) or how a turning kick (**Mawashi Geri**) is similar to **Yokomen Uchi.**

Mae Geri Soto Kokyunage

As the Uke kicks Nage moves in on the **Ura** or **Soto** side of the kick and delivers an **atemi** to Uke's face at the same time as he reaches underneath Uke's leg. The combination of the **atemi** and the raising up of Uke's leg will totally unbalance him.

Nage continues to move through Uke's centre line at an oblique angle to the rear. He can also flip the leg up into the air if needed, but generally simply continuing to move through while extending energy forward through the arms should be sufficient to give Uke enough impetus to fall.

Note that this is not pushing Uke over but simply of one body (Nage's) moving through the central space of another (Uke's). Uke will fall because his body is unstable with his position having been taken by Nage.

Mae Geri Uchi Kokyunage

This time entering inside (**omote** or **Uchi**) of the kick, the **atemi** is delivered with the elbow with the whole of Nage's body following behind. The elbow could strike the sternum or the jaw — either way will do serious damage — while raising the attacking leg from underneath will help topple Uke. For safety reasons we allow the atemi to pass by the side of Uke's head and cut down at the same time as raising the leg. The cut down would be equivalent to **kesa giri** or **gyaku yokomen**...

This same entry and throw can be used if the kick is a **Mawashi Geri** or turning kick.
Other applications can be made from this attack as well, **Kaitenage** for example, which has *been described on page 128*. **Mawashi Geri** can be equated with **Yokomen Uchi** since the circular attack is virtually the same. The kick is simply much lower down and usually much stronger. Nage's response in both attacks would for all practical purposes be the same.

Using Weapons as an aid to study Movement and application...

Weapons in Aikido are not usually studied as weapons systems, but are used selectively to study distance and timing, as well as a means of refining focus and movement. *If one requires a proper study of a particular weapon then one should find a teacher who teaches that specifc weapons system within a school that specializes in such systems of study.*

Because the weapon is of a fixed length it is easier to study **maai** (*combative distance*) than when both partners are unarmed and have to deal with different heights, length of arms, legs, torso and all the variables that affect distance and timing.

O-Sensei spent many years refining his study of weapons, and though he didn't systematically teach weapons techniques; he often used Bokken or Jo while teaching. This created awareness in his **Uchi Deshi** (*live-in students*) of the importance of weapons on a fundamental level.

The use of weapons in the development of Aikido was equally as important as the unarmed techniques adapted and evolved from AikiJutsu and other unarmed systems.

Many of his **Uchi Deshi** have taken this very seriously and have gone on to develop their own interpretation of weapons use in Aikido. Some in fact have evolved distinct systems of classification of techniques and have structured their systems with levels testing and grading.

Notable amongst these students are Saito Sensei who spent 28 years with O-Sensei at Iwama while the Founder's intense study and use of weapons was paramount in his later development of Aikido. Others from this period include Nishio Sensei, Chiba Sensei, Saotome Sensei, and Gaku Homma Sensei, all of whom have developed unique insights into the use of weapons and include them in their Aikido training.

Others have studied existing weapons systems but don't teach these systems integrated into Aikido. They teach them but keep them separate from Aikido.

Some use the odd weapon taking technique from time to time but it is often out of context and doesn't make a lot of sense in the way it is used. And there are many who eschew the use of weapons altogether, never teaching them: focussing strictly on the unarmed aspects of Aikido that evolved from Aikijutsu and jujutsu.

There is room for all of these approaches and what teachers teach usually reflects what they think about Aikido.

Those who don't use weapons in their training perhaps miss some of the essential elements involved in Aikido: for example the concept of Irimi is fundamental in Aikido.

Irimi derives from one of the many forms of **Kenjutsu** (*fighting sword arts*).

Finding an opening and instantly entering with a sword is pure Irimi.

In Aikido every response is initiated with Irimi. Studying Irimi with bokken against bokken is the best way to understand the conceept of Irimi.

Bokken against **Bokken**, **Jo** against **Jo**, **Bokken** against **Jo**, **Jo** against **Bokken**, are just some of the combinations where **Irimi** and timing are practiced, and where we begin to understand the reasons why in Aikido we move in certain specific ways. Dealing with a **tanto** (*knife*) is also part of weapons training and perhaps this is more applicable to modern times, but then even with **tanto** practice the training is formalised and focussed more on entering and timing rather than knife fighting methods.

None the less, for a deeper understanding of Aikido some form of weapons training is a good thing.

Without going into basic weapons training and covering aspects of **suburi** with **Bokken** and **Jo**, or examining various kata and forms practiced with one weapon against another such as **Bokken** against **Bokken**, **Jo** against **Jo**, **Bokken** against **Jo** or **Jo** against **Bokken** — *these are matters for additional volumes* — let us take a few examples of weapons taking and a few techniques such as **Iriminage**, **Kokyunage** and **Shiho Nage** done with Nage taking the **Bokken** or the **Jo** away during the execution of the technique to give us an idea of the relationship between training with a weapon and without it.

Facing a person attacking with a weapon sharpens one's focus.

Movement needs to be precise both in relation to the initial **Irimi** as well as the angle used to enter in order to avoid the weapon.

Shomen Uchi, *a sword cut vertically down in a straight line to cut through an opponent's head,* **is the most difficult attack to avoid, and this is why it is practiced so much in Aikido.**

Learning how to enter against Shomen Uchi is of primary concern in Aikido.

> ### Shomen Uchi Iriminage

As Uke moves forward to cut **Shomen Uchi** with the **Bokken** Nage, is already entering to the **Ura** side in preparation for the technique. At this point he is already in harmony with Uke's movement.

This is only one of a number of ways of approaching Iriminage and taking the bokken away.

Nage's movement here is **Irimi Ashi** with a half **Tenkan**.

Nage positions his leading hand above the grip Uke has on the descending **bokken** so he can grasp it by the hilt in between Uke's hands. His hand follows this movement down until he can grasp the hilt while his other hand reaches for Uke's neck. At the same time, as he finishes the **Irimi** and is behind Uke in an oblique position where Uke would find it difficult to counter respond, Nage should have a grip on the **bokken** as well as the back of Uke's neck.

This closer view shows the way Nage takes hold of the Bokken. By the time Uke has finished the cut Nage should have a firm grip.
It is important that Nage does not attempt to grab the Bokken too high but allows his hand to rest on top of Uke's (Ura) wrist and simply follows it down to the point where the cut finishes. By doing this he has plenty of time to position his hand and take a firm grip. This is harmonising with Uke's downward movement.

The instant the sword cut finishes Nage immediately rotates his wrist up in a small spiral which raises the hilt of the **bokken** up along Uke's centreline. It also makes Uke's grip on the **bokken** weaker and allows Nage to extend the hilt towards Uke's face.

At the same time Nage has a strong grip on Uke's neck and he uses this to draw Uke's head down in a backwards spiral against his shoulder.

With the base of the **bokken** coming towards his face and his head locked against Nage's shoulder Uke is completely unbalanced to the rear.

With a simple **Kaiten** twist of his hips, a downward extension of the hilt of the bokken into Uke's face, and simultaneously allowing the shoulder and arm holding Uke's head to drop — **gravity does the work here**— Uke will have no way to stop falling.

After taking a fall Uke should not move until Nage has moved away some distance, because the technique could be finished with a further cut or strike from Nage using the **bokken**. This could be an **atemi** with the hilt of the sword straight into Uke's face, or a spear like stab using the point after turning the weapon over, or even a step back followed by a strong cut to Uke's neck.

If Uke thinks that Nage has moved away he could inadvertently be injured by trying to get up too soon...

Alternate finish to Shomen Uchi Iriminage.
Note how the Katana is held.
Uke isn't going to move until Nage moves away.

Training with a live blade such as a Katana requires confidence and trust with both partners being extremely careful and focussed.   It is not recommended for beginners but is shown here purely as a matter of interest for more senior students...

Shomen Uchi Iriminage

This is still a form of I**riminage** although the **Katana** is not being taken.
As the attack comes Nage prepares to step offline. His foot is moving out but his body remains where it is until Uke begins to cut.

Nage moves to the **Ura** side entering with his body sideways and parallel to the cut with the **Katana**. He reaches for Uke's elbow to hold the cutting arm in place so Uke can't twist and cut sideways or backwards. Maintaining his firm hold against Uke's elbow Nage enters further behind to the position needed for **Iriminage** if it was being done without a

weapon involved. He reaches for Uke's forehead as he enters behind, and continuing to move behind while restraining Uke's elbow to prevent a backwards cut, Nage tips Uke's head over to the rear.

As Uke falls Nage mainatains his extension against Uke's elbow to keep the **Katana** well away. The moment Uke hits the mat Nage delivers a blow to Uke's ribcage still keeping the arm with the **Katana** well away.

Kokyunage while taking the Bokken from the Ura side

With any technique where Nage takes away a weapon, timing of the entry is extremely important. If Nage enters too soon, Uke will change the attack and Nage will get hit. If Nage enters too late he will get hit or cut. He needs to move only when he is certain that Uke is committed to the strike; that the sword cut is on the way and Uke is convinced he will hit the target. Only then can he safely move to enter because the strike can not be easily changed in mid flight.

Because the right arm (*Ura side*) is higher than the left arm (*Omote side*) holding the **bokken**, Nage has fractionally more time to enter on this side so timing is not quite as critical as it is for the same technique done from the **Omote** side.

The entry is either **Tsugi Ashi Tenkan** or **Irimi Ashi Tenkan** depending upon which **hanmi** Nage was standing in when Uke attacked with the **bokken**. The entry needs to gain sufficient space to finish parallel with Uke at the midway point of the strike. By the time the strike is finished the **Tenkan** part of the move has put Nage slightly behind Uke.

Note that as Nage makes his **Irimi**, his leading arm (*Left*) enters beneath Uke's both arms, while simultaneously Nage's right hand reaches up and rests softly on Uke's right wrist, and it follows the downward movement of the cut, perhaps even adding some slight energy to the downward movement.

By the time the cut has come fully down Nage has had plenty of time to take a solid grip on the hilt of the **bokken** between Uke's hands.

Nage draws Uke's wrist — and consequently his right arm — across his centreline so the hand gripping the hilt rests against Nage's right hip.

This drawing of the arm across combined with the downward movement of the cut has caused Uke to be completely unbalanced and as can be seen, he is leaning forward ready to fall over.

All Nage has to do now is shift his centre forward (similar to the movement used in the **Funekogi Undo** exercise and Uke will have to let go and take **mae kaiten ukemi** or else fall on to his head.

Note the forward extension is not forward and parallel to the ground but forward and downward at an angle that will convince Uke to let go for safety and take the fall.

Nage holds the Bokken firmly against his right hip.
As Uke begins to take his forward ukemi he will have to let go of the Bokken which leaves it in Nage's right hand.

Kokyunage while taking the Bokken from the Omote side

This is essentially the same technique as described on the previous two pages for taking the **Bokken** from the Ura side. The body movement is the same, but the timing here is more critical.

Because of the way the **bokken** is held Uke's left arm is lower than the right. **Nage will need to enter (Tsugi Ashi Tenkan) sooner than he would for the Ura side or he will not get his lead (right) arm underneath both of Uke's arms.**

Nage must not try to grab the hilt of the **bokken** too soon but simply rest his left hand between both of Uke's hands holding the **bokken**, to follow it down, only taking it firmly when the strike has reached the bottom.

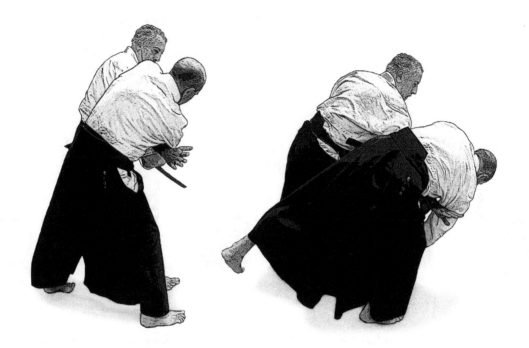

Again Nage draws the **bokken** across his centre until his hand grasping it is resting this time against his left hip. This will have tipped Uke over so he is completely unbalanced and ready to fall.

And again Nage shifts his centre forward while extending down.

Uke will of course let go of the **bokken** to take forward rolling **ukemi** in preference to falling directly down onto his head.

There are many different ways of taking a Bokken away from Uke, or a Jo for that matter, — and there are countless books, DVDs and videos explaining and demonstrating these ways — so the few techniques included in this section are to engage your curiosity, and perhaps induce you to explore more deeply this aspect of Aikido.

Once again entering (**Tsugi Ashi Tenkan**) **Omote** there is the possibility of a strike to the attacker's face, after which Nage allows his hand to follow the downward movement of the **bokken**, only grabbing and extending forward when the **bokken** has reached its lowest point, by which time Nage should be parallel to Uke.

Extending forward Nage leads Uke in a line down to a spot which is basically about an arm's length away on the mat between them.

If you visualise an imaginary triangle connecting at its base both Nage's and Uke's hips with the apex of the triangle being the point where Nage has gripped the hilt of the bokken, then stepping forward slightly and rotating this point down towards the mat will take Uke down very quickly. He will of course let go of the **bokken** to save himself with a forward **ukemi**.

Nage will finish holding the bokken.

> ## *Some aspects of Ikkyo worth having another look at...*

Migi... Gyaku Hanmi Katatori

Taking **Katatori** as a starting point for **Ikkyo** application, if we study the movement we find we are stepping back at an oblique angle to the outside (**ura**) after distracting Uke with an **atemi** to the face.

As Nage steps back he draws his hand back along Uke's grabbing arm to draw Uke forwards. Bringing Uke forwards unbalances him. Nage sinks his weight and reaches for Uke's elbow from underneath.

With the hand that has drawn Uke forward helping to bend Uke's elbow Nage then allows that hand to grasp Uke's wrist gripping his shoulder, not to take it off but to hold it there so he can easily shift Uke when he moves his whole body forward into Uke's centre .

This further destabilizes and tips Uke over.

As Nage enters the space occupied by Uke's centre (*basically where his hips are*) Uke has no option but to twist his body in an attempt to accommodate Nage's entry. If he doesn't he will find himself falling over backwards. By twisting in the direction Nage is moving he can at least control how he takes the **ukemi** leading into **Ikkyo Uder Osae.** (*See pages 81 to 87 for explanantions of the katame waza for Ikkyo.*)

The question that arises here is why do we step back the way we do when a grab is involved? It doesn't matter whether the grab is to the shoulder (Katatori), the elbow (Hijitori), or the wrist (Katatetori or Tekubi Mochi), the movement is the same, and of course the result should be the same.

One possible explanation is that it comes from the art of fighting with a sword (katana), and the need to be able to draw the sword to cut no matter how you are grabbed or held. In order to draw the sword from its scabbard in a confined space you need to step back so there is enough space for the sword to come free from its scabbard, hence the movement shown here.

Hidari...Gyaku Hanmi katatori ... Ikkyo

The instant Uke reaches out and Grabs the shoulder, instead of striking an **atemi** with his empty hand, Nage reaches down and takes the hilt of his **bokken**. He draws it partially out and strikes Uke's face. As Uke pulls his head back to avoid the strike Nage steps offline to his rear enabling the **bokken** to be fully drawn.

With cutting edge naturally up Nage raises the **bokken** to cut under Uke's elbow. With his other hand, instead of taking the elbow *as shown on the previous page for Katatori Ikkyo*, he takes the underside of the **bokken** with his palm and uses the **bokken** to cut upwards under Uke's elbow. This tips Uke over as he twists in an attempt to escape Nage's entry.

Note: the bokken is used as a training weapon rather than using a live blade which can have disastrous consequences if used incorrectly, but it should be kept in mind at all times that the bokken represents a live katana and it should be treated with equal respect and proper focus.
In its own way a bokken is a dangerous weapon and so proper etiquette should be used at all times.

Nage enters while cutting up thtough Uke's elbow, This tips Uke over even more and he reaches for the floor to help support himself.

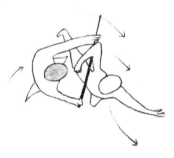

Eventually as Nage continues to enter while cutting through the elbow Uke can not hang on any longer and lets go of his grip on Nage;s shoulder.

As Uke collapses onto the floor Nage steps away slicing along his elbow as he moves back.

Migi...Gyaku Hanmi katatori ... Ikkyo

Stepping back again to draw Uke forward Nage uses his right leg because his right shoulder is grabbed. This opens a wide space allowing him to draw the **bokken** and slice across Uke's midriff. The movement is a mirror image of that done for **Hidari** side.

But the **bokken** is drawn with the right hand from the left side. This time the hilt isn't used to strike Uke's face but the blade is used to cut. Naturally Uke tries to pull away as he sees the **bokken** cutting towards him. So Nage grabs Uk's wrist to hold it in place on his shoulder thus preventing Uke from escaping the cut.

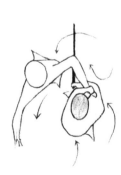

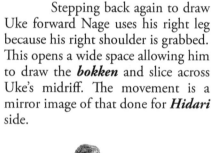

Once Nage has cut through he turns the **bokken** upwards and slices back up into Uke's elbow. He enters whils still holding the hand gripping his shoulder not allowing Uke any chance to escape.

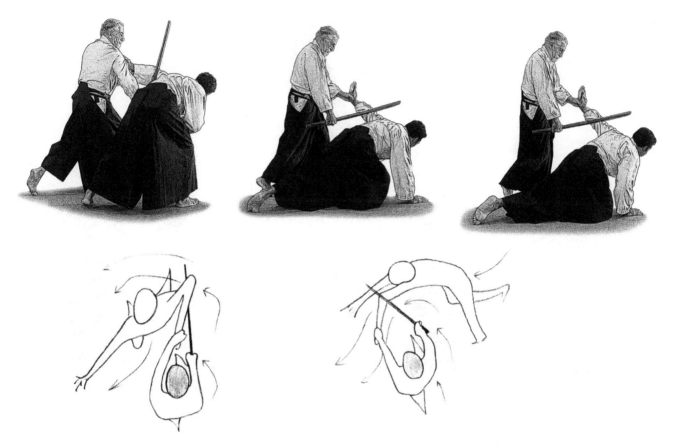

Cutting down as he enters and displaces Uke's centre compells Uke to reach down to the mat to support himself.

Nage can let go at this point and step back while slicing through Uke's elbow, or he can follow him down to the mat almost as if finishing with **Ude Osae** (arm lock) which he does by slicing forwards slong the elbow to drop Uke to the floor. Nage can then move away once Uke is incapacitated.

Shomen Uchi ... Ikkyo

One example of a bokken exercise that could explain why we move in certain ways when doing Ikkyo from a shoulder, elbow or wrist grabbing attack.

Nage begins with the bokken lowered to give Uke an opportunity to see an opening for an attack.

...from an attempted shoulder grab...

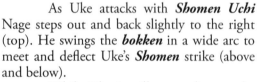

As Uke attacks with **Shomen Uchi** Nage steps out and back slightly to the right (top). He swings the **bokken** in a wide arc to meet and deflect Uke's **Shomen** strike (above and below).

While Uke is still responding to the deflection, Nage begins to raise his **bokken**.

As Uke reaches for Nage's shoulder, Nage steps this time slightly left offline and back to the rear while cutting down with his **tegatana** on Uke's wrist.

He allows his hand to sled forward anough to be able to grip Uke's hand from on top.

Raising the bokken up and over the shoulder it becomes a kesa giri cut, or gyaku yokomen towards Uke's neck and face.

Taking a firm grip on Uke's hand, Nage raises it up keeping it at the end of Uke's reach to maintain Uke lean-

At the same time as he cuts Nage steps forward to further enter into Uke's space.

ing forward with his weight on his front leg. Nage continues the circular movement as if cutting ***kesa giri*** or ***yokomen*** with a ***bokken*** to lead Uke over and

Nage finishes by cutting through Uke who will fall backwards to receive...

down into the ***Ikkyo*** application. ***Note: this much more fluid than a static shoulder grab.***

Shomen Uchi ... Ikkyo

The same exercise with **bokken** against **bokken** to create **Ikkyo**, but this time instead of knocking the **bokken** aside Nage reaches for Uke's **bokken**, and when contact is made he

Reaching towards Uke's shomen, Nage blends with the downward movement of the strike adding some slight weight to Uke's arm to make sure the cut continues. Note, Nage uses

guides it down without disturbing the line of the cut. As he enters **omote** he then cuts up

tegatana which is the same hand position as that used with the bokken.

At the bottom of the cut he allows his hand to rotate over so the palm is facing downwards in preparation for a grab.

towards Uke's neck and steps forwad at the same time to enter towards Uke's centre. As Uke pulls his head back to avoid the cut he is forced to lean backwards. He will lose balance and fall if Nage continues to cut downwards.

However in this case he does not grab Uke's wrist, he slides that hand back up along Uke's extended arm to make a *gyaku yokomen* strike to the side of Uke's head. Nage's other hand reaches out and grasps Uke's wrist from underneath. Continuing to cut Uke's head down, Nage takes a firm grip of Uk'es wrist and extends it up and over to tip Uke right over into a suitable position for *Kaitenage* instead of *Ikkyo*.

All Nage needs to do now is to step forward while extending Uke's raised arm across his shoulders to project him into a forward rolling *ukemi*.

Continuing to extend Uke's head down while pushing Uke's raised arm forwards across the shoulders maintains Uke in a position from which he can't escape.

Note: the hand position of Nage in this example is **Gyakute** and not the usual **Honte** (*Junte*) that one would use normally when doing **kaitenage** from a wrist grab or even from strikes such as **Shomen** or **Chudantsuki**.

The reason for this in this example is because Nage is on the inside of the strike, the **Omote** side, and not on the outside or **Ura** side of the strike as would normally be the case. And this position is where he would be if the exercise was **bokken** against **bokken** as shown on the previous page.

Note that this is also the exact same hand position used for **Kaitenage** from **Yokomen uchi.** *See page 127 for details regarding this application.*

Also see page 232 for Kubinage or Men Nage. The initial entry and starting point is exactly the same except that the instant the head is cut down Nage enters close enough to grasp Uke's head from the other side with his other hand, and then dropping to his kness he guides Uke down towards the mat while at the same time protecting Uke's head from damage. Uke will finish rolling over his shoulders without his head touching the floor at all.

Kaitenage from Kata Tori...

If by some chance Uke gets a firm grip on Nage's shoulder, as one would if the practice was static rather than moving, the exact same body movement used for the exercises with **bokken** angaist **bokken** (*page 272*), is used. ***Note however that the maai is very much closer.***

Nage reaches for Uke's face this time instead of for the **bokken**, to disturb balance. And the instant Uke draws his head back Nage cuts down with his **tegatana** through Uke's elbow.

He reaches for the elbow with his other hand from underneath, but instead of holding Uke's grip against his shoulder as he would for Ikkyo application with his hand on top, he cuts with **gyaku yokomen** towards Uke's head.

Above: Kaiatenage projection. Note the hand position on the wrist is honte (junte).

Below: Kaiatenage projection. Note the hand position on the elbow is gyakute.

Striking the head as he enters towards Uke's centre he tips Uke over far enough for either **Ikkyo** application or **kaitenage** but this time the hand grip on Uke's wrist would he from underneath as for normal **kaitenage** (*that is honte or junte and not gyakute as shown on page 274.*) *Also see pages 118 to 128 for kaitenage applications*

Above: Reaching for Ai Hanmi Katatetori to prevent Uke from drawing bokken.
Reading from left to right: Ai Hanmi Katatetori Ikkyo

Ai Hanmi Katatetori Ikkyo

The moment Uke tries to stop Nage from drawing his **bokken** Nage enters with *atemi* to Uke's face to disturb Uke's balance.

Having disturbed balance Nage makes **Kaiten** so he is facing side on (**hantai**) in relation to Uke who is still trying to stop the **bokken** from being drawn. Nage has no trouble drawing the **bokken** because Uke is in a weak position with balance disturbed. The **bokken** is drawn straight up and as soon as it clears, Nage turns back, reversing his **kaiten**, to face Uke having raised him up and further disturbed

balance. Nage now cuts down across the back of Uke's neck with the **bokken** parallel to Uke's outstreched arm to take Uke down to the mat for **Ikkyo** finish. When Uke is on the floor Nage steps back slicing across Uke's neck at the same time. As Nage moves away (*maintaining **Zanshin***) Uke is allowed to get up.

Without the **bokken**, **Ai Hanmi Katatetori Ikkyo** works exactly the same way... Nage enters to the side and turns **kaiten** while dropping his centre slightly to disturb Uke's balance. He immediatelt raises his arm as if drawing **bokken**. This stretches Uke Upwards so he is floating with balance gone. Nage turns back towards Uke (***kaiten** reversed*), then enters directly into Uke's centre to tip him over. Uke twists to avoid falling flat onto his back and thus ends up in a position for a takedown into **Ikkyo** *Ude Osae*.

Gyaku Yokomen Uchi Shihonage

If Uke is striking **gyaku yokomen uch**i with the **bokken** timing of the entry is critical. There is a very narrow window in which Nage can enter in order to take the appropriate grip. Nage must enter at the instant the strike commences or he will not get his hand in between the attacker's hands to properly grasp the hilt.

Note that the hand positions Nage adopts are reversed from the hand position for the standard omote form usually practiced from **Yokomen Uchi**. (*See pages 163-164*) In that other form the left hand is above facing palm down so it can rest on top of the attacker's right hand while Nage's right hand is below facing palm up ready to grasp the hilt of the bokken from underneath.

In this form from **gyaku yokomen uchi** the right hand is above facing palm down so the **tegatana** part of the hand can slice in between the attacker's hands to grasp the hilt of the **bokken**, while the left hand is below facing palm up ready to grasp the attacker's lower (left hand) where it holds the base of the bokken.

Nage must of course allow enough room so he can swing the bokken across in between the two of them. This will twist the attacker completely around and he will find his arms crossed and locked similar to **Jujinage** (cross arm throw)

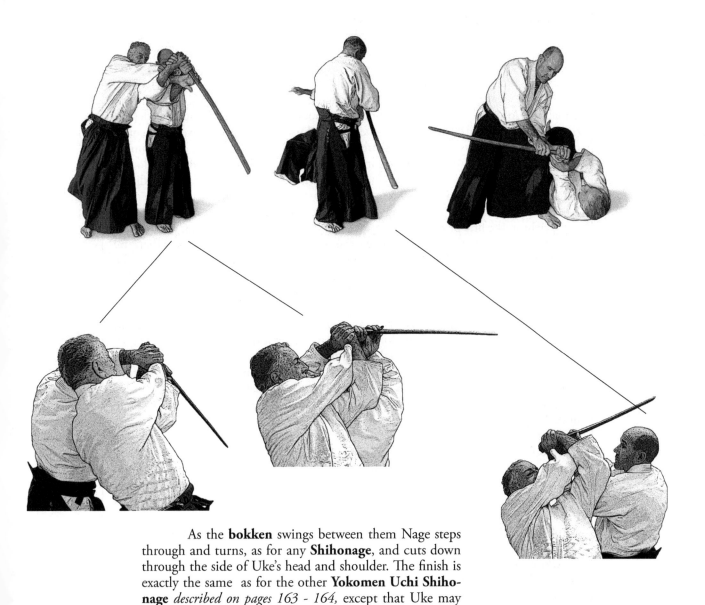

As the **bokken** swings between them Nage steps through and turns, as for any **Shihonage**, and cuts down through the side of Uke's head and shoulder. The finish is exactly the same as for the other **Yokomen Uchi Shiho-nage** *described on pages 163 - 164,* except that Uke may have his hands trapped and crossed over as in **Jujinage**.

In order to receive safely the attacker will have to let go of the **bokken** with his left hand so he can take a breakfall, *(middle picture above),* or else if he leaves it too late to let go of the base of the **bokken** his arms will be trapped in the cross arm lock and he will have to receive falling flat onto his back. *(right hand picture above).*

There are several other ways of taking the **bokken** while doing **Shiho-nage** from **Shomen Uchi,** but these are more difficult to do and consequently would appear in a volume where more complex interactions between Uke and Nage are examined. There is no space for them here...

Summing up...

> **We should keep in mind that Aikido is a martial art.**
>
> Unfortunately it is not often practiced with that in mind.
>
> Too often it has come down to a series of exercises where one person allows the other to do something, and often the person doing something acts more like bully and bashes the other into the mat. Then they change roles and the situation is reversed. In time both go away after practicing, perhaps for years like that, thinking that they can actually do Aikido as a martial art if something should happen and they need to defend themselves. Then a day comes when they try to do something they have done confidently for many years with someone they haven't trained with before and it simply doesn't work. They cannot get it to work. They try again and again, and still it doesn't work. They may even justify it by saying to themselves that this person is from a different school, or club, and is not used to us, or we are not used to them.
>
> But they never think that perhaps it doesn't work because they were simply not doing it right in the first place. There are a thousand ways to do it, (referring to any technique), and certainly there appear to be a thousand ways, or as many ways as there are people who practice Aikido, but the truth is, there is only one way, one position to be in, to make that technique work. It may appear different from one person to another because physique varies, but unless the principle underlying that particular technique is applied, the technique will not work.
>
> This is okay in a dojo because they can then try to understand what they were not doing right, but in a real life situation, if they cannot get it to work that one time they need it to work, they are finished, injured, perhaps maimed, or worse still, dead.
>
> People study Aikido for many different reasons, but whatever the reason, they should not delude themselves that they are studying a martial art.
>
> If they are studying it as a martial art then they need to be constantly aware of some underlying principles and these are what they must be studying. These principles apply in every situation.
>
> Another consideration is that Uke often does not attack with sufficient commitment to convince Nage of the threat implied by the attack. After all they are in a dojo, and no one wants to hurt their training partner — unless they are a bully, and there are plenty of those when they get the chance to be Nage — because injuring partners means after a time you have no one to practice with.
>
> However Uke must attack with such force as to make Nage believe there is some danger.
>
> Uke must also not fall down or give in the instant Nage responds. If Uke does this Nage will never learn how to do a technique properly, or even whether he is in the correct position to do a technique. (*And this is a major problem with a lot of people training today.*) Certainly Uke needs to absorb Nage's response and take some form of ukemi for self-protection, but this doesn't mean simply falling over for Nage. Uke should also be looking for the possibility of an opening to apply a counter attack (***kaeshi waza***) if Nage hasn't applied principles correctly. After all, you would be doing this if you really were trying to attack someone; you wouldn't give up the moment they countered your initial attack, you would keep trying.
>
> **The idea, that Aikido is an art of self-defence, should be abandoned.**
>
> *Nage's response in any situation must be to attack Uke the instant Uke attacks him. This makes Aikido as offensive as any other martial art. It should work against punches, kicks, strikes with and without weapons, grabbing and grappling. If it can't do this then you are not practicing Aikido.*

Aikido embodies certain principles some of which are:

Do not be where Uke expects you to be when the attack arrives, but move offline enough for the attack to just miss. (This embodies timing as well as *Maai* or combative distance.)

Do not try to block or stop the attack. Allow it to continue so it can be redirected if possible. (This is *Musubi* or blending.)

The instant you are attacked or contact is made you must take Uke's balance away. (The art of taking balance away is called *Kuzushi*.)

At the instant you take balance you must attack Uke's centre to further destabilize him.

Enter directly into Uke's centre to displace it with your own.

At this point a technique will become available, and you can apply it as a follow through.

There should not be a preconceived idea of doing something specific because this leads to a focus on technique rather than principle, but only the idea of taking balance and attacking Uke's centre directly. This can be from any angle from the front to the side or from behind, but there is usually only one spot where Uke cannot get back at you, and this is where you need to be to make a technique effective. If you are not in this spot you can be counter-attacked and may find yourself in a worse situation than the prevailing one when you were first attacked.

(*This spot is directly behind Uke's shoulder at an oblique angle, and if you are there and extending Uke forward with his balance gone you cannot be reached with either arm as Uke simply cannot respond effectively. This spot is called* **Shikaku**, *which means dead corner. Think of it as a blind spot similar to the spot behind the driver of a car where the following vehicle can't be seen in the rear view mirror inside the car, or from the side rear view mirror.*)

To sum up you need proper *Maai* (for distance), *Kuzushi* (for balance dissipation), *Musubi* (for blending, harmonizing and redirecting), *Irimi* (to enter and attack the centre) and *Zanshin* (as follow through awareness).

At least two of these must be applied simultaneously (*Kuzushi* and *Musubi*).

Focus should not be on the finishing technique or application which should take care of itself. Focus instead should be widened to include your surroundings (*Zanshin*) in case there as another attacker lurking about ready to attack you while you are occupied. And before any attack occurs there should be *Awase*, which simply means awareness of your surroundings and what they may contain.

If every time you practice something you think *'this is the only chance I am going to get to do this. There will be no second chance. I'd better get it right...'* then you will experience a marked improvement in your training. You will to a degree be experiencing 'beginner's mind' and with this comes the excitement of discovery. It probably means then you are practicing Aikido as a martial art and not simply as a series of exercises.

My hope is that this volume will have given you some insight into what Aikido is about and that you will use it as a reference guide after training to clarify things that may have escaped your notice while in the dojo.

Gambatte Kudasai.

GLOSSARY

AI Harmony, coming together, blending, meeting.

AI HANMI Mutual stance. Partners face each other with same foot forward.

AIKI The blending of two or more energies to harmonise, integration.

AIKI BUDO One of the names used before the second World War to describe Aikido.

AIKIDO The Way of Harmony, the art founded by Morihei Ueshiba, O'Sensei.

AIKIDOKA A person who practices or studies Aikido (Also Aiki Deshi.).

AIKI JO Short staff techniques according to Aikido principles.

AIKI JUJUTSU / AIKIJUTSU Martial system based on Aiki timing and control.

AIKIKAI Largest Aikido organisation headed by Moriteru Ueshiba, grandson of the founder. Moriteru Ueshiba is referred to as Doshu. He is the third Doshu following his father the late Kisshomaru Ueshiba who was the second Doshu (leader of the way).

AIKI KEN Swordsmanship according to Aikido principles.

ASHI Leg or foot.

ATEMI Strike. A blow aimed at a weak spot, usually defensive.

AWASE Blending to draw out one's partner by initiating a technique.

BO Long staff.

BOKKEN Wooden practice sword

BOJUTSU Techniques / Art of the staff.

CHUDAN mid level position of hands, sword, staff, or area of opponent to attack.

DAITO RYU (Aiki Jujutsu) A martial system taught by Sokaku Takeda.

DAN Ranking system in Japanese martial arts. (Shodan -1st degree to Judan 10th degree)

DESHI Serious student of Aikido, Disciple.

DO The path or way to physical and spiritual refinement.

DO GI Training uniform. Also known as a GI, or KEIKOGI.

DOJO Place of training.

DOKA Songs of the way. Often difficult to understand poems by Morihei Ueshiba.

DOMO ARIGATO GOZAIMASHITA Thank you very much.

DORI or tori. Hold or grab.

DOSA Basic movements. Kihon Dosa.

DOSHU Head or Grand master, Highest position in the AIKIKAI. (Previously Kisshomaru the son of the Founder Morihei Ueshiba was the 2nd Doshu. Upon his death Moriteru Ueshiba, the Grandson of The Founder became the third and present Doshu.)

EN NO IRIMI A circular entry used to get behind an attack so as to control it.

FUDO NO SHISEI Rocklike steady posture. Immovable posture.

FUKOSHIDOIN First level instructor. Assistant instructor.

FUNEKOGI UNDO Rowing exercise, moving meditation.

FURI TAMA To shake down the spirit. A meditation technique from Shinto ritual.

GEDAN lower level. (eg. Gedan Uchi, strike to lower level such as knee.)

GERI Kicking.

GI Training uniform.

GOKYO Pinning technique number five.

GYAKU HANMI Reverse stance. Partners have opposite foot forwards.

HAKAMA Samurai culottes (Wide pleated trousers) worn by Aikidoka and Kendoka.

HANMI Open triangular stance with even weight distribution.

HANMI HANDACHI Techniques where Nage sits while Uke stands.
HANTAI Reverse, opposite.
HAPPO UNDO Eight directions exercise.
HENKA WAZA Variations of a technique.
HIDARI Left
HIJI Elbow.
HIJI TORI Elbow hold.
HIZA Knee.
HOMBU (Dojo) Aikikai headquarters in Tokyo.

IAI DO Art of drawing and cutting with a sword.
IKI Breath. See Kokyu.
IKKYO 1st pinning technique or principle in Aikido. (Arm pin.)
IRIMI Entering. One of the most important movements in Aikido: entering into an attack in order to neutralise and defuse it. A movement adapted from Kenjutsu.
IRIMI NAGE Entering throw. A basic but difficult throw to master.
IRIMI TENKAN Entering and pivoting around a stable centre.

JIYU WAZA Free style techniques both for attack and defence.
JO Short staff
JODO / JOJUTSU Ways of using techniques with the short staff.
JODAN Upper level position. Upper area to attack or defend.
JO DORI Defence against short staff. ie. Taking the Jo away from the attacker.
JO DOSA Exercises with the Jo.
JO TAI KEN Practice with Jo against Bokken.
JUJI NAGE Crossed arm throw.
JUJI GARAMI another name for crossed arm throw.

KAITEN Open and turn (180 degrees so you are facing the opposite direction).
KAMAE Ready stance. A stance exhibiting awareness and readiness for combat.
KAMI Gods, Deities, Divine Spirits, Guardian Angels, enlightened human being.
KAMIZA The front of the dojo where scrolls, photographs of O'Sensei are displayed.
KATA Fixed forms used to teach movement and technique.
KATA Shoulder.
KATA DORI Shoulder grab.
KATA TE single hand (Kata te tori single hand grab)
KEIKO Training.
KEIKO GI Training uniform.
KEN Sword.
KENDO Swordplay as competitive sport.
KENJUTSU The martial art of swordplay.
KI Energy, Spirit, universal energy, a vital aspect in Aikido techniques.
KIAI Piercing shout which assists in the releasing of energy while applying techniques.
KIKAI TANDEN (also Seika Tanden or Hara) Physical and spiritual centre about 2 inches below the navel. All movement emanates from here.
KI NO NAGARE Free flowing techniques.
KIMUSUBI Linking of Ki and blending of energies.
KOGI FUNE UNDO (or Funekogi undo) Rowing exercise, a moving, voiced meditation adopted from Shinto Misogi ritual.
KOKYU The breath of life. Technically good timing.

KOKYU HO Exercises to develop breath power.

KOKYU ROKU Breath power as distinct from raw physical power. A great power that can be produced when consciousness and body are relaxed and unified. At higher levels kokyu roku is understood as spiritual energy that translates into physical energy.

KOSHI Lower back or hips.

KOSHI NAGE Hip throw.

KOTE Wrist (Also Tekubi)

KOTE GAESHI A throwing technique using an outward turn of the wrist.

KOTE MAWASHI Wrist in turn.(Also Kote Hineri) used with Nikkyo and Sankyo.

KUMI JO Exercises where both partners are training with Jo, or short staff.

KUMI TACHI Exercises with both partners using swords.

KYU levels or grades below Dan rank.

MA AI The correct distance between two partners. MA AI is constantly changing with the flow of action created by attack and defence. It cannot be learned through theory. The sense of MA AI is a matter of practical experience and can only be developed through practice.

MARUI Circular or round. A principle employed in Aikido techniques.

MEN UCHI Strike to the head.

MEN TSUKI Punch to the head or face.

MIGI Right

MOCHI Grab firmly. (ie Tekubi mochi - wrist grab)

MISOGI Purification of mind and body.

MOKUSO A command to meditate. (Used to clear the mind at the start of training.)

MOROTE DORI One arm held by two hands.

MUNADORI (MUNEDORI) Chest grab. Hold lapel in front.

NAGARE Flow of Ki during execution of technique.

NAGE the one who throws. The defender against an attack.

NIKKYO Pinning technique number two. (2nd principle).(Wrist twist inwards.)

OBI Belt used on training uniform. (Kuro obi is black belt.)

OMOTE Front or technique done to the front of Uke.

ONEGAI SHIMASU means I ask you please. Used when asking a partner to train with you. Used at the beginning of class by students to instructor, asking him to help them train.

OSAE WAZA Pinning techniques.

O'SENSEI Great teacher, a respectful way in which Aikidoka refer to Morihei Ueshiba, founder of Aikido.

OYO WAZA practical application of techniques for self defence.

RANDORI Free style techniques against multiple attackers.

REI Bow. The formal gesture of respect used in all martial arts.

REIGI Etiquette.

RIAI The relationship between methods of using ken, jo, and taijutsu.

RIYOTE Both hands

RIYOTE DORI Term used when both Nage's arms are held by both of Uke's hands.

ROKYO Sixth principle of Aikido (arm twist with attack to elbow.)

SABAKI motion.

SANKAKU IRIMI Triangular entering (Issoku Irimi or one step entering).

SANKYO Third pinning technique or principle. (Arm twist and pin.)

SEIZA Formal seated position with legs tucked beneath the buttocks.

SENSEI Teacher, respectful term added to name of instructor.

SHIDOIN Senior instructor.

SHIHAN Master instructor.

SHIHO GIRI Four directions cut. An aiki ken exercise.

SHIHO NAGE Four directions throw.

SHIKKO Knee walking. Used to develop leg and hip strength, also to teach one to move from one's centre or Tanden.

SHIME A lock as in Kansetsu shime waza, or joint locking techniques.

SHOMEN The front of the dojo where the Kamiza is located.

SHOMEN UCHI A direct frontal strike to the head (originating from Kenjutsu).

SODE TORI sleeve hold.

SOTO Outside.

SUBURI Individual sword or jo movements. Repetitive cuts with sword or jo.

SUMI OTOSHI corner drop.

SUWARI WAZA seated techniques.

TACHI DORI Techniques to counter a sword attack.

TAI JUTSU Unarmed body techniques.

TAI NO HENKO Pivoting the body around one's centre, tanden or one point.

TAI SABAKI Body movements.

TANDEN The body's centre just below the navel.

TANTO DORI techniques used to defend against knife attack.

TANTO Knife.

TATAMI mats used to cover the dojo floor.

TE Hand

TEGATANA side of hand used in a manner similar to striking with a sword.

TEKUBI wrist.

TENCHI Heaven and Earth.

TENCHI NAGE Heaven and Earth throw.

TOBU UKEMI Flying breakfall.

TSUKI Punch.

UCHI Inside.

UCHI Strike or blow to vital part of body.

UCHI DESHI Live in disciple or full time student under a senior instructor.

UCHI GATAME Pounding the body with fists, a warm up exercise to stimulate skin and muscles.

UKE another name for Tori, the one who receives the defence after attacking Nage.

UKEMI Breakfall. Mae-ukemi breakfall or roll to the front. Ushiro-ukemi breakfall or roll to the rear. Yoko-ukemi breakfall to the side

URA Back, or to the rear opposite of omote.

USHIRO DORI grasped or held from behind.

USHIRO behind, from the rear.

USHIRO WAZA Techniques from behind.

WAZA Techniques

YOKOMEN UCHI A diagonal strike to the side of the head, temple, or neck.

YONKYO Pinning technique number four. (Fore-arm pin.)

YUDANSHA A person with a Dan ranking, a black belt.

ZANSHIN The constant awareness of what is going on around you even when you have completed a technique. It is maintaining unbroken concentration and the continuity and flowing of Ki, the mental bridge between one action and another.

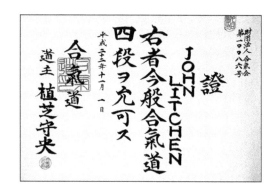

About the Author...

John commenced studying Aikido in 1990, the year of his 50th birthday, in Santiago, Chile while on an extended visit. His first teacher was Jorge Rojo (6th Dan and Technical Director of Aikikai Chile) who was such an inspiration that John and his son trained every day for the three months they were in Chile.

After returning to Australia he continued with his studies of Aikido with Aiki-Kai Australia under the direction of the late Sugano Shihan 8th Dan, (who was Founder and Technical Director of Aiki-Kai Australia) and his appointed senior instructors in Melbourne, training 5 days per week.

On retirement John moved to the Gold Coast where he continues to study and teach Aikido. In recent times he has also travelled across to New Zealand a number of times to study under the direction of Takase Shihan (7th Dan) and other visiting senior instructors from Japan.

John also writes about Aikido and other matters. He is the editor of Aikido in Australia, the official newsletter for Aiki-Kai Australia, and has contributed articles to that journal as well as Aikido Today magazine in the USA, Bujutsu International in Australia, and several websites.

He is the author of Cinematography Underwater (Oceans Enterprises), Convergence – Aspects of the Change (Zeus Publications), Attributes a Writer Needs (Yambu), Fragments from a Life in both English and Greek translation (Yambu), Fragments that remain (Yambu), and a novel 'and the waters prevailed' (Yambu).

He is also a keen photographer and in that capacity has contributed articles and photographs to Australian Photography, Neville Coleman's Underwater Geographic, and Blitz Martial Arts.

All the illustrations in this book were taken with digital cameras, and modified in Adobe Photoshop 7 Photoshop CS5. The drawings and sketches were also scanned into Adobe Photoshop, cleaned up and combined.

John can be contacted by post at PO Box 3503, Robina Town Centre, Queensland, 4230, Australia, or by email at jlitchen@bigpond.net.au
website: aikidogoldcoast.com

Graham Morris Sensei 6ᵗʰ Dan Shidoin

Having commenced his training with British Aiki Kai under both Chiba Sensei and Kanetsuka sensei, he became at 21 the youngest 2ⁿᵈ Dan in Europe at that time, and was awarded *Fuku-Shidoin* certificate for teaching.

Shortly after this, in collaboration with Allan Ruddock he founded the Isle of Mann Aikido Club. (1978)

Leaving Britain in 1983 he migrated to Australia, settling in South East Queensland on the Gold Coast. In 1984 he established a dojo and an association, Aikido Queensland Aikikai. He was appointed to the position of State Area representative for Queensland by Sugano Shihan and Aiki Kai Australia, (*a position he still holds today*). He is the senior instructor for Aikido in Queensland, and travels regularly to teach special training courses at all Queensland dojos, although primarily teaching at the Gold Coast dojo presently located in Mudgeeraba at the edge of the Gold Coast Hinterland.

Over the years he has instructed at local schools, taught Fisheries Department Officers and Police Officers self defence, as well as providing ongoing consultation for security courses with the Gold Coast Skill Centre.

He has always been one of the most highly regarded instructors in Australia and his willingness to be Uke for the author is a reflection of his outgoing personality and his sincere desire to teach Aikido both from the viewpoint of Nage as well as Uke.

Once again I would like to thank my various Ukes, who appear in many of the images in this book, for their ongoing assistance and their willingness to help, as well as their dedication to their training. They are Russell Cosby, Dave Robinson, Lam Nguyen, Jerry Ormsby, Yusuke Komiya, Clifford Coetzee, and Roland Stettler. Domo Arrigato Gozaimas...